1878 S Morgan Dollar
Attribution Guide

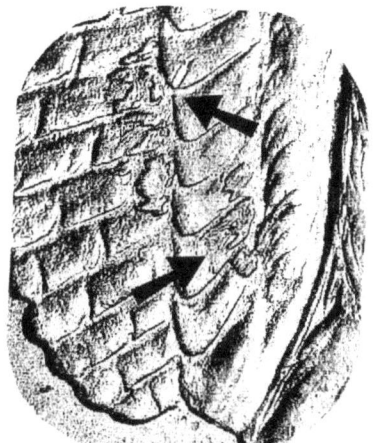

Acid Treated Wing Middle

Two Engraved Upper TF

Cap Band Gouge

by

Leroy Van Allen

&

Craig Lickenbrock

July 2006
Revised September 2012

Engraved Lines Wing Middle

Engraved Sagging Jaw

Acid Treated Wing Feather

Engraved Wing Feather

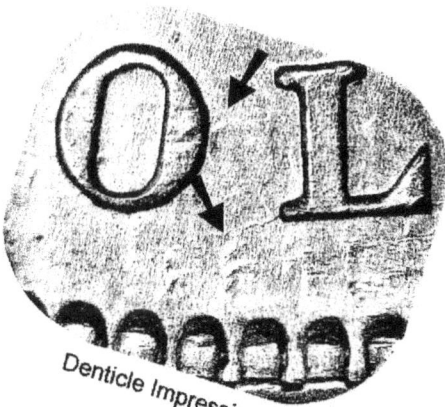

Denticle Impressions

Published by

Rare Coin Investments (RCI)
P.O. Box C
Ironia, NJ 07845

Copyright © 2022 by Michael S. Fey, Ph.D.

Authors: Leroy C. Van Allen and Craig Lickenbrock.

Library of Congress Catalog Number: 2023904390

ISBN

Printed in the United States

TABLE OF CONTENTS

LIST OF FIGURES

LIST OF CHARTS

ACKNOWLEDGMENTS

The authors would like to thank the many collectors and dealers who have reported new and revised 1878 S Morgan dollar varieties. It is through their sharing of knowledge and coins for examination and photographing that made this 1878 S Attribution Guide possible.

A **special thanks** goes to **David DeRuiter** who first reported the rare 1878 S B[1] long nock or arrow shaft reverse in November 1979 and at that same time, discovered and reported the engraved wing feather on the 1878 S between the eagle's right wing and leg. This feature makes the 1878 S interesting and unique in many cases. David DeRuiter reported many of the listed engraved wing feather varieties.

A **special thanks** also goes to **Brian Raines** who in September 2010 pointed out the possibility of acid treated on an obverse die of 1879 S and 1878 S VAM 76. Since then, the unique San Francisco Mint acid treatment of many dies has been confirmed.

It should also be noted that some of the later rare B[1] long nock varieties were first reported by Michael Fey, Jeff Oxman and Larry Briggs. In addition, much appreciation is given to the following collectors who each reported many new and revised 1878 S B[2] short nock varieties: Pete Bishal, Larry Briggs, Calvin Cherry, Martin Field, Michael Fey, Bill Fivaz, Guy Messing and many others listed below. A special thanks is given to Jeff Seawell for his tireless efforts in tracking down the shared dies and multiple obverse die varieties.

The following are the discoverers of each of the 1878 S varieties, plus those that reported significant revisions to the known varieties.

Leroy Van Allen
Craig Lickenbrock   June 2006 (Revised November 2006, March 2009 and August 2012)

1878 S DISCOVERERS HALL OF FAME

1	George Rice	June 1898	9revise	Craig Lickenbrock	Dec 05	26	David DeRuiter	Nov 79
1A	Lewis Rosenbaum	Mar 77	10	Charles Wallace	May 66	26revise	Jeff Oxman	Apr 95
1B	Martin Field	Mar 83	11	Bill Rawlings	Jul 67	27	David DeRuiter	Nov 79
1Brevise	Craig Lickenbrock	Dec 05	12	Guy Messing	May 73	27revise	Leroy Van Allen	Dec 99
1C	Calvin Cherry	Feb 02	13	Leonard Hinckley	Feb 74	28	David DeRuiter	Nov 79
1D	Michael Fey	Mar 02	14	Bill Deterline	Dec 77	28revise	Richard Carlson	Oct 07
1Drevise	Mike Torgrimson	Mar 03	14revise	David DeRuiter	Nov 79	29	Leroy Van Allen	Dec 79
1Drevise	Jeff Seawell	Aug 06	15	Bill Fivaz	Feb 74	29revise	Craig Lickenbrock	Dec 05
1E	Larry Briggs	Aug 02	15revise	David DeRuiter	Nov 79	29revise	Jim Bailey	Apr 10
1F	" "	Nov 02	15revise	Michael Fey	Jan 03	30	David DeRuiter	Nov 79
1G	" "	Aug 03	15revise	Clayton Christiansen	Jul 04	30revise	Craig Lickenbrock	Dec 05
1Grevise	" "	July 04	16	Guy Messing	May 73	30A	Jason Henrichsen	Feb 10
1Grevise	Hank Habenicht	Aug 10	16revise	David DeRuiter	Nov 79	31	David DeRuiter	Nov 79
1H	(eliminated, same as 1B)		17	Bill Fivaz	Feb 74	31revise	Larry Briggs	Nov 02
1I	Larry Briggs	Sep 10	17revise	Larry Briggs	July 04	31revise	George Delfico	July 03
2	Howard Newcomb	Feb 1913	17revise	David Johannesen	Mar 11	32	David DeRuiter	Nov 79
2revise	Craig Lickenbrock	Dec 05	17A	John Roberts	Dec 01	32A	Larry Briggs	May 04
3	Leonard Hinckley	Feb 74	17B	Brian Raines	Aug 09	33	David DeRuiter	Nov 79
4	George Mallis	Mar 68	17C	Jason Henrichsen	July 09	33revise	Larry Briggs	Aug 03
5	Paul Williams	Aug 66	18	Bill Fivaz	Jul 76	33A	Mike Emswiler	July 12
5revise	David DeRuiter	Nov 79	18A	Jason Henrichsen	Oct 11	34	David DeRuiter	Nov 79
5revise	John Wilson	Oct 99	19	Lewis Rosenbaum	Mar 77	34revise	Craig Lickenbrock	Dec 05
5revise	Hartley Cole	Feb 08	19revise	Calvin Cherry	July 02	35	David DeRuiter	Nov 79
6	Francis Klaes	Jun 63	19A	" "	July 02	35revise	Jym Braun &	Mar 00
6revise	David DeRuiter	Nov 79	20	Leroy Van Allen	June 77		Marc Serafine	Apr 01
7	George Mallis	Mar 68	20revise	David DeRuiter	Nov 79	35revise	Mark Kleimen	Jan 02
7revise	Craig Lickenbrock	Dec 05	21	Jim Baxter	Sep 77	36	David DeRuiter	Nov 79
8	George Mallis	Mar 68	21revise	Craig Lickenbrock	Dec 05	36revise	Benjamin Underwood	Sep 09
8revise	David DeRuiter	Nov 79	22	Jim Baxter	Sep 77	36revise	Leroy Van Allen	Apr 11
8revise	Jeff Seawell	Feb 03	22revise	Jason Henrichsen	Apr 10	36A	Craig Lickenbrock	July 04
8revise	Craig Lickenbrock	May 06	23	Bill Fivaz	Nov 77	36B	Michael Ash	Jun 06
8A	Michael Ash	Mar 06	23revise	Craig Lickenbrock	Dec 05	37	David DeRuiter	Nov 79
9	Bill Fivaz	Jul 72	24	Martin Field	Mar 79	37revise	Laurence Galbraith	Oct 05
9revise	David DeRuiter	Nov 79	24revise	Craig Lickenbrock	Jan 06	37revise	Craig Lickenbrock	Dec 05
9revise	Leroy Van Allen	Feb 03	25	Martin Field	Mar 79	37A	Jason Henrichsen	May 12

38	David DeRuiter	Nov 79	
38revise	Larry Briggs	Aug 03	
38revise	Craig Lickenbrock	July 04	
39	David DeRuiter	Nov 79	
39revise	Logan McKechnie	Apr 06	
40	David DeRuiter	Nov 79	
41	David DeRuiter	Nov 79	
42	Martin Field	Jan 80	
42revise	Jim Bailey	Apr 10	
42A	Jason Henrichsen	Apr 10	
43	Martin Field	Jan 80	
44	" "	Aug 80	
44revise	Craig Lickenbrock	July 04	
45	Leroy Van Allen	Oct 80	
45revise	Calvin Cherry	Oct 01	
45revise	Leroy Van Allen	May 10	
46	Martin Field	Oct 80	
46revise	Craig Lickenbrock	Dec 05	
46A	Calvin Cherry	July 02	
47	Pete Bishal	Jan 81	
47revise	Craig Lickenbrock	May 06	
48	Leroy Van Allen	Apr 81	
48revise	Calvin Cherry	Feb 03	
48revise	Jym Braun	Aug 03	
48revise	Craig Lickenbrock	July 04	
48revise	Brent Fogelberg	Mar 12	
49	Pete Bishal	Jul 81	
49revise	Craig Lickenbrock	Aug 06	
49revise	Leroy Van Allen	Apr 11	
50	Martin Field	Aug 81	
50revise	Jeff Seawell	Aug 06	
50revise	Leroy Van Allen	Apr 11	
51	Leroy Van Allen	Dec 81	
51revise	Larry Briggs	Aug 03	
51revise	Hartley Cole	Feb 06	
52	Pete Bishal	Dec 81	
52revise	Larry Briggs	Aug 03	
53	Martin Field	Sep 82	
53revise	Craig Lickenbrock	Dec 05	
54	Martin Field	Mar 83	
55	Leroy Van Allen	Mar 83	
55revise	Calvin Cherry	Mar 02	
55revise	Craig Lickenbrock	Aug 06	
55revise	Leroy Van Allen	Aug 12	

56	Leroy Van Allen	Aug 89	
56revise	Jeff Oxman	Apr 95	
57	Michael Fey &		
	Charles Nowack	Apr 95	
58	Jeff Oxman	Apr 95	
59	" "	June 97	
60	Michael Fey	Apr 98	
61	Herb Walter	Oct 99	
62	Michael Fey	Dec 99	
63	Marc Serafine	Apr 01	
63revise	Logan McKechnie	Oct 07	
63revise	Michael Fey	Dec 09	
64	Calvin Cherry	Oct 01	
64revise	Hartley Cole	Feb 08	
64revise	Leroy Van Allen	July 11	
65	Calvin Cherry	Feb 02	
66	" "	Feb 02	
66revise	Larry Briggs	July 04	
66revise	Craig Lickenbrock	Sep 04	
67	Calvin Cherry	Feb 02	
68	" "	Feb 02	
69	Michael Fey	Mar 02	
69revise	Michael Ash	Feb 11	
70	Calvin Cherry	Mar 02	
71	(old eliminated, same as 35)		
71	Craig Lickenbrock	Dec 05	
72	Larry Briggs	July 02	
73	Calvin Cherry	July 02	
74	" "	July 02	
74revise	Craig Lickenbrock	Dec 05	
74A	Craig Lickenbrock	Dec 05	
75	Calvin Cherry	July 02	
75revise	Craig Lickenbrock	Aug 06	
75A	" "	Aug 06	
75Arevise	Leroy Van Allen	Aug 12	
76	Larry Briggs	Aug 02	
76revise	Brian Raines	Sep 10	
77	Robert Bruce	Oct 02	
78	Michael Fey	Oct 02	
78revise	Craig Lickenbrock	Dec 05	
78revise	Hank Habenicht	Aug 10	
79	Craig Lickenbrock	Dec 05	
80	Michael Fey	Jan 03	
80revise	Craig Lickenbrock	July 04	

80revise	Craig Lickenbrock	Jan 11	
81	Logan McKechnie	Jan 03	
81revise	Leroy Van Allen	Apr 11	
82	Calvin Cherry	Feb 03	
82revised	Layton Pitts	July 12	
83	" "	Feb 03	
84	Jym Braun	Oct 99	
84revise	Brent Fogelberg	Mar 12	
85	Brian Raines	Sep 03	
86	Larry Briggs	May 04	
86revise	Logan McKechnie	Sep 06	
86revise	Larry Briggs	Sep 07	
86 Die 3	Benjamin Underwood	Jun 09	
87	Larry Briggs	May 04	
88	Jeff Seawell	June 04	
89	Craig Lickenbrock	July 04	
89revise	Craig Lickenbrock	Jan 11	
90	" "	July 04	
91	Larry Briggs	July 04	
91revise	Brent Fogelberg	Mar 12	
91A	" "	May 04	
92	" "	July 04	
92revise	Craig Lickenbrock	Sep 04	
93	Larry Briggs	July 04	
94	" "	July 04	
94revise	Russell James	Jun 11	
95 (old one eliminated, same as 46)			
95	Craig Lickenbrock	Dec 05	
95revise	Russell James	June 11	
96	John Roberts	Apr 05	
97	Calvin Cherry	Nov 05	
98	Craig Lickenbrock	Dec 05	
99	John Baumgart	Jan 06	
100	John Roberts	Dec 05	
101	Craig Lickenbrock	May 06	
102	" "	May 06	
103	" "	May 06	
103revise	" "	Aug 06	
104	Larry Briggs	July 06	
105	John Coxe	July 06	
106	Jeff Seawell	Aug 06	
107	Logan McKechnie	Aug 07	
108	" "	Oct 07	
109	Brian Raines	Nov 07	
110	Brent Fogelberg	July 11	
111	Logan McKechnie	Sep 11	

Craig Lickenbrock & Leroy Van Allen
May 2006

1878 S MORGAN DOLLAR ATTRIBUTION GUIDE

INTRODUCTION

Welcome to the *fascinating* world of the 1878 S Morgan dollar die varieties! The 1878 S, struck at San Francisco Mint, has been the ***neglected step-child*** common date of the 1878 year of Morgan dollars. They are relatively available for that year and they don't have the appeal of the Carson City mint mark. The 1878 S has always taken a **back** **seat** to the 1878 P die varieties of 8 Tail Feather (TF), 7/8 TF, 7 TF Reverse of '78 and 7 TF Reverse of '79 in popularity and price.

Note that there are 17 1878 P, three 1878 CC and only one 1878 S listing (All of the B[1] long nock varieties are lumped together.) in the 1996 booklet, *The Top 100 Morgan Dollar Varieties: The VAM Keys,* by Michael Fey & Jeff Oxman. Of course, the varieties listed for the 1878 P and 1878 CC are spectacular and desirable. The same trend is also evident in the book, *SSDC Official Guide to the Hot 50 Morgan Dollar Varieties* by Jeff Oxman, 2000, where 13 1878 P varieties, one listing of two 1878 S varieties and no 1878 CC varieties are listed. The book, *Official Guide To The Morgan Dollar Hit List 40,* 2009, has 12 1878 P, four 1878 S and no 1878 CC varieties listed. So the **Top 100, Hot 50** and **Hit List 40** have 42 1878 P varieties total and **only seven 1878 S varieties** and three of 1878 CC.

Currently, there are **four 1878 P Guides** available that cover all known die varieties, **one 1878 CC Guide** and **one 1878 S Guide** for **long nock** and this **1878 S Guide**:

- *1878 Morgan Dollar 8-TF Attribution Guide* by Jeff Oxman & Les Hartnett, 1998.
- *The 1878 Morgan Dollar 7/8-TF Attribution Guide* by Jeff Oxman & Les Hartnett, 1999.
- *1878 P 7 Tail Feather Morgan Dollar Attribution Guide* by Leroy Van Allen, 2002.
- *Official Guide to the 1878 Reverse of '79 Varieties* by Mark Witkower with Jeff Oxman, 2008.
- *1878 S Morgan Dollar Attribution Guide* by Leroy Van Allen & Craig Lickenbrock, 2006.
- *Long Nock A Guide to the 1878-S B1 Reverse Varieties* by John Roberts, 2008.
- *A Guide to the Varieties of the 1878 Carson City Morgan Dollar* by John Roberts, 2010.

Previously, the only detailed listings and photographs on the 1878 P, S & CC die varieties was the book, *Comprehensive Catalog and Encyclopedia of Morgan & Peace Dollars* by Leroy C. Van Allen & A. George Mallis, DLRC Press, third edition, 1992, & WorldWide Ventures reprint in 1998 (Known as the VAM book.) plus the yearly *VAM Varieties Supplements* by Leroy Van Allen. Thus, the 1878 S listings and photos had been scattered in a number of documents.

Previous revisions to this book had added VAMs 36B, 75A, 104, 105, 106 & 107. The March 2009 update added VAMs 108 & 109 plus revisions to VAMs 5, 28, 63, 64 & 86. **This major revision** adds VAMs 110 & 111, sub-varieties 1I, 17B, 17C, 18A, 30A, 33A, 37A, 42A, 86 Die 3, engraved 9 upper TF of 45 & 68, 8 engraved upper TF of 64 & 110 and acid treated dies of 1G, 36, 48, 49, 50, 55, 75A, 76, 78, 81, 84, 91, plus revisions to 1C, 17, 22, 29, 36, 42, 63, 69, 94, 95, 80, 89.

This Guide is **consolidates** all the known 1878 S listings and photographs into one convenient document. It aids in the **quick identification** of the die varieties, as many are very similar in appearance and can be **difficult** and **time consuming** to attribute. New and larger photographs plus special charts are presented to help in the variety identification process. A prime objective is to **highlight** the spectacular, different and highly desirable 1878 S die varieties. The unique branch mint engraving and acid treatment of the 1878 S working dies is examined and illustrated.

The authors can be contacted about new and revised 1878 S die varieties at:

Leroy Van Allen
P.O. Box 196
Sidney, OH 45365

Craig Lickenbrock
P.O. Box 997
O'Fallon, IL 62269-0997

Or via e-mail: vams@woh.rr.com

Or via e-mail: vams1878s@msn.com

BACKGROUND

The **1878 S mintage** of **9.8 million** is almost as much as the **1878 P mintage** of **10.5 million** coins and much larger than the **1878 CC mintage of 2.2 million**. All of the **1878 S** coins are of the **second B reverse design type** with parallel arrow feathers and flat eagle's breast. The **1878 P** have **much more varied design types** and varieties of 8 TF, 7/8 TF, 7 TF B type reverse of '78 and 7 TF C type reverse of '79 plus dual, triple and quadruple hubs of the reverse dies and I, II, III type and dual hubs of the obverse dies. The **1878 S** only has a single **II obverse** design hub and a single **B reverse** design hub which has the rare B^1 sub-type with long center arrow shaft or nock and the common B^2 sub-type with short or flush nock center arrow feather.

Since the 1878 S and 1878 P each have a total mintage of about the same of around 10 million coins, the **1878 S has nearly as many die varieties listed**. The **1878 P** currently has **135 die varieties** (41 8 TF, 15 7/8 TF, 59 B 7 TF, 20 C 7 TF), not including any sub-varieties, whereas the **1878 S** has **111 B 7 TF** currently listed. But the 1878 S has more 7 tail feather varieties listed at 111 compared to 79 for the 1878 P, even though the 7 TF mintage is comparable at both mints at around 9 to 10 million.

A possible explanation for the larger number of 1878 S 7 TF varieties is that the San Francisco Mint **engraved and acid to touched up** a **large number of reverse dies, 44,** that had portions of the eagle's feathers missing. This was due to the **die basining** (Lapping the die face on a zinc disc with compound to give a radius of curvature to the die face.) and polishing which removed some wing feathers on the B reverse design on the working dies. Each touched-up engraved and acid treated reverse dies are listed as die varieties. Only eight such cases of added engraved wing feather are known for the 1878 P 7 TF. But 1878 P also has a large number of dual hub obverse dies (over 40) that were used with the 7 TF reverse dies that make up a substantial number of the listed 7 TF varieties.

The years after 1878 have large numbers of **doubled date varieties** because some or all of the date digits were punched into each working die by hand. In 1878, the **entire date** was in the **working hubs and dies**. So doubled date digits only happened in 1878 if other portions of the working die were also die doubled during the hubbing operations. This is a rarer occurrence than doubled date digits when they were punched into the working die by hand.

1878 S Obverse and Reverse

SOME 1878 S HIGHLIGHTS

Touched-up Engraved Wing Feather

The added **engraved wing feather** between the eagle's right wing lower portion and leg is a **significant** die feature on many of the 1878 S reverse dies. As previously mentioned, the basining and polishing steps on the working dies removed some shallow wing feathers in this area. This was a defect in the 7 TF B design type with parallel arrow feathers that was corrected in the 7 TF C reverse design type with the slanted arrow feathers. The San Francisco Mint workman touched up this over polished area by engraving a wing feather in this area on 37 working dies. (The five known 1879 S engraved wing feather dies were likely engraved in 1878.) The Philadelphia Mint also engraved somewhat smaller and fainter feather in this same area on eight 1878 P 7 TF B type dies, and also small feathers were added between the lower wings and legs on sixteen 8 tail feathers reverse dies. The San Francisco Mint also performed touch-up engraving on the wreath leaves on some 1879- 1882 S reverse dies The San Francisco Mint is the only **branch mint** that performed touch-up engraving on working dies.

Another engraving feature of the 1878 S reverse dies is the touch-up engraving between the eagle's right wing and body where a flat long gap occurred from the over polishing of the die. There are 13 known cases of this unique engraving to strengthen this wing and body gap. These were extensions of the engraved wing feather between the lower wing and leg and generally are connected with continuous engraving. Many of these wing and leg--body engravings extend almost the entire length of the eagle's inner wing making them the **longest** known engraved areas of the Morgan working dies.

The Philadelphia Mint also had difficulties with this lower wing feather being polished away. But for the most part, the 7 TF dies used at the Philadelphia Mint were not touched up by engraving a feather back into the working dies. Only eight 1878 P die varieties with an engraved wing feather for the 7 TF design are known, including seven at the wing-leg with four of these also with engraved bars at wing-body and one with only engraving at wing-body. This compares to 37 dies with engraved wing-leg for the 1878 S. The Philadelphia Mint did add small feathers at the lower part of the eagle's left and right wings for 16 of the 8 TF design working dies.

Some of the 1878 S altered wing-leg gap are quite **spectacular** with either very smooth or rough surfaces with raised dots of VAM s 49, 50, 76 & 81. These four special die varieties have been designated as **"Funky Feathers"** and were acid treated as discussed in a later section. A typical **smooth engraved feather** at the wing-leg junction is shown for **VAM 8** in Figure 1. **VAM 64** shown in Figure 2 has very **unusual** series of **horizontal engraved lines** across the usual engraved wing feather area.

Because of the many very similar looking engraved areas, it is often time consuming and tedious to attribute these engraved wing feather varieties. This Guide points out other features to look for that are helpful in die identification. Large photographs of each engraved wing feather are grouped together for easy comparison in the Die Attribution section. Also, procedures are given in this Die Attribution section to narrow down the possible varieties to consider.

Touched-up Engraving on Wings

A **unique** feature of the 1878 S varieties is **touch-up engraving** on the **middle** of the eagle's wings and even the **tail feathers** above the olive branch. Excessive die basining and polishing of the B type reverse dies often left missing or weak wing feathers in the middle of the eagle's wings and near the eagle's body on the eagle's left wing. The Philadelphia Mint also experienced trouble with over polished feathers in the same middle wing areas but never added feathers back by touch-up engraving of the working dies.

The San Francisco Mint was **unique** in it's efforts to salvage and repair the working dies by **touch-up engraving** of the **middle** of the wings. It was only done in 1878 on the B reverse design type working dies and not on the later years C reverse design type dies. VAMs 6, 8, 18, 64/110, 45/68 and 105 are the six examples of attempts to fill in missing wing feathers in the middle of the wings by

Figure 1 VAM 8 Engraved Wing Feather

Figure 2 VAM 64 Engraved Wing Feather
With Lines

Figure 3 VAM 6 Engraved Wing Middle

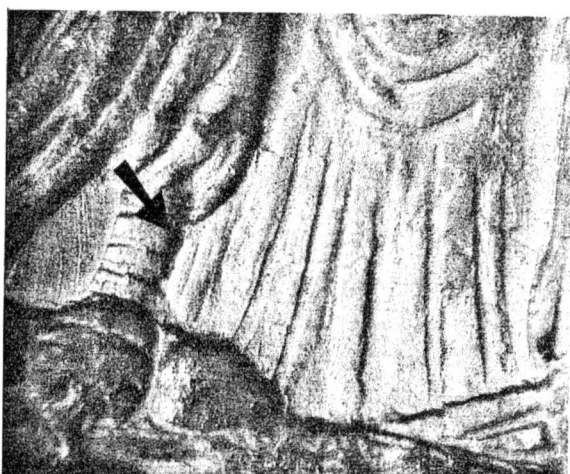
Figure 4 VAM 45/68 Two Engraved Upper TF

Figure 5 VAM 64/110 Engraved 8th Upper TF

Figure 5 VAM 64/110 Engraved 8th Upper TF

Figure 6 VAM 49 Smooth Acid Treated Feather

touch-up engraving. An example of touch-up engraving on the middle of the wing is shown in Figure 3 for **VAM 6.**

Engraved 8 & 9 Upper Tail Feathers

The die basining and polishing of the B^2 type revere dies often resulted in shallow or missing portions of the lower ends of the **left side of the upper tail feathers.** This also occasionally happened on the later C type reverse dies. The first report of the San Francisco Mint engraving on some of these left upper tail feathers was in mid-May 2010 for an 1879 S VAM 74 of C type reverse. Two of the left upper tail feathers had engraving to **strengthen** the weak vertical feathers there.

In late May 2010, **two added engraved far left upper tail feathers** on the B^2 type reverse was reported for the reverse die used for the 1878 S **VAMs 45 & 68** and the later 1879 S VAMs 9 and a new VAM 77. This engraving resulted in **nine upper tail feathers** instead of the normal seven as shown in Figure 4. The reverse die was later polished in 1879 that eliminated the far left engraved feather and weakened the one engraved next to it. The two extra upper tail feathers that were added to the normally blank area was likely done by the San Francisco Mint workman who mistakenly thought it was an over polished area.

An added **eighth engraved vertical feather** on the **left side of the upper tail feather** was reported in June 2011 for the 1878 S **VAM 64 & 110** reverse die as shown in Figure 5. Again, a vertical bar was engraved in the normally blank area of the die to make eight upper tail feathers. No other mint engraved extra feathers in the upper tail feathers. That is a **unique die alteration** by the San Francisco Mint!

Acid Treated Dies

It was reported in September 2010 that an 1879 S obverse die with over polished lower hair had subsequently possibly been treated with acid like an 1878 S VAM 76 "Funky Feather". This was confirmed and all the four 1878 S "Funky Feather" reverse dies of **VAMs 49, 50, 76 & 81** are now understood to have been **treated with acid** at the eagle's right wing lower wing-leg gap. They typically have **flat raised smooth surfaces** with **sharp ragged edges** and **sometimes tiny raised dots.** Normal die polishing and engraving didn't leave well defined raised areas with sharp edges.

Both **nitric acid** and **sulfuric acid** was used to refine bullion at the San Francisco Mint for many years, including 1878- 1882. Apparently the San Francisco Mint workers experimented with the two acid types with varying strengths and duration of application in **unique** attempts to **fill in over polished areas** of the working dies. An example of a **smooth** acid treated wing-leg area is shown for **VAM 49** "Funky Feather" in Figure 6. **VAM 49** is a **special unique case** of a reverse die without touch-up engraving or acid treatment being used to strike coins as VAM 103 Die Combo 3 and then polished and acid treated as VAM 49 to strike more coins. An example of **raised dots and ragged edges** is shown for **VAM 81** "Funky Feather" in Figure 7. Acid was also used extensively on the 1878 S **VAM 36** in the middle of the wings and upper tail feathers as shown in Figure 8. It has the **most touch-up engraved and acid treatment** on the working die in the entire Morgan dollar series.

Acid treatment was used on one 1878 S obverse die, VAM 78, at the over polished lower hair edge plus two 1879 S obverse dies. Acid treatment was also used on 1878 S VAMs 48/84/91 and VAM 55 plus possibly on other reverse dies. In addition, acid treatment was used on a number of 1879 S to 1882 S C type reverse dies to strengthen over polished leaves of the left wreath. Using acid on dies in attempts to fill in over polished areas was **unique** to the San Francisco Mint and likely an **unauthorized** procedure on working dies.

Touched-up Engraving on Liberty Head Jaw Edge

A highly **unusual** case of engraving of the 1878 S obverse die is **VAM 29/31.** Fine lines were **scratched** into the bottom **edge** of the **jaw cavity** to remove die doubling on the jaw bottom as shown in Figure 9. This obverse die has strongly doubled eyelid, nostril and hair above the date. The engraving of the jaw edge extended the jaw line down in the middle and caused a **"sagging jaw"** appearance! It is the **only** known case of **engraving** on an **obverse working die** of the **1878 S.** The

Figure 7 VAM 81 Dots Acid Treated Feather

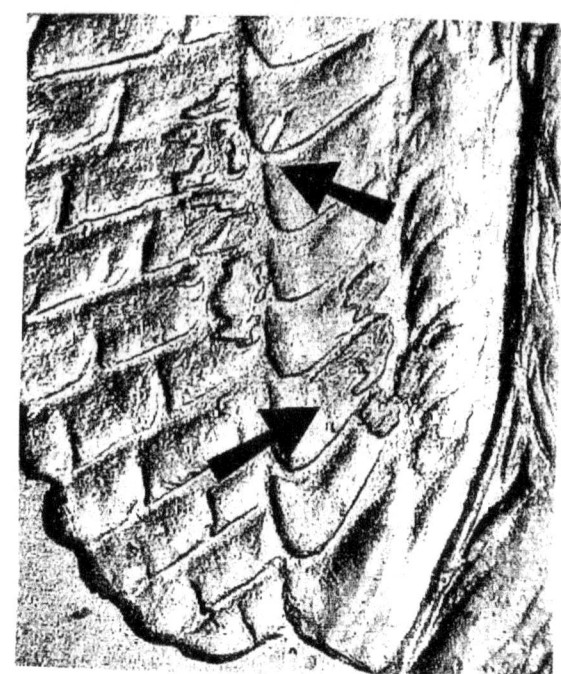

Figure 8 VAM 36 Acid Treated Wing

Figure 9 VAM 29/31 Engraved Sagging Jaw

Figure 10 VAM 1C Lightly Engraved Wing Feather

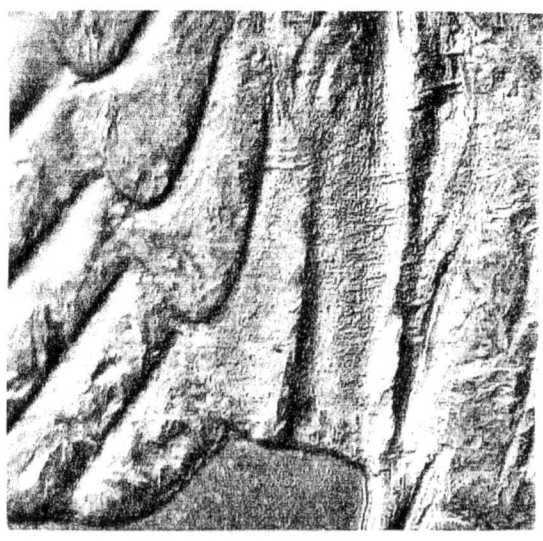

Figure 11 VAM 45 Engraved Wing Feather

Figure 12 VAM 17B Denticle Impressions Neck

1904 O VAM 41/44 with engraved jaw and neck was reported in 2009, the only other known case of engraving of an obverse die of the Morgan dollar series.

Use of 1878 S Reverse Working Dies in 1879

Another almost unique feature of the 1878 S is the use of 1878 S reverse working dies known to have struck 1878 S coins that were used later in 1879 for striking of coins with 1879 S obverse dies of VAMs 4/23/25 and 9/77. Two 1878 S reverse working dies have so far been identified that were used in 1879, the reverse dies of **VAMs 1C/95** (1879 S VAMs 4/23/25) and **VAMs 45/68** (1879 S VAMs 9/77). The engraved wing area is shown in Figure 10 of **VAM 1C** and in Figure 11 of **VAM 45**. The 1878 Proof die of the C reverse design type was used again in 1879 and 1880 to strike proofs. But no other Morgan dollar **reverse working dies** have yet been identified so far that were **used for more than one year** to strike coins.

Denticle Impressions

Denticle impressions have been reported on the Morgan dollar reverse dies where the **obverse denticle edges contacted** into the **reverse die fields**. This type of die variety with denticle impressions is known for a number of reverse dies from 1878 thru 1921 but **only one 1878 S die**. The **most spectacular denticle impressions** on the obverse and reverse dies is that of the **1878 S VAM 17A/B/C,** dubbed **King of Denticle Impressions**. The VAM 17B has **13 obverse and over 43 reverse denticle impressions** for the earliest denticle contact die state. The obverse has five denticle impressions at the Liberty head neck edge as shown in Figure 12 plus eight at the date. The reverse has 18 around OLL in DOLLAR, four below the tail feathers, 13 at STATES and eight at UNITED for the most denticle impressions, by far, of any Morgan dollar reverse die. In addition, this 1878 S variety is the **only** confirmed **denticle impressions** on a Morgan dollar **obverse die**. Some denticle impressions at LO are shown in Figure 13. The VAM 17A was the **first** identified reverse die with denticle impressions for the Morgan dollar series and was reported by John Roberts in December 2001. It remains the **strongest** denticle impressions variety in the Morgan dollar series.

Die Gouges

The 1878 S also has an unusually high number of heavy gouges on dies including VAMs 1D/73, 1E, 1I, 15/80/89, 16/28, 19, 38/90, 41, 63, 91A, 92 & 97. **VAM 19** shown in Figure 14 has a **very wide and long horizontal die gouge** in the form of a cap band across the wheat leaves, top cotton leaf and the upper part of the Phrygian cap. It is the **largest** and **most spectacular** die gouge of the 1878 S die gouges and of the entire Morgan dollar series. It is three times longer and also wider than the notorious 1890 CC VAM 4 Tail Bar die gouge or the 1921 S VAM 1B Thorn Head with die gouge in the top right of the Phrygian cap. The 1880 P VAM 1A1 has a little longer but narrower die break or gouge in the wreath bow and lower right wreath, but it is fairly well hidden there.

Doubled Dies

There are a few strong doubled dies for the 1878 S including VAMs 6, 10/65/100 & 11/22/77/111 with VAMs 6 and 22 listed as **Hot 50** varieties. But these take a back-seat to some spectacular doubled dies known for the 1878 P & CC. Figure 15 shows some strong die doubling on the letters UM of UNUM of **VAM 22**. This die has all of the motto letters, stars and date digits doubled. It should be noted that a weak strike can cause the doubling on letters to be weak or not visible. In many cases, where possible, die markers have been provided to confirm a given variety.

B¹ Reverse with Long Nock or Center Arrow Shaft

There are nine known varieties with **eight B¹ reverse design type reverse dies** with **long nock** or center arrow shaft for 1878 S. (An example long nock is shown in Figure 16 for **VAM 26**.) They are a **scarce** and **desirable Top 100** die variety with only a few known uncirculated specimens. The first 10 die pairs sent to the San Francisco Mint on April 16, 1878 were of the B¹ design type with the long center arrow or nock. Only four days later it was reported that eight reverse and three obverse dies were condemned by the San Francisco Mint. Fifteen more pairs of Morgan dollar dies arrived at the San Francisco Mint about April 25 or 26 with some of these undoubtedly being the B¹ reverse design type.

Figure 13 VAM 17B Denticle Impressions OLL

Figure 14 VAM 19 Cap Band Gouge

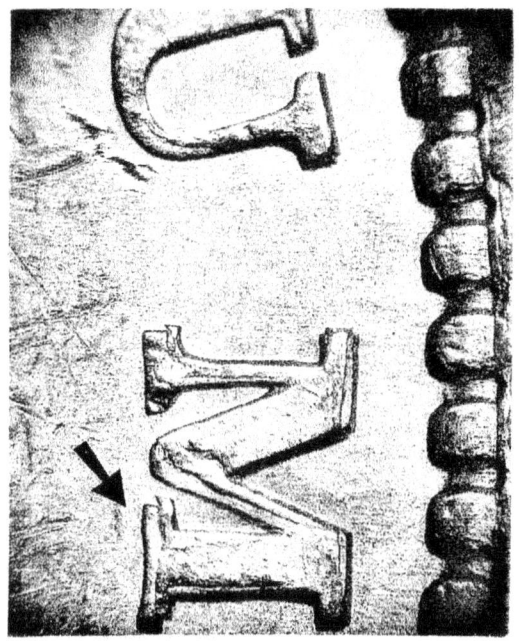

Figure 15 VAM 22 Doubled UM

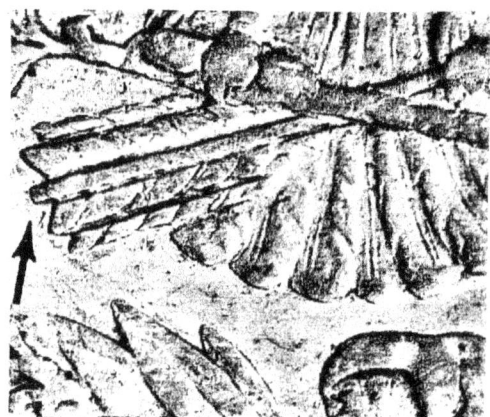

Figure 16 VAM 26 B¹ Long Nock

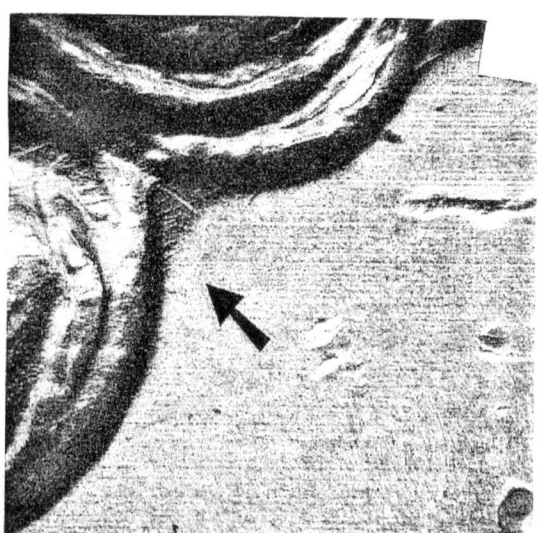

Figure 17 VAM 42A Clashed st

Apparently most of the first coins struck at the San Francisco Mint with the B¹ design type reverse were released into circulation.

The 1878 P has five known B¹ reverse design type die varieties. But they are not especially scarce and BU coins are readily available, since they were not the first Morgan dollars struck at the Philadelphia Mint in 1878. The 1878 CC has at least eight B¹ reverse design type die varieties but they are not as scarce as the B¹ type of the 1878 S and BU specimens are readily available. So the 1878 S with B¹ reverse with long nock has the distinction of being **scarce** in circulated condition and a true **rarity** in BU.

Clashed Dies

Strangely, there is **only one obverse die** reported with **clashed die letters** for the 1878 S, **VAM 33A/42A**, that share the same obverse die. This is compared to hundreds known for the Morgan dollar series. It has fairly weak clashed st at the lower right hair vee and no clashed n at the Liberty head neck. Likely the San Francisco Mint had different coining presses than the other mints that seldom had the die clashing together, as there are few clashed letters that have been reported for 1878 S- 1904 S. Figure 17 shows the clashed st of **1878 S VAM 33A/42A**.

Highlights Summary

In summary, the 1878 S has some very **unusual** and **unique** die varieties:
- 37 working dies with touched-up **engraved wing feather** between eagle's lower right wing and leg. 1878 P has eight 7 TF reverse dies with an engraved wing feather and sixteen 8 TF reverse dies with added small feathers between lower wings and legs.
- **Unique** engraving in the **middle** of the eagle's wings on seven working dies and **between** the eagle's right wing and body on 17 working dies.
- **Unique** case of a Morgan reverse die **VAM 103 Die Combo 3** used to strike coins without any touched-up engraving or acid treatment and then being polished and the acid treated wing feather added as **VAM 49** with Funky Feather, and used to strike coins again. **Only case** of acid treatment performed on a *used* die which was used again to strike coins!
- **Largest series** of **touched-up engraved and acid treated areas** on any Morgan working die of **VAM 36** with two acid treated areas on both wings, added engraved feather between wing and leg, acid treatment between eagle's right wing and body, plus added acid treated upper tail feathers.
- **Engraving** of **obverse working die** jaw cavity of **VAM 29/31** that resulted in "**Sagging Jaw**", the only case of engraving on an 1878 S obverse working die. The 1904 O VAM 41/44 is the only other reported engraving on obverse jaw/neck.
- Two 1878 S reverse working dies of **VAMs 1C/95 & 45/68** that were used again in 1879 to strike coins. These are currently the only known examples of **working dies used** to strike Morgan business coins in **two different years**.
- Most **spectacular** case and largest number of **denticle impressions**, 43, on a Morgan dollar reverse die **VAM 17B**, with **unique** denticle impressions also on obverse die of 13.
- **Longest** and **widest**, most **spectacular die gouge** on any Morgan dollar obverse die that is in the Phrygian cap of **VAM 19**.
- **B¹ reverse** design type with **long nock** or center arrow shaft that is much **scarcer** than 1878 P or CC with B¹ reverse. Very rare in BU and scarce in circulated.
- **Two engraved extra** vertical feathers in left side of upper tail feathers for **9 total** on reverse die of **VAMs 45 & 68** that was later used in 1879 S for VAMs 9 & 77 & **one extra** engraved for **8 total** on 1878 S VAMs 64/110. Engraving on upper tail feathers was **unique** for San Francisco Mint.
- **Unique** use of **acid** to strengthen over polished wing feathers of so-called Funky Feathers for **VAMs 49, 50, 76 & 81**. Acid also used extensively on **VAM 36** middle of both wings and

upper tail feathers. Two other 1878 S reverse dies were acid treated on the eagle's feathers and possibly other reverse dies. The lower obverse hair of 1878 S **VAM 78** was acid treated as was two obverse dies of 1879 S. A number of C type reverse dies were acid treated to strengthen some leaves in the left wreath for 1879 S- 1882 S.

● There is only **one weak clashed die letter st** reported for 1878 S, **VAM 33A/42A** and very few reported for 1878 S- 1904 S.

ENGRAVING OF EAGLE'S WINGS & LIBERTY HEAD

David DeRuiter sent some 1878 S Morgan dollars for examination in November 1979 pointing out that the ends of the eagle's bottom right wing feathers next to the leg were different. He stated that many of them had been **re-touched** on the working die. He had also seen similar re-touching of the 1879 S with the B^2 parallel arrow feather reverses. Examination of the coins confirmed that many of the 1878 S reverse working dies had been **engraved** at the San Francisco branch Mint, a very **unorthodox** branch mint procedure.

Trouble with the Dies

The Philadelphia Mint prepared the Morgan dollar design and manufactured all of the Morgan dollar working dies for the branch mints. The only work that the branch mints were suppose to do on the working dies was to basin and polish the die face to enable various types of coining presses used to properly strike-up the design. Basining of the die face was performed by placing the die face against a rotating disk that had the desired radius of curvature. Polishing grit and compound mixed with water or oil on the basining disc gave a slight curvature and polish to the die face.

The eagle's wing center and the feathers between the eagle's right wing and leg would not basin properly for the B^2 reverse dies with **parallel** arrow feathers and **flat** eagle's breast. Engraver George Morgan had indicated this trouble in his letter to the Director of the Mint, Dr. Henry R. Linderman on April 17, 1878:

...The reverse dies now fill up quickly while striking the coin. I am finishing this hub so that I believe this filling will be avoided.

I noticed that some places in both dies are apt to get rubbed too low in the polishing....

The Philadelphia and Carson City Mints used these B^2 reverse dies with the weak or missing feathers between the eagle's right wing and leg. There are eight dies for the 1878 P that has some weak engraving between the eagle's right wing and leg or body. The San Francisco Mint used some B^2 working dies in 1878 with weak or missing feather details. However, there are currently known 37 dies of the 1878 S (plus four acid treated dies) and five 1879 S B^2 reverse '78 dies that were engraved to touch-up and add or strengthen the feather between the eagle's right wing and leg to give the appearance of complete feather(s).

Since each of these dies was **individually** engraved by **hand** using engraving tools, these touched-up dies each have a **unique** raised feather design in that area. This created a whole series of die varieties unique to the 1878 S and 1879 S (Dies left over from 1878 and likely engraved in 1878.). They are not different design types, but rather, special touched-up engraving of individual working dies of the B^2 design type.

The San Francisco Mint had **trouble** with these early B reverse design dies. The first Morgan dollars were struck at the San Francisco Mint on April 17, 1878. After nearly one thousand coins were first struck on April 17, the die cracked and the press was stopped. In a letter from the Director of the Mint, Linderman, to the Superintendent of the Philadelphia Mint, James Pollock, on April 20, 1878, Linderman reported:

Supt. Dodge telegraphs the 8 reverse and 3 obverse new silver dollar dies have been condemned...

...It will be necessary for the Engraver to get ready as soon as possible another lot of silver dollar dies for shipment to S.F.

Thus, the San Francisco Mint experienced difficulties with the dies early in the striking of the Morgan dollars and took **extraordinary** measures to **salvage** many of the dies by performing touch-up engraving on them.

Engraving Tools

It isn't known exactly which San Francisco Mint workman performed the touch-up engraving on the working dies or exactly what kind of tools were used. It's likely that several different workman touched-up the dies at different times in 1878 because of the staggered shipment of dies to that facility throughout 1878 and the various kinds of engraving appearances. They range from crude lines and rough surfaces to very smooth surfaces that blend into the surrounding feathers. This is likely due to the differences in the workman's skills and tools used.

During the late 1970s, the author visited the Philadelphia Mint and toured the Engraving Department and the Die Manufacturing Division. The tools and procedures used for touching up the dies in the 1970s are likely similar to those used in 1878 at the San Francisco Mint for touch-up engraving of the die wing feathers.

In the Engraving Department, in the late 1970s, the coin design on a large copper plated plaster model, or Galvano, was reduced using a three-dimensional pantograph to the final coin size on the face of a steel cylinder hub. The design on the coin size hub had to be touched up with engraving tools to eliminate the cutting tool lines and to sharpen the design features. The engraver used a variety of engraving tools including a honing stick, Sulphur bonded stick and abrasive stick. Abrasive paper and polishing cloths were used to smooth the field areas. All engraving tools, cloths and papers were dipped in oil to aid in the sanding and polishing process. Small, narrow strips of various grades of sanding paper and cloth were placed on the end of a small stick to sand and polish small areas. Figure 18 shows some of the engraving tools used in the Engraving Department in the 1970s.

The dies were inspected and touched up in two separate steps in the Die Manufacturing Division in the 1970s. The first inspection was before the dies were hardened as shown in Figure 19. A three-power magnifying glass was used to check for imperfections and some were corrected by the inspector through hand touch-up. Burnishing tools, hardened steel, 500 grade paper and Arkansas stones were used as shown in Figure 20.

A final inspection was made of the dies in the 1970s after they were hardened and received the final machining, as shown in Figure 21. A ten power stereo microscope was used for the inspection. India and Arkansas abrasive stones were used to touch-up defects in the hardened dies. Areas were smoothed up using 500 grade paper on flat rubbing blocks.

The Morgan dollar working dies received by the San Francisco Mint in 1878 were already hardened. The over polished feather between the eagle's right wing and leg had to be made deeper on the die. A ten power microscope was likely used to view the small elongated area. Abrasive stone, such as India and Arkansas, had to be used on the hardened steel to remove much of the metal to form a feather cavity. Hardened steel chisels and pointed tools were likely used to touch-up the blunt feather end and other areas. Abrasive paper and polishing cloths on the end of a stick could have been used to smooth out the engraved area.

Examples of Wing Die Engraving

The **normal** appearing area between the eagle's **right wing and leg** is shown in Figure 22. The wing feather next to the leg is weak but still raised on the coin. An example **over polished** wing next to the leg and eagle's body is shown in Figure 23 for VAM 22. There is a long, flat area at the same level as the field where there should be a raised feather. The working die is a flipped or reversed cavity of this feather area. Figure 24 shows a **simulated die** photograph of this area from the flipped and negative photograph of VAM 22 over polished wing. This is the area that the San Francisco Mint workman touched up and had to remove metal to form a feather.

Nice **smooth** examples of an engraved wing feather is shown of VAM 38 in Figure 25 and VAM 47 in Figure 26. The added feather blends into the normal design feathers smoothly, it's top is relatively smooth and it has a well defined end. There are many examples of carefully engraved feathers for the 1878 S, but each one has a slightly different appearance because they were done by hand. A somewhat rough engraved feather with vertical lines is shown for VAM 69 in Figure 27.

There are also four examples of **crudely** looking **acid treated feathers** designated as "**Funky Feathers**"which may have been done by a different workman and are discussed in a separate section. Figure 28 shows a raised engraved wing feather of VAM 64 that has numerous **horizontal lines scratched** across this area. It isn't known why such **obvious** scratch lines would be placed there!

Figure 18 Engraving Tools for
Galvano Touch-up, 1970 s

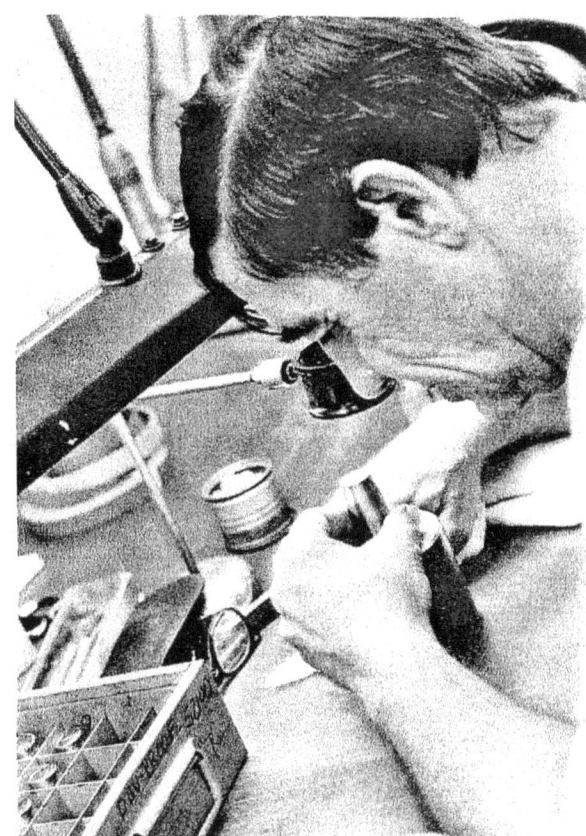

Figure 19 Initial Inspection of Dies, 1970 s

Figure 20 Die Touch-up Tools, 1970 s

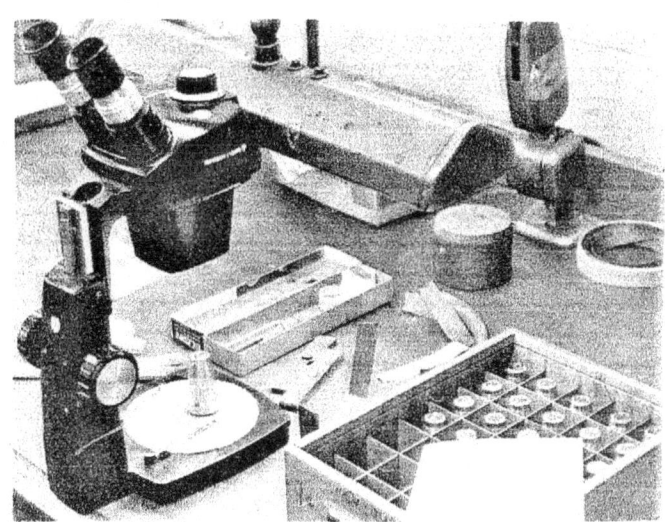

Figure 21 Die Inspection Station,
with Box of Dies, 1970 s

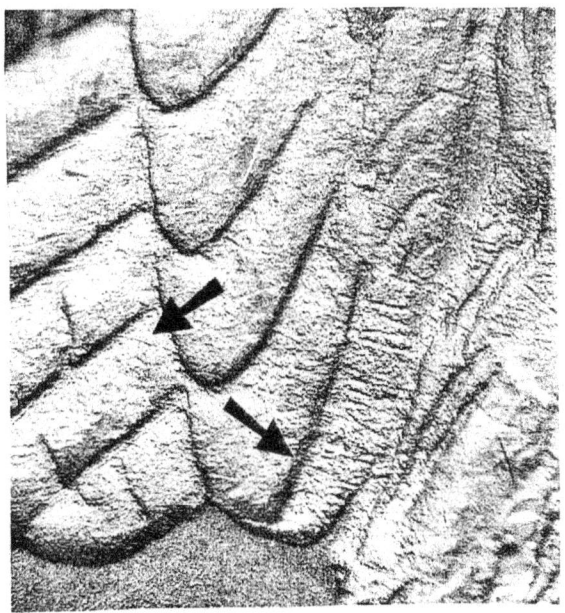

Figure 22 VAM 109 Normal B^{2}a Reverse

Figure 23 VAM 22 Over Polished Wing

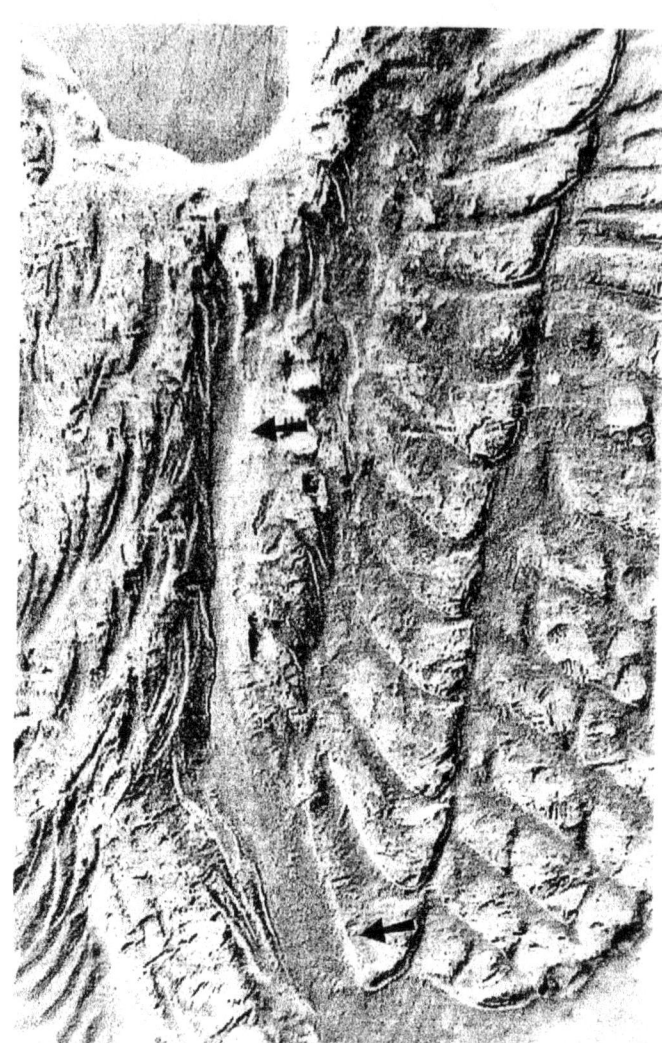

Figure 24 VAM 22 Over Polished Wing
Simulated Die

Figure 25 VAM 38 Smooth Engraved Wing Feather

Figure 26 VAM 47 Smooth Engraved Wing Feather

Figure 27 VAM 69 Engraved Wing Feather
With Lines

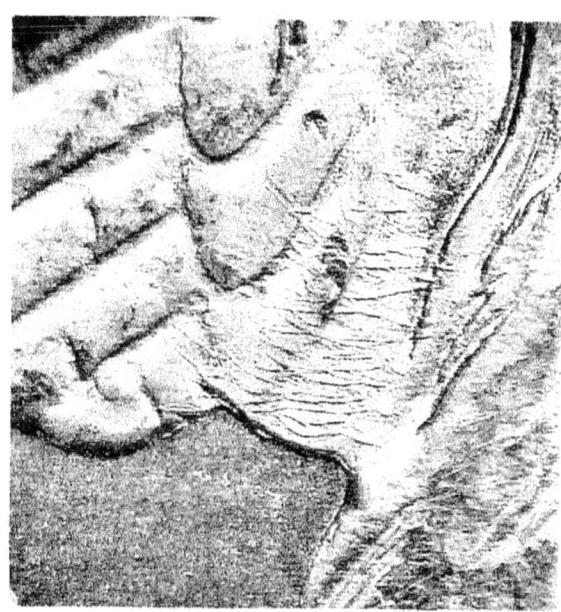

Figure 28 VAM 64 Engraved Wing Feather with Lines

Figure 30 VAM 93 Double Engraved Vertical Bars

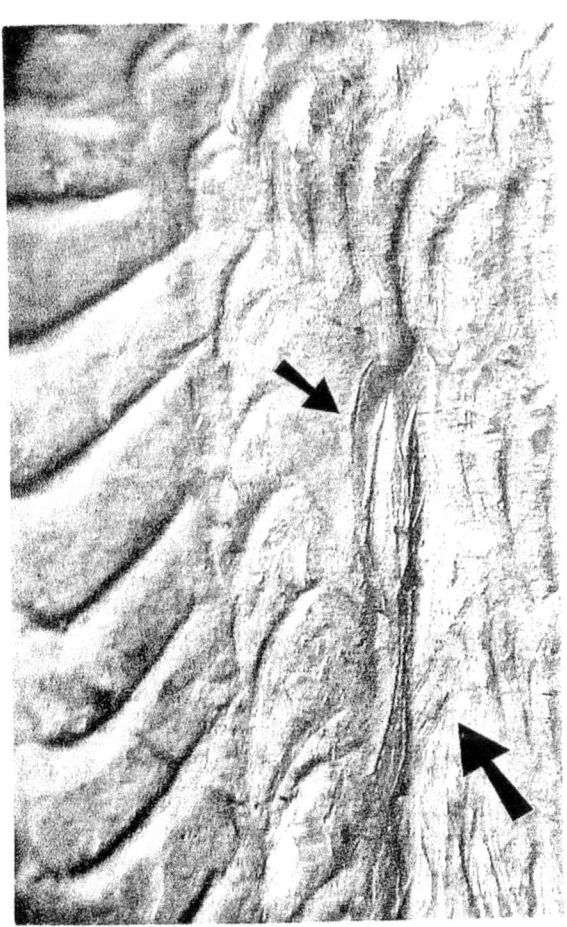

Figure 29 VAM 21 Engraving Lines, Wing-Body, Gouge

Figure 31 VAM 101 Over Polished Middle
Wing Feathers

These broad and long engraved wing feathers are unique to the 1878 S and some 1879 S reverse of '78 dies. **Thirty-seven** different 1878 S engraved wing feather dies have been identified. There are also known **five** different dies with the engraved wing feather for the 1879 S reverse of '78. One 1879 S Rev '78, VAM 9/77, has the same 1878 S reverse die of VAM 45/68 and the another 1879 S Rev '78 is VAM 4/23/25 with same reverse die as 1878 S VAM 1C/95. These 1879 S Rev '78 with engraved wing feather were likely engraved in 1878 and were left over reverse dies that were used the next year in 1879.

The Philadelphia Mint added **tiny short** feather points to the inside bottom of the eagle's wings on 16 of the 8 tail feather dies of 1878 because of the weak feather detail from die polishing. The Philadelphia Mint engraved some small vertical bars between the eagle's right wing and leg plus body where the wing feathers were weak on eight 1878 7 tail feather B^2 type dies, but these weren't the long broad feather of the 1878 S engraved type.

Some 1878 S show engraving touch-up between the **eagle's right wing and body** to strengthen the feather detail that had been over polished, as was shown for VAM 22 in Figure 24. An example of **engraved lines** in this **wing-body** narrow area is shown in Figure 29 for VAM 21 and an example of double engraved vertical bars is shown in Figure 30 for VAM 93. There are **13** currently known 1878 S dies with engraving between the eagle's right wing and body of VAMs 6/44, 8/85, 9, 19/35/74/93, 21, 23/37, 29, 31, 38/90, 39, 40, 52/79 & 53.

The **center** of the eagle's wings occasionally had over polished and missing feathers as shown for VAM 101 in Figure 31. There are **six** 1878 S dies with touch-up engraving in the middle of the eagle's wing of VAMs 6, 8, 18, 45/68, 64/110 &105. An example of engraved bars in the middle of the eagle's wing is shown for VAM 6 in Figure 32. An extreme example of **crude lines** in the middle of both wings is shown in Figures 33 & 34 for VAM 18. Smooth engraved bars in the middle of the wings are also shown in Figure 35 for VAM 105.

Engraved Liberty Head Jaw

In July of 2003, George Delfico reported an 1878 S Morgan dollar with a very unusual appearing jaw line which he called "**Sagging Jaw**". It had a fairly obvious more rounded bottom line to the jaw and was determined to be the VAM 29/31 obverse die variety as shown in Figure 36. Since the Delfico specimen was a lightly circulated VAM 31 variety, it was thought at that time that the more rounded jaw line was caused by a form of die doubling since the nostril and eyelid were strongly doubled.

It was not until May, 2006, when the authors examined an early die state uncirculated VAM 29 obverse, that it was discovered that the lower jaw and edge had many die file or scratch lines. This was a case of the San Francisco Mint performing fairly crude engraving on the jaw edge cavity to presumably remove some obvious die doubling there. It resulted in a somewhat distorted jaw line that extended down more in the middle than normal. This is a highly **unusual** case of the Morgan dollar **obverse working die** that had been **engraved**– and it was performed at a branch mint! The only other known case of engraving on the obverse is the 1904 O VAM 41/44 with engraving lines on the jaw and neck reported in 2009.

Figure 33 VAM 18 Engraved Lines in Wing

Figure 34 VAM 18 Engraved Lines in Wing

Figure 32 VAM 6 Engraved Wing Middle

Figure 35 VAM 105 Engraved Wing Middle

Figure 36 VAM 29/31 Engraved Lines Jaw

ENGRAVED 8 & 9 UPPER TAIL FEATHERS

Another chapter to the San Francisco Mint performing touch-up engraving on the 1878 S and 1879 S reverse dies has recently been reported. This is the **engraving** of **added** or **strengthened** feathers at the left side of the **eagle's upper tail feathers**. The touch-up engraving of feathers on the eagle's wing-leg junction on the B^2 type reverse dies has been known since 1979 and the added feathers at the wing bottom of the 1878 P 8 TF die varieties has been known since the early 1960's. But it has only recently been reported in May 2010 and July 2011 that an 8th and 9th upper tail feathers had been added to one 1878 S reverse die that was later used for 1879 S and a second 1878 S die had an added 8th upper tail feather. It was also reported in May 2010 that an 1879 S with a C type design reverse of 1879 had engraving to strengthen the two left upper tail feathers.

Parts of the eagle's feathers were frequently removed on the B^2 type reverse when the working dies were basined and polished at the Philadelphia, Carson City and San Francisco Mints in 1878 and also the latter mint for some B^2 dies used in 1879. The lower feathers of the eagle's right wing next to the leg and middle of the wing became weak or missing altogether. This area was touched-up by engraving back a feather there on some Philadelphia Mint working dies and many San Francisco working dies as discussed in a separate section of **Engraving of Eagle's Wings & Liberty Head**.

In addition, the **far left upper tail feathers** would frequently become **very shallow** or with lower portions of the **left feather missing**. The full upper tail feathers is shown in Figure 37 for **VAM 111** and a typical over polished upper and lower tail feathers is shown in Figure 38 for **VAM 105**. The Philadelphia and Carson City Mints didn't engrave on these B^2 reverse design upper tail feathers. But the San Francisco Mint engraved on the upper left tail feathers on two known 1878 B^2 type reverse dies and one 1879 C type reverse die. The **first reported engraved upper tail feather** was reported by Leroy Van Allen in mid-May 2010 from examination of a 1879 S new variety coin of Brian Raines that he stated had strong polishing lines between legs in tail feathers. It was a C type reverse designated a VAM 74 with strengthened far left two upper tail feathers. The other known engraved upper tail feathers are on B^2 reverse type for 1878 S dies.

Added 8th & 9th Engraved Upper Tail Feathers

In late May 2010, some 1879 S Rev '78 coins of David Mitchell were forwarded for examination that were thought to be a new die combination. They were indeed found to be a new die combination of VAM 77 with obverse die of VAM 34B and reverse die of VAM 9. Although not mentioned by Mitchell, it was discovered by Leroy Van Allen that there were **two added engraved vertical feathers** at the far left on the upper tail feathers to make a total of **nine upper tail feathers**. One of the coins had the reverse die polished removing the extreme left engraved vertical feather and the engraved one next to it was made thin and shallow for **eight upper tail feathers** designated VAM 77A.

The reverse die of 1879 S Rev '78 VAM 9 and 77 with 9 upper tail feathers was first used for 1878 S as **VAMs 45 & 68**. These die varieties have the full 9 upper tail feathers with the two added engraved feathers at the left side as shown in Figure 39 for the 1879 S VAM 9. The die was later polished in 1879. Why these two vertical extra feathers were engraved in the normally far left blank area of the upper tail feathers is a mystery. Perhaps the San Francisco Mint workman mistakenly thought this was an over polished area on the die. The touched-up engraved reverse die was used in combination with two 1878 obverse dies and two 1879 obverse dies. An **unusual** case of only the San Francisco Mint engraving on the upper tail feathers!

Added 8th Engraved Upper Tail Feather

It was late June 2011 that Brent Fogelberg sent for examination an 1878 S that John Roberts had stated was a new obverse die combined with the engraved wing feather of VAM 64 reverse die. Upon examination, it was discovered by Leroy Van Allen and not mentioned by Roberts or Fogelberg that there was a long vertical bar of an 8th engraved feather at the extreme left of the upper tail feathers. It was similar to the recently discovered 8 and 9 upper tail feathers of VAMs 45 & 68. This new **VAM**

110 reverse die has a total of **8 upper tail feathers** as shown in Figure 40. The reverse die is shared with VAM 64 with different obverse die that has an engraved wing feather with **unusual horizontal engraved lines** on it on the eagle's right wing next to the leg. This die also has smooth engraved feathers in the middle of the eagle's left wing and engraving lines in the middle of the eagle's right wing. Quite an **amazing** 1878 S engraved reverse die by the San Francisco Mint.

Note: Touch-up engraving has been reported on the left wreath over polished leaves opposite ON, U & IT for the C type revere dies for 1879 S VAMs, 29, 81, 82 & 83. Many left wreaths were likely touched up for 1879 S- 1882 S reverse dies.

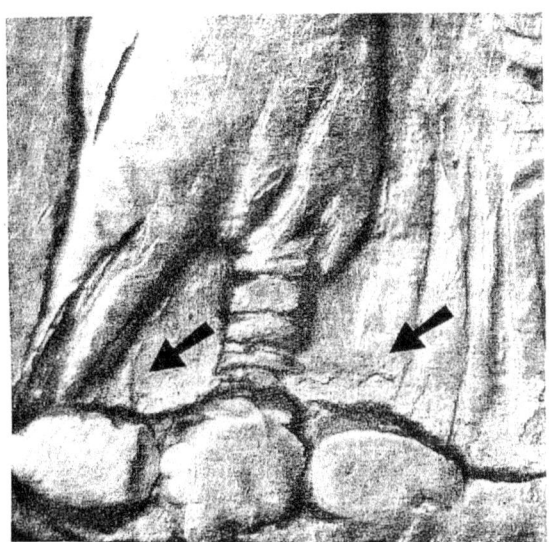

Figure 37 VAM 111 Full Upper Tail Feathers

Figure 38 VAM 105 Over Polished Upper & Lower TF

Figure 39 VAM 45/68 (1879 S Rev 78 VAM 9) Two Engraved TF

Figure 40 VAM 64/110 Engraved 8th Upper TF

ACID TREATED DIES

Another chapter has recently been added to the **modification** of the 1878 S- 1882 S Morgan dollar obverse and reverse dies by the San Francisco Mint. New findings reported in 2010- 2012 and re-examination of some features of the 1878 S, 1879 S, 1880 S, 1881 S and 1882 S coins has confirmed the **astonishing practice** that **acid etching** was used in an attempt to fill in over polished areas on some of the obverse and reverse dies of these years. This **unique** practice was used **only by the San Francisco Mint** for those five years, and possibly other years yet to be reported. Acid was not used on dies at the other mints that struck the Morgan dollars.

A New Practice at San Francisco Mint

The addition of an engraved feather between the eagle's right wing and leg was reported way back in November 1979 by David DeRuiter. Some of these modified dies had different and strange smooth or dotted surfaces with four were dubbed **"Funky Feathers"**. The earliest of these were VAM 49 reported by Pete Bishal in July 1981 and VAM 50 reported by Martin Field in August 1981. It had long puzzled the author why or how these odd and crude looking engraved feathers were made compared to other smooth normal-like looking engraved feathers made with traditional engraving tools of burnishing sticks, Arkansas stones and abrasive paper. It is now known that **acid** was used to treat these strange looking added feathers.

In early September 2010, Brian Raines sent an 1879 S with the comment, *"...lower hair severely polished like V34b, but filled back in, possibly with acid (like 1878 S V76)...."*. It was confirmed that the smooth slightly raised areas in gaps in the lower hair looked like acid treated to fill in the hair gaps. It was listed as a new variety **VAM 1E** as shown in Figure 41. The **key to identifying** acid treated areas is the **flat raised smooth surface** with **sharp ragged edges** and sometimes **tiny raised dots**. Normal die polishing doesn't leave well defined raised areas with sharp edges. An acid drop applied to a small area would interact with the steel alloy and dissolve a layer.

A similar acid treated over polished lower hair obverse is shown in Figure 42 for the **1878 S VAM 78 Die 1.** Hank Habenicht had sent the coin in August 2010 with the comment, *"Thin flange of metal around Liberty's profile. Edge of flange is ragged like a torn sheet of paper."* At the time, it was thought the thin layer with ragged edge below the lower hair was from over polishing of the die. But a round dot is below the designer's initial M and very flat areas with sharp edges in the two adjacent hair gaps meets the criteria for acid treated die.

In May 2011 William Green sent an 1879 S with C type reverse that John Roberts had commented, *"Several leaves in left wreath have odd surfaces that suggest acid etching of die to fill weakened details from polishing similar to VAM 16A."* The leaves in the four top clusters of the left wreath die indeed have flat smooth areas with ragged edges of acid treatment as shown in Figure 43. It is a new **VAM 78** variety with the same obverse die as VAMs 50 & 68, but a different reverse die. The wreath leaves is a **new reported location for acid treatment** of dies. A number of other obverse and reverse dies of 1878 S- 1882 S have since been identified as being acid treated. Additional acid treated dies are likely to be reported.

Type of Acid

What kind of acid may have been used on the dies? The San Francisco Mint refined bullion for many years, including 1878- 1882. **Nitric acid** was used to extract and refine the silver from the gold and silver granulations made from the bullion deposited at the mints. Nitric acid dissolved the silver in the bullion as chloride of silver and **sulfuric acid** was used to aid the reduction of the chloride by zinc to extract the pure silver. (*Hutchings California Magazine*, October 1856, "Coining Money, at the San Francisco Mint", and *Report of the Director of the Mint*, 1896 pg 135.)

It is not known whether nitric or sulfuric acids available to the mint workers were used on the dies. Various strengths of the acid would react differently with the steel die surface. The mint workers likely experimented with the two acid types with varying strengths and duration on the die face to produce the different results shown in the following section.

Figure 41 1879 S VAM 1E Acid Treated Hair Areas

Figure 42 VAM 78 Die 1 Acid Treated Hair Edges

Figure 43 1879 S VAM 78 Acid Treated Leaves,
2nd Lower Cluster

Figure 44 VAM 49 Smooth Acid Treated
Wing Feather

Figure 45 VAM 50 Rough Acid Treated Wing Feather

Figure 46 VAM 76 Smooth Acid Treated
Wing Feather

Besides the previously mentioned obverse dies of 1878 S VAM 78 Die 1 and 1879 S VAMs 1E with acid treated lower hair and VAM 78 with acid treated wreath leaves, the four known 1878 S **"Funky Feathers"** reverses of **VAMs 49, 50, 76 & 81** show flat areas with sharp edges at the eagle's right wing and leg gap that look like they were acid treated. The feather at this B^2 reverse type wing-leg junction was frequently made weak or even erased when the reverse dies were basined and polished. This over polished feather was engraved back with a feather of various shapes on 37 working dies plus four working dies with acid treatment.

Figure 44 shows the **smooth top** of the acid treated missing feather area of **VAM 49** with sharp, ragged and curvy edges. It is relatively shallow compared to the typical raised engraved feather and two layers are apparent. Engraving a wing with typical tools of burnishing sticks, Arkansas stone and abrasive paper would produce straighter edges. There are also some tiny raised dots below the smooth area which wouldn't have been made by the typical engraving tools, but rather by tiny drops of acid. VAM 49 also shows a long narrow smooth acid treated area at the wing-body junction above the acid treated lower feather.

The **VAM 49 "Funky Feather"** is **unique** because the reverse die was first used to strike coins before it had acid treated reverse as the VAM 103 Die Combo 3. It was then used to strike coins as VAM 49 after being polished and acid treated. It is the **only known case** of a **used die having a later acid treatment**.

An **unusual** looking acid treated feather area is shown for **VAM 50** in Figure 45. The area extends vertically up into the wing-body junction and has a flat surface with sharp ragged edges and **raised dots and splotches**. A smaller shallow raised area with sharp lower edge is below the larger flat raised area and must have been a first application of acid. The larger area with dots and splotches could have been made with a different acid type or concentration which caused more violent bubbling reaction on the steel die surface. It is not known whether nitric or sulfuric acid was used on a particular die or the concentration and length of time left to etch the steel surface.

Figure 46 shows acid treated wing-leg area for **VAM 76** that looks similar to VAM 49 with smooth flat surface with ragged edges. However, this die has unusual flat smooth acid treated areas in the middle of both wings and above the eagle's right talon as shown in Figures 47, 48 & 49. It was an attempt to fill up some flat over polished areas. These additional acid treated areas have the same general appearance as the wing-leg area.

The fourth **"Funky Feather"** acid treated wing leg area is shown in Figure 50 for **VAM 81**. This has the similar appearance of VAM 50 with a long flat area with ragged edges and raised dots and splotches on the surface.

Another acid treated 1878 S reverse die is the **VAM 36** as shown in Figures 51, 52, 53 & 54. The wing-leg junction has a normal engraved feather, but the middle of both wings have some smooth raised areas with sharp curvy edges plus a few small round raised dots typical of the acid treated surface. The upper tail feathers show **unusual** elongated **smooth top areas** with **sharp edges** and a few vertical fine lines where a sharp tool must have been used during the acid application. It is the **strongest example** of **acid treated upper tail feathers**.

The other 1878 S example of a weaker acid treated upper tail feathers is **VAM 48/84/91/91A** recently reported Brent Fogelberg in March 2012. He stated that *"Engraved feather/acid tx. On eagle's left wing/body area as well as the upper tail feathers. That is so strong it is what is driving me crazy."* Other areas noted to be acid treated upon examination were eagle's right wing-body junction, some lower tail feathers, upper arrow feather (as shown in Figure 55.) and middle of eagle's right wing. Quite and **extensive acid treated die,** although light.

Another acid treated 1878 S reverse die is **VAMs 55/75A** that share this same reverse with raised dots, bands and lines with rough edges in the middle of the over polished eagle's left wing as shown in Figure 56. Additional possible acid treated 1878 S reverse dies, judging from their photographs, include VAM 1B on lower tail feathers and wreath, 8A in middle of eagle's left wing,

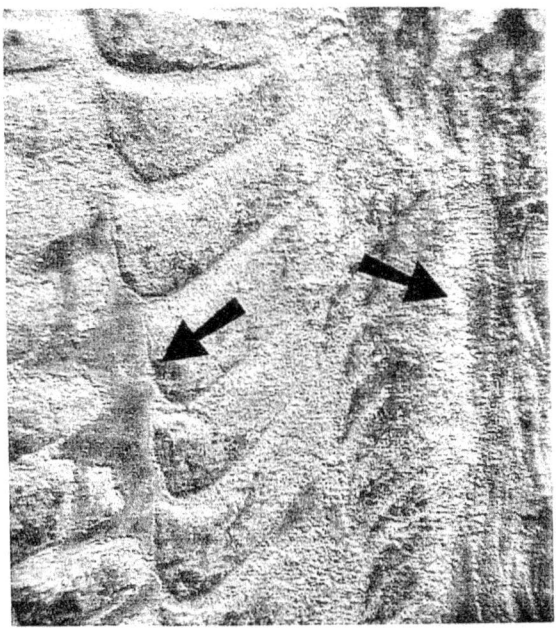

Figure 47 VAM 76 Acid Treated Wing Middle

Figure 48 VAM 76 Acid Treated Wing Middle

Figure 49 VAM 76 Acid Treated Leg

Figure 51 VAM 36 Acid Treated Wing Middle

Figure 50 VAM 81 Acid Treated Wing Feather

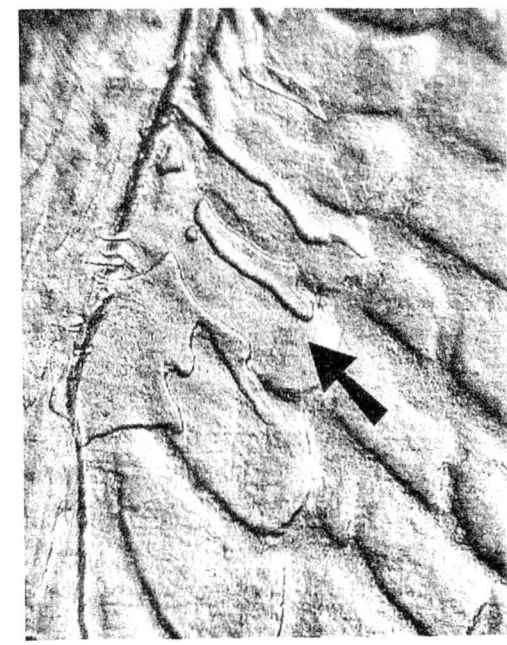

Figure 52 VAM 36 Acid Treated Wing Bottom

24/30/43 on eagle's right wing and 69/102 on engraved wing feathers.

The C type reverse frequently has over polished leaves in the left wreath opposite ON, U & IT. The San Francisco Mint used acid treatment on some 1879 S- 1882 S reverse dies in attempts to strengthen the weak leaves and also on the over polished lower obverse hair on 1879 S. Acid treated 1879 S obverse dies include VAMs 1E and 64 and acid treated 1879 S C type reverse dies include VAMs 45, 78 & 80. The 1880 S VAM 7 has acid treated leaves in both wreaths. The 1881 S VAM 76 has acid treated lower wreath leaves and bow to strengthen them. An 1882 S VAM 3 has acid treated wreath leaves and bow.

Summary

It is currently known that the San Francisco Mint used **nitric** and/or **sulfuric acid** on **two 1878 S obverse dies** and **seven reverse dies** in an attempts to fill in flat over polished areas on the die surface. Other acid treated dies include four more possible ones for 1878 S, and confirmed ones of five for 1879 S, one 1880 S, one 1881 S and one 1882 S. More are likely to be reported. It was of limited success because of ragged edges and smooth flat surface not typical of the over polished and missing hair edges or more rounded feathers. These **acid treated dies** are <u>amazing</u> examples of the San Francisco Mint applying un-authorized treatment on dies and are <u>unique</u> in the Morgan dollar series.

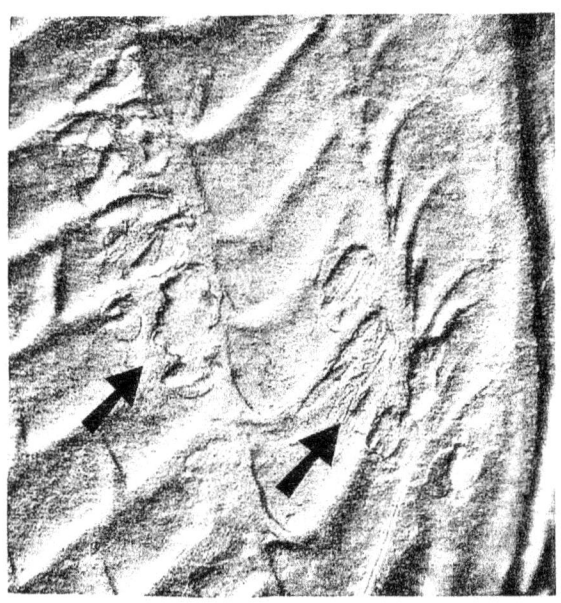

Figure 53 VAM 36 Acid Treated Wing Middle

Figure 54 VAM 36 Acid Treated Upper TF

Figure 55 VAM 84 Acid Treated
Upper Arrow Feather

Figure 56 VAM 55/75A Acid Treated Wing Middle

TOP 30 1878 S DIE VARIETIES

Some of the 1878 S die varieties are more interesting to collectors than others. To aid collectors in choosing these more interesting varieties, the authors have prepared a listing of what they consider to be the **Top 30** 1878 S die varieties. Of course collectors may have their own favorite 1878 S varieties and that is part of what makes the Morgan dollar series so fascinating, there are so many types and individual die varieties to collect!

The first obvious Top 30 die varieties are the earlier B[1] reverse with long nock or arrow shaft that are **Top 100** varieties listed in the 1997 book, *The Top 100 Morgan Dollar Varieties: The VAM Keys*, by Michael Fey and Jeff Oxman. These long nock varieties are very scarce in circulated grade and rare in BU and command large premium prices. There are eight presently known 1878 S B[1] reverse dies, VAMs 26, 27, 56/58 (shared reverse die), 57, 59, 60, 62 & 72.

The next obvious type of Top 30 die varieties are the **Hot 50** varieties listed in Jeff Oxman's 2000 book, *SSDC Official Guide to the Hot 50 Morgan Dollar Varieties*, of VAMs 6 and 11/22/77/111 with strongly doubled obverse motto letters. There are a few other **strongly doubled obverse** of VAMs 5 and 10/65/100. There are no comparable strongly doubled 1878 S reverse dies, only VAM 83 with doubled eagle's wing..

Another obvious type of 1878 S die variety that should be a Top 30 are the two known reverse dies that were also used to strike coins in 1879, VAMs 1C/95 and 45/68. So far, this is the only documented case of Morgan dollar **working dies striking coins** in **two different years**.

The 1878 S is the only case where a **branch mint engraver** touched up many Morgan dollar working dies. This was performed on 37 reverse dies to add back some feather detail that was removed on the B type dies during the basining and polishing steps. Four reverse dies were **acid treated** at the wing-leg junction, instead of engraving with very rough, long, odd looking feathers. These are termed "**Funky Feathers**", and VAMs 49, 50, 76 & 81 are included as Top 30.

There are also 1878 S dies with **engraved bars** and **lines** in the middle of the eagle's wings to add feathers back in areas made smooth by over basining and polishing. This is **unique** in the Morgan dollar series as the 1878 P dies didn't have any significant engraving in the middle of the eagle's wings. The Top 30 1878 S die varieties with engraved middle of the wings are VAMs 6, 8/85 and 18. The VAM 36 is an *amazing* case of **acid treatment** on the reverse die with patches in both wings and on the upper tail feathers. It also has an engraved wing feather next to the eagle's right leg plus between the eagle's right wing and body. It has the **most** touch-up acid treatment and engraving of a Morgan dollar die! VAM 8A engraved lines in the middle of the wing disappear with the **rusted die pits** in both eagle's wings and unusual dense **splotches** in the eagle's left wing of possible acid treatment.

Another **unusual** case of branch mint engraving is the VAM 29/31 obverse with **sagging jaw**. The die doubling on the jaw line edge was eliminated by engraving lines on the jaw edge cavity. This produced a bulge down on the middle of the jaw line making a distorted sagging jaw.

There are added two added **eighth and ninth engraved feathers** at the left side of the eagle's upper tail feathers of 1878 S VAMs 45/68 die that was later used in 1879 as VAMs 9/77. An added **eighth engraved feather** at the left side of the upper tail feathers is that for VAMs 64/110.

A spectacular case of **denticle impressions** on the reverse die from blows of the obverse die edge is VAM 17A, B, C. It has the **most** individual denticle impressions on the obverse and reverse dies of any known Morgan dollar and is included in the Top 30 for that reason.

A popular collector variety type is the **die gouges.** The 1878 S has more than its share of heavy, very visible die gouges. VAMs 1D/73, 15/80/89, 16/28, 19 and 41 are included in the Top 30 selection. VAM 19 is particularly outstanding and is the **largest** and **widest die gouge** known for the Morgan dollar obverse dies that forms a band in the Phrygian cap.

The Top 30 1878 S die varieties are each given a number of **Desirability Stars** from one to five, with five being the most desirable. The desirability number of stars is automatically five for the

Top 100 and Hot 50 varieties since they are widely collected with available price guides. The desirability stars for the other Top 30 1878 S die varieties is somewhat subjective. One of the factors is the **visibility** of the feature and how strong it is relative to other varieties of the same type for 1878 S and other Morgan dollar dates. A second factor is the **uniqueness** of the variety type that is only found on the 1878 S varieties. A third factor is the **rarity** of the variety. The rarity of many of the 1878 S varieties continues to be established with their increased wide-spread collecting.

The chart presented below lists the **Top 30 1878 S Die Varieties** in order of VAM variety number as selected by the authors. In some cases the obverse or reverse die is also found on another die combination variety as indicated by a second or third VAM number with a slash. Obverse or reverse die designations are included for each VAM number along with the main feature of each variety and the number of desirability stars assigned.

There are 20 VAM varieties with five desirability stars, five with four stars and five with three stars. The other 1878 S die varieties included in this guide have three or less desirability stars, except for VAMs 48/84/91 only recently assigned four stars. There are a large number of VAM varieties with five desirability stars, 20, because the eight **Top 100** B^1 long nock reverse varieties and the two **Hot 50** VAMs 6 and 22 doubled obverse die varieties. That only leaves ten other 1878 S varieties with five desirability stars which include four "**Funky Feathers**", one **denticle impression**, one cap band **die gouge**, one **acid treated middle** of eagle's wing, two **8 and 9 upper tail feathers** and one engraved obverse "**Sagging Jaw**"– not a large number with the spectacular nature of many 1878 S varieties.

TOP 30 1878 S DIE VARIETIES

VAM Variety #	Die Designations	Feature	Desirability
1C/95	II 1/II 40 • B^2a	Reverse die used in 1879	★★★★
1D/73	II 1/II 30 • B^2a	Heavy die gouges in tail feathers	★★★
5	II 4 • B^2i	Strongly doubled obverse	★★★★
6	II 5 • B^2j	Strongly doubled obverse (Hot 50)	★★★★★
8/8A/85	II 1/II 35 • B^2k	Lines middle of wings, rusted die	★★★★
10/65/100	II 8 • B^2b/B^2ap/B^2bd	Strongly doubled obverse	★★★
11/22/77/111	II 9 • B^2b/B^2g/B^2at/B^2a	Strongly doubled obverse (Hot 50)	★★★★★
15/80/89	II 11/II 32/II 38 • B^2n	Heavy die gouges in wing	★★★
16/28	II 12/II 1 • B^2o	Long die scratch in wing	★★★
17A,B,C	II 13 • B^2d	Denticle impressions on reverse	★★★★★
18, 18A	II 1 • B^2e	Lines in middle of wings	★★★★
19, 19A	II 14 • B^2w	Cap band die gouge	★★★★★
26	II 23 • B^1a	Long nock (Top 100)	★★★★★
27	II 1 • B^1b	Long nock (Top 100)	★★★★★
29/31	II 17 • B^2q/B^2s	Engraved sagging jaw, doubled die	★★★★★
36	II 1 • B^2x	Engraved wing feather, acid treated	★★★★★
41	II 19 • B^2a	Gouges in wing	★★★★
45/68	II 1/II 28 • B^2ad	Reverse die used in 1879, 9 upper TF	★★★★★
49	II 15 • B^2ag	"Funky Feather", acid treated	★★★★★
50	II 21 • B^2ah	"Funky Feather", acid treated	★★★★★
56/58	II 24/II 25 • B^1c	Long nock (Top 100)	★★★★★
57	II 23 • B^1d	Long nock (Top 100)	★★★★★
59	II 1 • B^1e	Long nock (Top 100)	★★★★★
60	II 23 • B^1f	Long nock (Top 100)	★★★★★
62	II 24 • B^1g	Long nock (Top 100)	★★★★★
64/110	II 1/II 45 • B^2ao	Lines in engraved feather, 8 upper TF	★★★★★
72	II 1 • B^1h	Long nock (Top 100)	★★★★★
76	II 21 • B^2as	"Funky Feather", acid treated	★★★★★
81	II 1 • B^2aw	"Funky Feather", acid treated	★★★★★
87	II 37 • B^2a	Spiked eye, doubled motto	★★★

HIGH INTEREST 1878 S VARIETIES

The Interest Factor has been changed in many cases in the current descriptive listings in this document from what is in the VAM book. The descriptions, photos and Interest and Rarity Factors in the 1992 VAM book and 1998 VAM book reprinting were prepared about 20 years ago. Since then the uniqueness and spectacular nature of some of the 1878 S varieties have become better known and appreciated. There were no I-4 or I-5 for the 1878 S in the VAM book. It is now realized that many of the 1878 S varieties are much more **incredible** and **spectacular** than most of the Morgan dollar varieties of later years and rank, in their own unique way, with the 1878 P varieties.

The 1878 S varieties will always stand out because of the amount of **touch-up engraving** the San Francisco Mint did on so many working dies. This did not happen in the later years (The 1879 S B² with reverse of '78 were likely left over from 1878 S.), except for minor touch-up engraving on some wreath leaves for 1879 S-1882 S. The 1878 S touch-up engraving surpasses, in many instances, even the incredible touch-up engraving performed on the 1878 P 8 TF working dies. The extensive touch-up engraving on 1878 S working dies is **unique** for a **branch mint** in the Morgan dollar series. The San Francisco Mint also experimented with **unusual** and **unique acid treatment** on a number of obverse and reverse dies for 1878 S-1882 S.

There is only one **Top 100** listing for the 1878 S, the B¹ reverse varieties which are all lumped together. There is also one **Hot 50** 1878 S listing that treats VAMs 6 & 22 doubled obverse dies.

The following sections summarize the main features of the high Interest Factor 1878 S varieties of I-5 and I-4 but not considering their current apparent rarity. Only the VAM numbers are given for the I-3 varieties.

Interest Factor 5

B¹ reverse with <u>long nock or center arrow shaft end</u>:

VAMs 26, 27, 56, 57, 58, 59 60, 62 & 72
All are scarce in circulated condition and rare in BU. Subtle differences in dies are shown in the later photographs at the end of the Guide and their main features are described in the Die Attribution Procedures section.

B² reverse with <u>short nock or flush center arrow shaft end</u>:

VAM 6	II 5 obverse. **Strongly doubled** motto letters on surface and stars. B²j reverse. Feather engraved between eagle's right wing and leg.
VAM 17A, B, C	II 13 obverse. Very over polished date and hair. B²d reverse. Four sets of denticle impressions below OLL of DOLLAR, thru OLL and below arrow feathers. **Largest amount of denticle impressions** on any Morgan dollar working die.
VAM 19	II 14 obverse. Thick broad horizontal die gouge across wheat leaves, top cotton leaf and Phrygian cap top. **Largest known obverse die gouge** in Morgan dollar series. B²w reverse. Feather engraved between eagle's right wing and leg.
VAM 19A	B²w reverse. Very over polished legend letters.
VAM 22/77/ 111	II 9 obverse. **Strongly doubled** motto letters stars and date. B²g reverse. Small S mint mark set left and slightly high.
VAM 29/31	II 17 obverse. Engraved jaw edge with "Sagging Jaw". **First example** reported of **engraving** on **obverse die** of Morgan dollar series. B²q & B²s reverses. Feather engraved between eagle's right wing and leg.
VAM 36	B²x reverse. Two **acid treated** areas on each wing, **acid treated** upper tail feathers and feather engraved between eagle's right wing and leg. **Largest amount of touch-up engraving** and **bold acid treatment** on any Morgan dollar working die.

VAM 36A	II 1 obverse. Small die gouge added at top of left wheat leaf.
VAM 36B	II 1 obverse. Radial die break at E.
VAM 45/68	B^2ad reverse. **Die later also used in 1879.** Added **8th & 9th engraved** upper TF.
VAM 49	II 15 obverse. Polished concave fields.
	B^2ag reverse. **Smooth** acid treated wing feather between eagle's right wing and leg with rough edges. A **Funky Feather.** **Unique** case of engraved **used** die.
VAM 50	II 21 obverse. Tripled eye front.
	B^2ah reverse. **Rough** acid treated wing feather between eagle's right wing and leg with dots on top. A **Funky Feather.**
VAM 64/110	B^2ao reverse. Feather engraved between eagle's right wing and leg. Fine **horizontal engraved lines** across engraved feather area. Added **8th engraved** upper TF.
VAM 76	II 21 obverse. Tripled eye front.
	B^2as reverse. **Smooth** acid treated wing feather between eagle's right wing and leg with rough edges and patches in wings and tail feathers. A **Funky Feather.**
VAM 81	II 1 obverse. Normal.
	B^2aw reverse. **Rough** acid treated wing feather between eagle's right wing and leg with dots on top. A **Funky Feather.**

Interest Factor 4

B^2 reverse with **short nock or flush center arrow shaft end**:

VAM 1C/95	B^2a reverse. **Die later also used in 1879.**
VAM 5	II 4 obverse. **Doubled** profile, date, eyelid, lower hair, cotton and wheat leaves.
	B^2i reverse. Feather engraved between eagle's right wing and leg.
VAM 8/8A/85	B^2k reverse. Feather engraved between eagle's right wing and leg and **engraved patch** on eagle's right wing.
VAM 18/18A	B^2e reverse. Fine **engraved lines** in middle of both eagle's wings.
VAM 41	II 19 obverse. Doubled nostril, eyelid, lips, chin and wheat grains.
	B^2a reverse. Heavy vertical die **gouges** in eagle's right wing.
VAM 48/84/ 91/91A	B^2af reverse. **Acid treated eagle.**

Interest Factor 3 (All with B^2 reverse)

VAMs 1D, 1E, 1G, 1I, 7, 15, 16, 20, 21, 23, 28, 35, 37A, 38, 46A, 51, 53, 55, 63, 65, 73, 74, 74A, 75A, 77, 78 Die 1, 80, 87, 88, 89, 96, 97, 98, 100 & 103 Die Combo 3, 107, 109

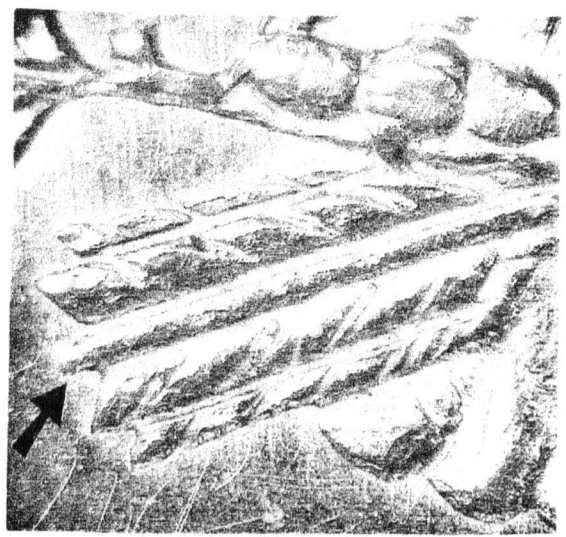

Figure 57 VAM 26 B^1 Long Nock

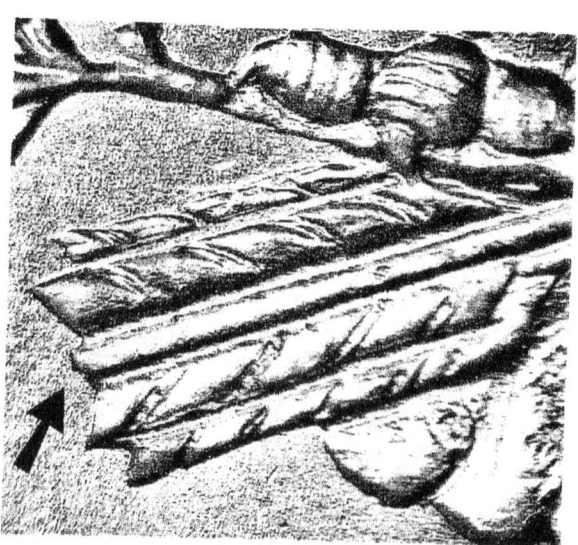

Figure 58 VAM 36 B^2 Short Nock

DIE ATTRIBUTION PROCEDURES

This section provides some procedures and aids for the attribution of the 1878 S die varieties.

The **first** attribution aid is an **1878 S Summary Chart**. Presented for all known 111 1878 S VAM varieties, in numerical order, are the obverse and reverse die designations, some die features, their availability and number of desirability stars. The availability is given in a scale of six terms from common to rare. Desirability is ranked with one to five stars as previously discussed in the Top 30 1878 S Die Varieties section. This Summary Chart is useful for obtaining concise information on each variety, but it is not as useful for attributing an unknown variety.

A **second** attribution aid are the **1878 S Die Combination Summary Charts**. A listing is provided for the B¹ long nock die combinations with short feature description noted for each one. Two charts are provided for the B² short nock or flush arrow shaft end– one with all varieties that have a **broken r in Trust** on the reverse and the other one with the **r in Trust not broken**. These two charts further branch into varieties with **no engraved wing feather** or with **an engraved wing feather**. These are in turn further divided into **normal II 1 obverses** and the obverses with **die designation features**. These charts allow some narrowing down of the possibilities when attributing an unknown variety. The short die designations and descriptions can further aid in the die and VAM number identification. Not all sub-varieties are listed however.

A **third** attribution aid are the **grouped** close-up **photographs of** all the known **engraved wing feather** reverse varieties. These are divided into those with a **broken r in Trust** and those with the **r in Trust not broken**. The photographs are useful for quick comparison and identification of the engraved wing feather features and reverse die designation.

A **fourth** attribution aid are the four **listings** of **die combinations** for the obverse and reverse dies. These cover the **Shared and Multiple Obverse Die Varieties, Obverse Die Designation to VAM Number** and the **B² Reverse Die Designation to VAM Number** for the **Broken r Varieties** or the **r Not Broken Varieties**. These listings are useful for quickly determining the obverse and reverse die designations of the VAM varieties and for checking if specific obverse or reverse dies occur for multiple VAM number varieties. Also presented are the known obverse die progression sequences, with the obverse die **II 15** occurring with **seven** different **reverse dies**– the highest number of die pairings of the 1878 S!

A **fifth** attribution aid are the detailed **Descriptive Listings** for each VAM variety. These include for each VAM number, in numerical order, the obverse and reverse die designation with descriptions, reeding count, Interest Factor of 1 thru 5, and the Rarity Factor of 1 thru 5 as described in the VAM book.

A **sixth** attribution aid are the enlarged **photographs** of each obverse and reverse die variety at the back of the Guide. These photographs are presented in numerical order of VAM number.

The following are some suggested steps for the attribution of the 1878 S die varieties. These steps will help to quickly narrow down the possible number of varieties to consider when trying to attribute an unknown variety.

1. Determine if **center arrow nock or shaft** is **long and protruding** to left of B¹ reverse design type as shown in Figure 57 or **short and flush at end** of B² design type shown in Figure 58.
2. For B¹ type reverse with **long nock or center arrow shaft end**, there are 9 known varieties with 8 different reverse dies and 7 different obverse dies.
   - VAM 26 has spike at bottom of eye front with S mint mark centered.
   - VAM 27 has unique broken denticle above second S in STATES.
   - VAM 56 has 2 short spikes below eyelid front with missing tail feather detail above olive branch.
   - VAM 57 has same obverse as VAMs 26 & 60 but with unique die chip at lower right outside of S mint mark with small die chips below it.

- VAM 58 has a single heavy spike below eyelid front.
- VAM 59 has thick diagonal line at front tip of eyelid.
- VAM 60 has same obverse as VAMs 26 & 57 but with S mint mark set high to left with diagonal polishing lines in left tail feathers above olive branch.
- VAM 62 has same obverse as VAM 56 but with unique S mint mark set far to left.
- VAM 72 has no spikes at front of eye but with tiny die chips below eyelid front and S mint mark tilted to left without any die chips below it.

3. For B^2 type reverse with **short nock or flush arrow shaft end**, determine if **right arm** of **r in trust** on reverse is **complete** at same height as vertical shaft as shown in Figure 59 or is **broken** and shallow below height of vertical shaft as shown in Figure 60. A few reverse dies show the r arm completely missing from over polished dies as shown in Figure 61.

4. The next step, for either the case of r in trust not broken or with broken r, is to determine if an **engraved wing feather** exists between the eagle's lower right wing and leg. Figure 62 shows a B^1 reverse of VAM 26 with no engraved wing feather that is not very over polished. The feather between the wing and leg has a notch on the right side of the end and is fairly shallow. Figure 63 shows a B^2 reverse of VAM 103 Die combo 3 with no engraved wing feather but with a typical over polished shallow and missing portions of the feather. The touched-up engraved wing feathers have a full raised feather with a shelf-like end all across the bottom in most cases or an obvious raised engraved area. The bottom end of the engraved feather can be straight, curved or with several angles. Since they were hand engraved by the San Francisco Mint personnel after basining and polishing of the die face, each engraved feather is **unique** in appearance. The **key feature** is the raised **shelf-like feather end** as shown in one example in Figure 64 for VAM 39. The **grouped photographs** of all known **engraved wing feather** varieties allow quick comparison of features.

5. A final general sorting of the varieties can be made, after the presence or non-presence of an engraved wing feather is determined, by **examining the obverse**. Those with some obvious **die doubling** of motto letters, LIBERTY, profile or date digits would have a variety designation of **II 2, 3 etc**. Those without obvious die doubling would be designated as **II 1 normal**. The accompanying **Die Combination Charts** have separate listings of VAM variety numbers for II 1 Normal and II Other. Then the photographs at the back of the Guide of these narrowed down possible varieties can be compared to the coin being attributed. A weak strike can make the doubling on peripheral letters weak or not visible.

6. A further sorting can be made as shown in the chart for the varieties with r in trust not broken and no engraved wing feather. The **B^2 reverse varieties** with some die doubling, S mint mark not in a normal position or S mint mark with doubling are listed in one column while those with a **normal B^2a reverse** are listed in another column.

7. The above steps are a general procedure to narrow down the possible die varieties of 10 to 20 out of the 111 total of listed 1878 S die varieties. Of course some varieties have a feature that is instantly **recognizable** and can be quickly attributed. The examiner can also get familiar with certain varieties which enables quick attribution of them.

8. Another aid to attribution are a series of die combinations and shared dies charts. One chart shows the **shared obverse die varieties** with some known die progressions. This first chart shows which VAM varieties share a common obverse variety die. The second chart further breaks down the obverse dies by **VAM designation** and which VAM numbers they are each associated with. This is useful to check the VAM number(s) that a particular identified obverse die variety is found with.

Similar charts are provided for the **reverse dies** with one chart for **broken r varieties** with the VAM numbers for each known reverse die. A separate chart is for the reverse varieties that **do not have a broken r** and also shows the VAM numbers for the listed reverse dies.

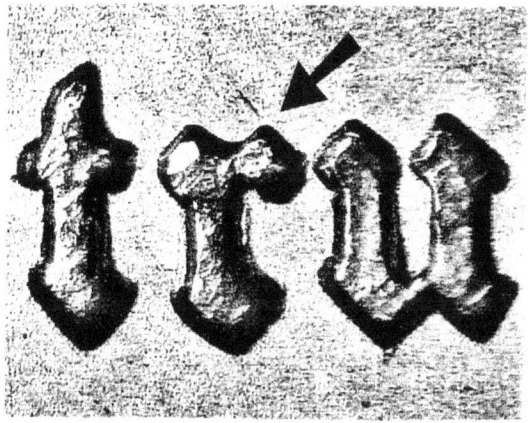

Figure 59 VAM 55 r Not Broken

Figure 60 VAM 36 Broken r

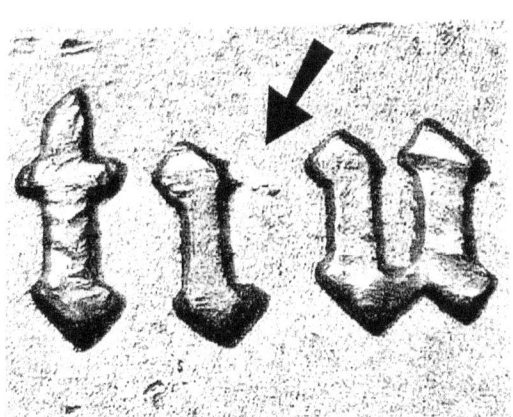

Figure 61 VAM 19 r Completely Broken

Figure 62 VAM 26 No Engraved Wing Feather

Figure 63 VAM 103 Die Combo 3
Over Polished Feather

Figure 64 VAM 39 Engraved Wing Feather

Again, this is helpful in determining if several VAM number photographs or descriptions need to be checked for an identified reverse die.

9. Many variety descriptions identify whether the **fourth right obverse star** has a broken left point. This is another useful feature to categorize the die varieties, although not all listed obverse varieties yet mention this feature. Figure 65 shows the normal fourth right star, Figure 66 shows a broken star and Figure 67 has the point completely missing.

10. It should be noted that some of the **low** VAM number 1878 S varieties may actually **not exist** or may be a **higher listed** VAM number. In November 1979, David DeRuiter pointed out that many 1878 S and some 1879 S had a touched-up engraved wing feather between the eagle's right wing and leg. Some of the varieties listed before November 1979, namely VAMs 1-25, were revised to include the engraved wing feather while those of VAM 26 and later have been checked for the engraved wing feather.

Some low number VAM numbers have not been confirmed as not having an engraved wing feather such as VAMs 2, 10, 11, 12, & 25. VAM 2 with broken r in trust may not exist, but may always occur in combination with the engraved wing feather. VAMs 3 & 4 are actually the VAM 29/31 obverse. VAM 10 may actually be VAM 65 or 100 and VAM 11 is possibly VAM 22 or 77. VAM 13 has been eliminated since it is the same as VAM 33. VAM 25 may not exist but may be a later variety with engraved wing feather with S mint mark set slightly high and to the right. Further study is required to determine the true status of some of these low VAM number 1878 S varieties.

Figure 65 VAM 26 Fourth Rt. Star Not Broken

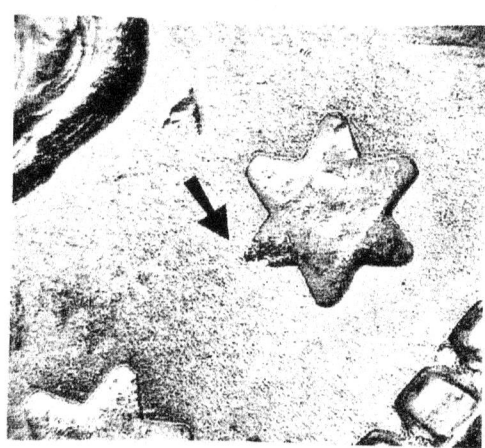

Figure 66 VAM 36 Broken Fourth Rt. Star

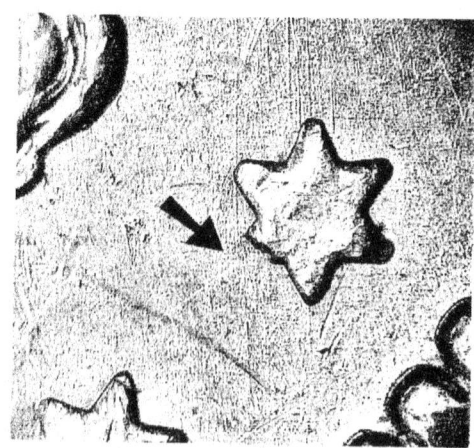

Figure 67 VAM 17A Fourth Rt. Star Point Missing

1878 S SUMMARY CHART

EWF= Engraved Wing Feather   **RB**= R in Trust Broken   **RNB**= R in Trust Not Broken

Availability Terms:

Common: Readily available variety likely seen at even the smallest local coin show.

Available: A little bit harder to find than common. May take a couple small shows or a larger one to locate.

Somewhat Scarce: Could take several visits to larger shows to locate. Some premium for attributed coins.

Scarce: Could take months of searching even at larger shows to locate. Larger premium for attributed coins.

Very Scarce: Difficult to locate even at larger local or regional shows. Premium could be substantial for attributed coins depending on desirability of variety.

Rare: Thought to have such a low population that years of searching regional and national shows may be required to "Cherry Pick". Attributed coins should bring a substantial premium.

VAM #	Die Designations	Key Features	Availability	Desirability
1	II 1 obverse. B²a reverse. Normal without die doubling, gouges.		Scarce	★
1A	(Eliminated, same as VAMs 16 or 28)			
1B	II 1 Lines in hair at back of neck.		EDS Rare	★★
	B²a Gouges between eagle's rt wing & leg. RNB	LDS Rusted Scarce circ, Very Scarce BU		
1C	Same as VAM 95, but still used.		Available AU, BU	★★★★
1D	II 1 Normal. (Also 106) B²a Doubled D. Lines in tail feathers. RNB (Also 73)		Rare BU	★★★
1E	II 1 Normal. B²a Gouges right wreath. RNB		Rare	★★★
1F	(Not used, same as VAM 63)			
1G	II 1 Die 1: Lines in LIB. (Also 96) B²a Lines top eagle's left wing. RNB		Scarce circ, Rare BU	★★★
	Die 2: Missing nostril, gouge rt side rt cotton boll. Light acid treated lower hair edge.			
	(Also 78 Die 1)			
1H	(Eliminated, same as VAM 1B.)			
1I	II 1 Over polished nostril.		Scarce	★★★
	B²a Gouges eagle's left wing. RNB			
2	II 1 Normal. B²b Arm of r in Trust partially broken or completely missing, a hub defect.			
	(May always exist with EWF & therefore probably not a separate variety.)			
3	(Eliminated, same as obverse of VAM 29/31)			
4	(Eliminated, same as obverse of VAM 29/31)			
5	II 3 Doubled rt inside 8's, lower hair, nostril, lips. Die chip cheek middle.		Available MS 63 up	★★★★
	B²i EWF RB (Also 7, 46)			
6	II 5 Doubled motto letters, 6 & 7 left & 4-6 rt stars. B²j EWF RB (Also 44) **Hot 50**		Available BU	★★★★★
7	II 6 Doubled top left Liberty head, hair below LIBERTY, wheat leaves. (Also 24)		Common	★★★
	B²i EWF RB (Also 5, 46)			
8	II 1 Die 1: Die scratch forehead front. (Also 28)		Common	★★★★
	Die 2: Die chip below cap fold. (Also 47 Die 1)			
	B²k EWF RNB Engraved patch middle eagle's rt wing. (Also 85)			
8A	II 1 Die 2 B²k Die rust pits and splotches on eagle's wing.		Scarce	★★★★
9	II 7 Die flakes on E-P, broken B. Lines below cap ribbon. (Also 21, 53, 79)		Available	★★
	B²l EWF RB Tiny chip bottom eagle's rt wing.			
10	II 8 Doubled motto. B²b (Likely VAM 65 or 100)			
11	II 9 Doubled motto, stars, date. B²b (Likely VAM 22, 77 or 111)			
12	II 10 Slightly doubled motto. B²b (Probably VAM 93)			
13	(Eliminated, same as VAM 33)			
14	II 11 L & R doubled left side. Lines & dots in hair at jaw-neck. (Also 15, 44)		Available	★★
	B²m EWF RNB Wings middle over polished.			
15	II 11 L & R doubled left side. Lines & dots in hair at jaw-neck. (Also 14, 44)		Scarce	★★★
	B²n EWF RB Two vertical gouges bottom both wings, lines wing middle. (Also 80, 89)			
16	II 12 Doubled E PLURIB and ear.		Available	★★★
	B²o EWF RNB Long vertical die scratch eagle's right lower wing. (Also 20, 28)			
17	II 13 Very over polished lower hair & date. LDS		Scarce EDS	★★
	B²d RNB Doubled D. Lines below tail feathers. EDS (Also 66)		Common LDS	
17A	II 13 Slanted dash below 7.		Available	★★★★★
	B²d Raised denticle impressions thru OLL, below OL & below tail feathers.			

17B	II 13 Raised denticle impressions neck & date.	Scarce	★★★★★
	B²d Raised denticle impressions thru OLL, UN, STAT & below tail feathers.		
17C	II 13 Slightly polished die.	Scarce	★★★★★
	B²d Die wear weakened denticle impressions.		
18	II 1 Normal. **B²e** Fine engraving lines middle both wings.	Very Scarce	★★★★
18A	II 1 Radial die break first right star.	Scarce	★★★★
19	II 14 Doubled motto, nostril eyelid, profile. Broad horizontal die gouge across	Very Scarce	★★★★★
	wheat leaves & top cotton leaf. **B²w** EWF RB Doubled D (Also 35, 74, 93)		
19A	**B²w** Very over polished with shallow UNITED STATES. Arm of r in Trust missing.	Somewhat Scarce	★★★★★
20	II 15 Concave field near rim. (Also 49, 83, 101, 103)	Available	★★★
	B²o No die scratch eagle's right wing. (Also 16, 28)		
21	II 7 Polished with slightly concave fields near rim. Lines below cap ribbon. (Also 9, 53, 79)	Available	★★★
	B²f EWF RNB Doubled legend, left & right wreaths.		
22	II 9 Strongly doubled motto, stars, date. (Also 11, 77, 111) **Hot 50**	Scarce Circ	★★★★★
	B²g RNB S mint mark set left.	Rare BU	
23	II 43 Doubled profile, motto, cap top. Flaked hair surface above second rt star. (Also 34)	Available	★★★
	B²y EWF RB S/S with lines in loops. (Also 37)		
24	II 6 Doubled top left Liberty head, hair below LIBERTY, wheat leaves. (Also 7)	Very Scarce	★★
	B²r EWF RNB Over polished shallow UNITED. Die chip back top arrow head. (Also 30, 43)		
25	II 1 Normal. **B²c** S mint mark set slightly high & to right.	Rare	★★
	(May not exist– listed before EWF known. Possibly VAM 33)		
26	II 23 Doubled eye lid and spikes. (Also 57, 60) **Top 100**	Rare	★★★★★
	B¹a Long Nock. S m/m set slightly rt with slight left tilt.		
27	II 1 Normal. 3 spikes below eyelid. **Top 100**	Rare	★★★★★
	B¹b Long nock. S m/m centered. Broken denticle above second S in STATES.		
28	II 1 Normal. **B²o** EWF RB Die scratch eagle's rt wing (Also 16, 20)	Available	★★★
29	II 17 Tripled LIBERTY. Doubled eyelid, nostril, lower hair, 18-8 at bottom. Engraved	Available	★★★★★
	sagging jaw. Die gouge top first U in PLURIBUS. (Also VAM 31, LDS) **B²q** EWF RNB		
30	II 18 Quadrupled LIBERTY. Doubled nostril, eyelid.	Common	★★
	B²r EWF RNB Over polished shallow UNITED. Die chip back top arrow head. (Also 24, 43)		
30A	II 18 Radial die break U..	Scarce	★★
	B²r EWF RNB Over polished shallow UNITED. Die chip back top arrow head. (Also 24, 43)		
31	II 17 Tripled LIBERTY. Doubled eyelid, nostril, lower hair, 18-8 at bottom. Engraved	Available	★★★★★
	sagging jaw. Die gouge top first U in PLURIBUS. (Also VAM 29, EDS)		
	B²s EWF RNB Line in vee between eagle's neck and wing.		
32 (Eliminated, same as VAM 48.)			
32A (Eliminated, became VAM 91A.)			
33	II 20 Dbld L-R-BU. Spike above eyelid. (Also 42) **B²u** EWF RNB S/S notches on serifs.	Common	★★
33A	II 20 Clashed die st (Same as VAM 42A.)	Scarce	★★
34	II 43 Doubled profile, motto, cap top. Flaked hair surface above second rt star. (Also 23)	Available	★★
	B²v EWF RNB Doubled UNITED STATES OF.		
35	II 26 Doubled profile. Doubled & tripled stars, PLURIBUS UNUM. Triangular die chip	Common	★★★
	at jaw-neck near curl. (Also 55) **B²w** EWF RB Doubled D. (Also 19, 74, 93)		
36	II 1 Two raised dots inside ear. **B²x** EWF RB Engraved wing. Acid treated wings & TF.	Scarce	★★★★★
	(Most extensive engraved and acid treated of all Morgan dies.)		
36A	II 1 Small die gouge top left wheat leaf.	Very Scarce	★★★★★
36B	II 1 Radial die break at E.	Very Scarce	★★★★★
37	II 41 Doubled US UNUM, cap top & front of hair.	Common	★★
	B²y EWF RB S/S with lines in loops. (Also 23)		
37A	II 41 Beveled field at denticles 1-2 rt stars..	Scarce	★★★
	B²y Beveled field at S-OF.		
38	II 32 Tripled US UNUM. Doubled profile, lower hair, 8's. Dot chip in hair behind eye.	Very Scarce	★★★
	(Also 84, 89) **B²z** EWF RB Wide gouge top & lower middle eagle's rt wing. (Also 90)		
39	II 1 Tiny die chips in front of ear. **B²aa** EWF RB Light polishing lines left field.	Available	★★
	Line bottom of wing to olive branch. Gouge outside of eagle's left leg. Die chip back		
	of top arrow head. (Also 99)		
40	II 1 Die chips on cheek. Vertical line eye rear. (Also 45, 64) **B²ab** EWF RB	Available	★★
41	II 19 Strongly double cap fold front. Doubled nostril, eyelid, lips, chin.	Rare	★★★★
	B²a Heavy vertical gouges eagle's rt wing & lines in left wing.		
42	II 20 Doubled L-R-BU. Spike above eyelid. (Also 33) **B²ac** EWF RNB	Available	★★

42A	II 20 Clashed die st. (Also 33A)	Scarce	★★
43	II 1 Raised areas inside first 8. **B²r** EWF RNB Over polished shallow UNITED. Die chip back top arrow head. (Also 24, 30)	Common	★★
44	II 11 L & R doubled left side. Lines & dots in hair at jaw-neck. (Also 14, 15) **B²j** EWF RB (Also 6)	Common	★★
45	II 1 Die chips on cheek. Vertical line eye rear. (Also 40, 64) **B²ad** EWF RB Slightly doubled UNITED. 9 Upper TF. Die later used on 1879 S VAM 9/77. (Also 68)	Very Scarce	★★★★★
46	II 1 Worm-like die scratch behind eye. (Also 52) **B²i** EWF RB (Also 5, 7)	Common	★★
46A	**B²i** Die break left side second berry cluster from left wreath top.	Very Scarce	★★★
47	II 1 Die 1: Chip below cap fold. (Also 8 Die 2)	Die 1 & 2 Common	★★
	Die 2: Polishing line in top of ER in LIBERTY.	Die 3 Scarce	
	Die 3: Long horizontal scratch between hair locks back of neck. (Also 69) **B²ae** EWF RB Slightly doubled ITED STATES F. Tiny dig end third tail feather from rt.		
48	II 1 Slight doubling B, forehead edge, hair front, cap top. **B²af** EWF RB with triangle on arm. S m/m high, tilted rt. Acid treated eagle. (Also 84, 91)	Common	★★★★
49	II 15 Concave field near rim. (Also 20, 83, 101, 103) **B²ag** Acid treated wing feather added to VAM 103 Die Combo 3, smooth top & rough sides, "Funky Feather". RNB	Very Scarce	★★★★★
50	II 21 Tripled eyelid front. Die chip mouth corner. (Also 76) **B²ah** Acid treated wing feather with rough surface with dots, "Funky Feather". RNB	Rare	★★★★★
51	II 1 Over polished ear, spike below eyelid front. **B²ai** EWF RNB Notch top serif S m/m. Over polished wing centers & shallow STAT. Doubled tops ONE DOL. (Also 101)	Very Scarce circ. Rare BU	★★★
52	II 1 Worm-like die scratch behind eye. (Also 46) **B²aj** EWF RB Vertical line eagle's rt wing. (Also 79)	Scarce	★★
53	II 7 Die flakes on E-P, broken B. Same concave die as VAM 21. Lines below cap ribbon. (Also 9, 21, 79) **B²ak** EWF RNB Dbld left wreath & upper legend. Scratch above EWF.	Scarce	★★★
54	II 22 Doubled profile & first four left stars. **B²a** Normal.	Rare	★★
55	II 26 Doubled profile. Doubled & tripled stars, PLURIBUS UNUM. Triangular die chip at jaw-neck near curl. (Also 35) **B²al** Shallow EWF. RNB Slightly doubled UNITED STAT. Rusted die middle eagle's left wing. Acid treated wing centers. (Also 75)	Scarce	★★★
56	II 24 Two bars at eye front. (Also 62) **B¹c** Long nock. High S m/m. (Also 58) **Top 100**	Rare	★★★★★
57	II 23 Doubled eye lid and spikes. (Also 26, 60) **Top 100** **B¹d** Long nock. Small die chips lower right and below S m/m.	Rare	★★★★★
58	II 25 Thick spike eye front. **B¹c** Long nock. High S m/m. (Also 56) **Top 100**	Rare	★★★★★
59	II 1 Diagonal clash line eyelid tip. (Also 72) **B¹e** Long nock. S m/m left. **Top 100**	Rare	★★★★★
60	II 23 Doubled eye lid and spikes. (Also 26, 57) **Top 100** **B¹f** Long nock. S m/m set high & left.	Rare	★★★★★
61	II 1 Normal. **B²am** RB Slightly doubled UNITED STAT, top left wreath.	Very scarce	★★
62	II 24 Two bars at eye front. (Also 56) **B¹g** Long nock. S m/m set far left. **Top 100**	Rare	★★★★★
63	II 1 Normal. Diagonal scratch eye front. **B²an** RNB S/S Line in upper loop. Long horizontal line thru eagle's neck & rt wing.	Scarce circ Rare BU	★★★
64	II 1 Die chips on cheek. Vertical line eye rear. (Also 40, 45) **B²ao** EWF RNB Horizontal lines over EWF. 8 upper TF. (Also 110)	Scarce	★★★★★
65	II 8 Doubled motto. (Also 100 & 109) **B²ap** EWF RNB (Also 82)	Rare	★★★
66	II 27 Doubled ear. Line thru IB. (Also 92) **B²d** RNB Doubled D. Lines below tail feathers as in VAM 17 EDS. (Also 17)	Rare	★★
67	II 1 Normal. **B²aq** EWF RNB S m/m set left.	Rare	★★
68	II 28 Doubled hair front, eye front, chin. **B²ad** EWF RB Slightly doubled UNITED. 9 upper TF. Die later used on 1879 S VAM 9/77. (Also 45)	Rare	★★★★★
69	II 1 Normal. **B²ar** EWF with vertical lines. RB Slightly dbld UNITED S-TE. (Also 102)	Somewhat Scarce	★★
70	(Eliminated, same as VAM 31)		
71	II 1 Normal. **B²bc** High S m/m.	Rare	★★
72	II 1 Chips below eyelid front. (Also 59) **B¹h** Long nock. S m/m tilted left. **Top 100**	Rare	★★★★★
73	II 30 Doubled eyelid with spike below eyelid front. **B²a** Doubled D. Lines in tail feathers. RNB (Also 1D)	Scarce Circ, Rare BU	★★★
74	II 1 Line back of eye socket. **B²w** EWF RB Doubled D. Very over polished. Arm of r in Trust completely broken off. (Also 19, 35, 93)	Common	★★★
74A	**B²w** Die chip left wreath opposite NI.	Rare	★★★
75	II 31 Doubled L-BUS UNUM, left stars, chin. Comma die chip inside ear. **B²al** Shallow EWF. RNB Slightly doubled UNITED STAT. (Also 55)	Available	★★

| 75A | B²al Raised dots & splotches in wing centers from rusted and light acid treatment die with polishing lines in fields. | Scarce | ★★★ |

75A B²al Raised dots & splotches in wing centers from rusted and light acid treatment die with polishing lines in fields. — Scarce ★★★

76 II 21 Tripled eyelid front. Die chip mouth corner. (Also 50) B²as Acid treated wing feathers with very smooth surface and sharp edges, smooth spots in middle of wings. "Funky Feather" RNB — Very Scarce ★★★★★

77 II 9 Strongly doubled motto, stars, date. (Also 11, 22,111) B²at RNB Very high S m/m. — Hot 50 Rare ★★★★★

78 II 1 Die 1: Missing nostril. Gouge rt side rt cotton boll. Light acid treatment at lower hair edge (Also 1G Die 2) (3 stars) — Available Circ Scarce BU ★★
Die 2: Faint doubling below eyelid front. Die 3: Divided cap ribbon with chips at left. Die 4: Tiny die chips end of cap ribbon. B²au RNB S m/m set left & tilted left. (Also 98)

79 II 7 Die flakes on E-P, broken B. Fields not concave. Lines below cap ribbon.. (Also 9, 21, 53) B²aj EWF RB Vertical line eagle's rt wing. (Also 52) — Available ★★

80 II 38 Slightly dbld E PL-R-B. Fine line eye front. (Also 90) — Very Scarce ★★★
B²n EWF RB 2 vertical gouges bottom both wings, lines wing middle. (Also 15, 89)

81 II 1 Normal. B²aw Acid treated wing feather with granular surface, raised dots, splotches. "Funky Feather" RNB — Rare ★★★★★

82 II 1 Normal. B²ap EWF RNB (Also 65) — Very Scarce ★★

83 II 15 Concave field near rim. (Also 20, 49, 101, 103) — Scarce ★★
B²ax Doubled eagle's left wing upper feathers and motto.

84 II 32 Tripled US UNUM. Doubled profile, lower hair, 8's. Dot chip in hair behind eye. Polished with slightly concave fields. (Also 38, 89) B²af EWF RB with triangle on arm. S m/m high, tilted rt. Acid treated eagle. (Also 48, 91) — Common ★★★★

85 II 35 Doubling below eyelid, top of eye socket. B²k EWF RNB Engraved patch middle eagle's right wing. (Also 8) — Scarce ★★★★

86 II 36 Doubled ear. B²a Normal. Die 1: Die scratches in eagle's right wing and tail feathers. (Often found in Redfield collection holders.) — Somewhat Scarce ★★
Die 2: Die chips on upper tail feathers. Die 3: Two spikes at wing edge below In.

87 II 37 Two spikes below eyelid with one very thick. Doubled motto letters. B²a Fine raised dots all over eagle from rusted die. — Rare ★★★

88 II 1 Slightly doubled ear left inside, rt outside. B²ay EWF RNB S/S top left inside. — Rare ★★★

89 II 32 Tripled US UNUM. Dbld profile, lower hair, 8's. Dot chip hair behind eye. (Also 38, 84) — Available ★★★
B²n EWF RB Two vertical gouges bottom both wings, lines wing middle. (Also 15, 80)

90 II 38 Slightly doubled E PL-R-B. Fine line eye front. (Also 80) — Rare ★★
B²z EWF RB Wide gouge top & lower middle eagle's rt wing. (Also 38)

91 II 34 Slight doubling hair front, cap top, US UNUM. — Rare ★★★★
B²af EWF RB with triangle on arm. S m/m high, tilted rt. Acid treated eagle. (Also 48, 84)

91A II 34 Horizontal die gouge back of cap. — Very Scarce ★★★★

92 II 27 Doubled ear. Line thru IB. (Also 66) B²az RNB Doubled D. Wide vertical gouges and polishing lines in lower part eagle's rt wing. — Scarce ★★

93 II 39 Slightly dbld PL-R-B, hair front, left stars. B²w EWF RB Dbld D. (Also 19, 35, 74) Available — ★★

94 II 40 Doubled PLURIBUS UNUM, LIBERTY band front, cap top. (Also 95) B²a Normal. Scarce — ★★

95 II 40 Doubled PLURIBUS UNUM, LIBERTY band front, cap top. (Also 1C, 94) — Scarce ★★★★
B²a Lightly engraved wing feather. Die chip R. Rev die also use in 1879 S VAMs 4, 23, 25. RNB (Also 1C)

96 II 1 Lines in LIB. (Also 1G Die 1) B²ba RNB S/S Triangles inside loops. — Very Scarce ★★★

97 II 1 Normal. B²bb EWF RB Slanted gouge lower inside eagle's left wing. — Rare ★★★

98 II 42 Doubled 878, nostril, eyelid, lower hair, ear. Die chip back of cap below ribbon. B²au RNB S m/m set left & tilted left. (Also 78) — Rare ★★★

99 II 44 Doubled L-BUS UNUM, cap top, rt wheat leaf. 2 lines below lower left hair. (Also 102) B²aa EWF RB Light polishing lines left field. Line wing bottom to olive branch. Gouge outside of eagle's left leg. Die chip back of top arrow head. (Also 39) — Somewhat Scarce ★★

100 II 8 Doubled motto. (Also 65 & 109) B²bd EWF RNB — Rare ★★★

101 II 15 Concave field near rim. (Also 20, 49, 83, 103) B²ai EWF RNB Notch top serif. Very Scarce circ S m/m. Over polished wing centers & shallow STAT. Doubled tops ONE DOL. (Also 51) Rare BU — ★★

102 II 44 Doubled L-BUS UNUM, cap top, rt wheat leaf. 2 lines below lower left hair. (Also 99) B²ar EWF with vertical lines. RB Slightly dbld UNITED S-TE. (Also 69) — Somewhat Scarce ★★

103	**II 15** Concave field near rim. (Also 20, 49, 83, 101) **B²a**- Four dies:	Available	★★

Die combo 1: Obv not concave, die scratch ribbon end. Rev RNB Double vertical lines
        Middle eagle's left wing.

Die combo 2: Obv not concave, die scratch ribbon end. Rev RNB Line top middle
        eagle's left wing.

Die combo 3: Obv not concave, die scratch ribbon end. Rev RNB Line top of eagle's
        rt wing & leg, die gouge in eagle's mouth. Earlier die state of VAM 49.

Die combo 4: Obv polished, slightly concave, no scratch ribbon end. Rev RNB
        Double lines top inside eagle's rt leg.

104	**II 1** Die gouges in lower hair. **B²be** EWF RNB Long vertical die gouge eagle's left wing.	Scarce	★★
105	**II 1** Die scratch nose bridge. **B²bf** EWF RB Triangular die gouge top olive leaf. Triangle r arm.	Scarce	★★
106	**II 1** Normal. (Also 1D) **B²bg** RNB High S mint mark tilted left.	Scarce	★★
107	**II 30** Dbld eyelid with spike. (Also 73) **B²bh** RNB Dbld D, S m/m set left.	Scarce	★★★
108	**II 1** Die chip right of next to bottom cotton leaf. **B²bi** RNB S/S lines in loops.	Scarce	★★
109	**II 8** Doubled motto. (Also 65 & 100) **B²a** Normal.	Scarce	★★★
110	**II 45** Dbld US UNUM, cap top. **B²ao** EWF RNB Horizontal lines over EWF. 8 upper TF. (Also 64)	Scarce	★★★★★
111	**II 9** Strongly dbld motto, stars, date. (Also 11, 22, 77) **B²a** RNB Normal S m/m. **Hot 50** Two die chips rt of eagle's rt leg.	Rare	★★★★★

NOTE: Availability designations are estimates by the authors of the rarity of each variety. In some cases this was based on a limited amount of information or coin specimens. Collectors are encouraged to report the scarce or better varieties with the coin grade and grading service where applicable to:

Craig Lickenbrock   Or e-mail: vams1878s@msn.com
P.O. Box 997
O'Fallon, IL 62269-0997

1878 S DIE COMBINATIONS SUMMARY
(Number designates VAM variety)

B¹ Design
(Long center arrow nock)

II 1 Normal   **II 23** Doubled eyelid & spikes   **II 24** Two bars eye front   **II 25** Thick spike eye front

27 II 1 Spikes below eyelid   26 B¹a S tilted left   56 B¹c S set high (also 58)   58 B¹c S set high (also 56)
     B¹b Broken denticle S   57 B¹d Chips lower rt   62 B¹g S set far left
59 II 1 Clash eye (also 72)   & below S
     B¹e S slightly left   60 B¹f S set far left
72 II 1 Chips below eyelid (also 59)
     B¹h S tilted left

B² Design
(Short center arrow nock)

r in trust broken

Engraved wing feather

No engraved wing feather
(VAMs 2, 10, 11 & 12 may not exist)

2 II 1 Normal
     B²b Broken r
10 II 8 Dbld motto (also 65, 100)
     4th rt star not broken
     B²b Broken r
11 II 9 Dbld motto (also 11, 77, 111)
     B²b Broken r
12 II 10 Dbld motto
     B²b Broken r
61 II 1 Normal
     B²am Slightly dbld motto

II 1 Normal

36 B²x Acid treat feathers, wing centers
36A II 1 Gouge wheat leaf
39 II 1 Normal
     B²aa Eng wing feather
40 II 1 Chips on face, line on eye (also 45, 64)
     B²ab Eng wing feather
45 II 1 Chips on face, line on eye (also 40, 64)
     B²ad Dbld legend, 9 upper TF (also 68)
46 II 1 Worm eye break (also 52)
     B²i 5 short lines eng wing feather (also 5, 7)
46A B²i Break left wreath
47 B²ae Dbld legend
48 II 1 Dbld B, forehead
     B²af Scratch bow, acid treat eagle (also 84, 91)
52 II 1 Worm eye break (also 46)
     B²aj Eng wing feather (also 79)
69 B²ar Vertical lines eng wing feather (also 102)
74 II 1 Line behind eye
     B²w Eng wing feather (also 19, 35, 93)
74A B²w Chip left wreath
105 II 1 Scratch nose bridge
     B²bf Eng wing feather, triangle r arm

II Other

5 II 4 Dbld 878, nostril lower hair
     Chip cheek middle
     B²i 5 short lines eng wing feather (also 7, 46)
6 II 5 Dbld motto
     B²j Eng wing feather (also 44)
7 II 6 Dbld LIBERTY, wheat leaves (also 24)
     B²i 5 short lines eng wing feather (also 5, 46)
9 II 7 Broken B bottom (also 21, 53, 79)
     B²l Chip next to eng wing feather
15 II 11 Lines hair jaw-neck (also 14, 44)
     B²n Lines in wing middle (also 80, 89)
19 II 14 Broad gouge cap top
     B²w Eng wing feather (also 35, 74, 93)
19A B²w Shallow legend & motto
23 II 43 Dbld profile, flaked hair (also 34)
     B²y S/S left (also 37)
35 II 26 Dbld profile (also 55)
     B²w Eng wing feather (also 19, 74, 93)
37 II 41 Dbld UNUM
     B²y S/S left (also 23)
38 II 32 Dbld lower hair & 8-8 (also 84, 89)
     B²z Gouge rt wing (also 90)
44 II 11 Lines hair jaw-neck (also 14, 15)
     B²j Eng wing feather (also 6)
68 II 28 Dbld LIBERTY
     B²ad Dbld legend, 9 upper TF (also 45)
79 II 7 Broken B bottom (also 9, 21, 53)
     B²aj Eng wing feather (also 52)
80 II 38 Dbld E-PL-B (also 90)
     B²n Lines in wing middle (also 15, 89)
84 II 32 Dbld lower hair & 8-8 (also 38, 89)
     B²af Scratch bow, acid treat eagle (also 48, 91)
89 II 32 Dbld lower hair & 8-8 (also 38, 84)
     B²n Lines in wing middle (also 15, 80)
90 II 38 Dbld E-PL-B (also 80)
     B²z Gouge rt wing (also 38)
91 II 34 Dbld motto & cap
     B²af Scratch bow, acid treat eagle (also 48, 84)
93 II 39 Dbld motto & L
     B²w Eng wing feather (also 19, 35, 74)
99 II 44 Dbld motto
     B²aa Eng wing feather
102 II 44 Dbld motto (also 99)
     B²ar Vertical lines eng wing feather (also 69)

B² Design
(Short center arrow nock)

r in trust not broken

No engraved wing feather

B²a Normal design & S mint mark

II 1 Normal

1 II 1 Normal
  B²a Normal
1B II 1 Lines back of neck
  B²a Lines eagle's talons, rusted wreath
1C II 1 Normal
  B²a Chip top of R (also 95)
1D II 1 Normal (also 106)
  B²a Gouges in TF (also 73)
1E II 1 Normal
  B²a Gouges rt wreath
1G II 1 Lines in LIBERTY , acid treat hair
  B²a Lines eagle's left wing
1 II 1 Over polished nostril
  B²2 Diagonal lines wing bottom
41 II 19 Dbld LIBERTY up
  B²a Vertical lines eagle's rt wing
54 II 22 Dbld profile
  B²a Normal
73 II 30 Dbld eyelid
  B²a Gouges in TF (also 1D)
86 II 36 Dbld ear
  B²a Normal
87 II 37 Spiked eye
  B²a Normal
94 II 40 Dbld motto (also 95)
  B²a Normal
95 II 40 Dbld motto (also 1C, 94)
  B²a Chip top of R (also 1C)
103 II 15 Die chip E (also 20, 49, 83, 101)
  B²a Normal (also 49)
109 II 8 Dbld motto (also 65, 100)
111 II 9 Dbld motto (also 11, 22, 77)

Reverse varieties

II 1 Normal

18 B²e Lines in wings
25 B²c S high & rt
63 B²an S/S rt, scratch neck & wing
71 B²bc S set high
78 II 1 Acid treat hair edge
  B²au S left & tilted left (also 96)
96 B²a ba S/S triangles
106 II 1 (also 1D)
  B²bq S high tilted left
108 B²bi S/S lines

II Other

17 II 13 Shallow hair
  B²d Dbld D, lines below TF (also 66)
17A B²d Denticle impressions
22 II 9 Dbld motto (also 11, 77, 111)
  B²g S set left & high
66 II 27 Dbld ear & eyelid (also 92)
  B²d Lines below TF (also 17)
77 II 9 Dbld motto
  B²at S very high
83 II 15 Concave field (also 20, 49, 101, 103)
  B²ax Dbld wing tip
92 II 27 Dbld ear & eyelid
  B²az Heavy lines next to leg
98 II 42 Dbld 878 & nostril
  B²au S left & tilted left (also 78)

Engraved wing feather

II 1 Normal

8 B²k Some chip E in UNITED (also 85)
8A B²k Rusted die wings
28 B²o Scratch eagle's rt wing (also 16, 20)
43 B²r Chip arrow head (also 24, 30)
51 II 1 Over polished ear
  B²ai Shallow STAT
64 II 1 Chips on face (also 40, 45)
  B²ao Lines on eng wing feather
      8 upper TF (also 110)
67 B²aq S set left
81 B²aw Dots acid treat wing feather
82 B²ap Eng wing feather (also 65)
88 II 1 Slight dbld ear
  B²ay S/S top left inside
104 II 1 Gouges lower hiar
  B²be Eng wing feather.
  Vertical gouge wing

II Other

14 II 11 lines hair jaw-neck (also 15, 44)
  B²m Over polished wing middle
16 II 12 Dbld motto
  B²o Scratch eagle's rt wing (also 20, 28)
20 II 15 Concave field (also 49, 83, 101, 103)
  B²o No scratch wing (also 16, 28)
21 II 7 Dbld LIBERTY & B (also 9, 53, 79)
  B²f Dbld legend
24 II 6 Dbld LIBERTY (also 7)
  B²t Chip arrow head (also 30, 43)
29 II 17 Dbld nostril & eyelid
  sagging jaw (also 31)
  B²q Eng wing feather
30 II 18 Quadrupled LIBERTY, dbld nostril
  B²r Chip arrow head (also 24, 43)
31 II 17 Dbld nostril & eyelid
  sagging jaw (also 29)
  B²s Eng wing feather
33 II 20 Dbld L-R-BU (also 42)
  B²u S/S notches
34 II 43 Dbld profile, flaked hair (also 23)
  B²v Dbld legend
42 II 20 Dbld L-R-BU (also 33)
  B²ac Eng wing feather
49 II 15 Concave field (Also 20, 83, 101, 103)
  B²ag Smooth acid treat wing feather
50 II 21 Tripled eyelid (also 76)   (also 103)
  B²ah Rough acid treat wing feather
53 II 7 Dbld LIBERTY & B (also 9, 21, 79)
  B²ak Scratches eagle's rt wing
55 II 26 Dbld profile (also 35)
  B²al Eng & acid treat wing feathers (also 75)
65 II 8 Dbld motto (also 10, 100, 109)
  B²ap Eng wing feather (also 82)
75 II 31 Dbld UNUM
  B²al Eng & acid treat wing feathers (also 55)
76 II 21 Tripled eyelid (also 50)
  B²as Smooth acid treat wing feather
85 II 35 Dbld eyelid
  B²k Eng wing feather, chip E (also 8)
100 II 8 Dbld motto & ear (also 10, 65, 109)
  B²bd Eng wing feather
101 II 15 Concave field, Die chip E (also 20, 49,
  B²ai Eng wing feather (also 51)   83, 103)

110 II 45 Dbld motto
  B²ao Lines on eng wing feather,
      8 upper TF (also 64)

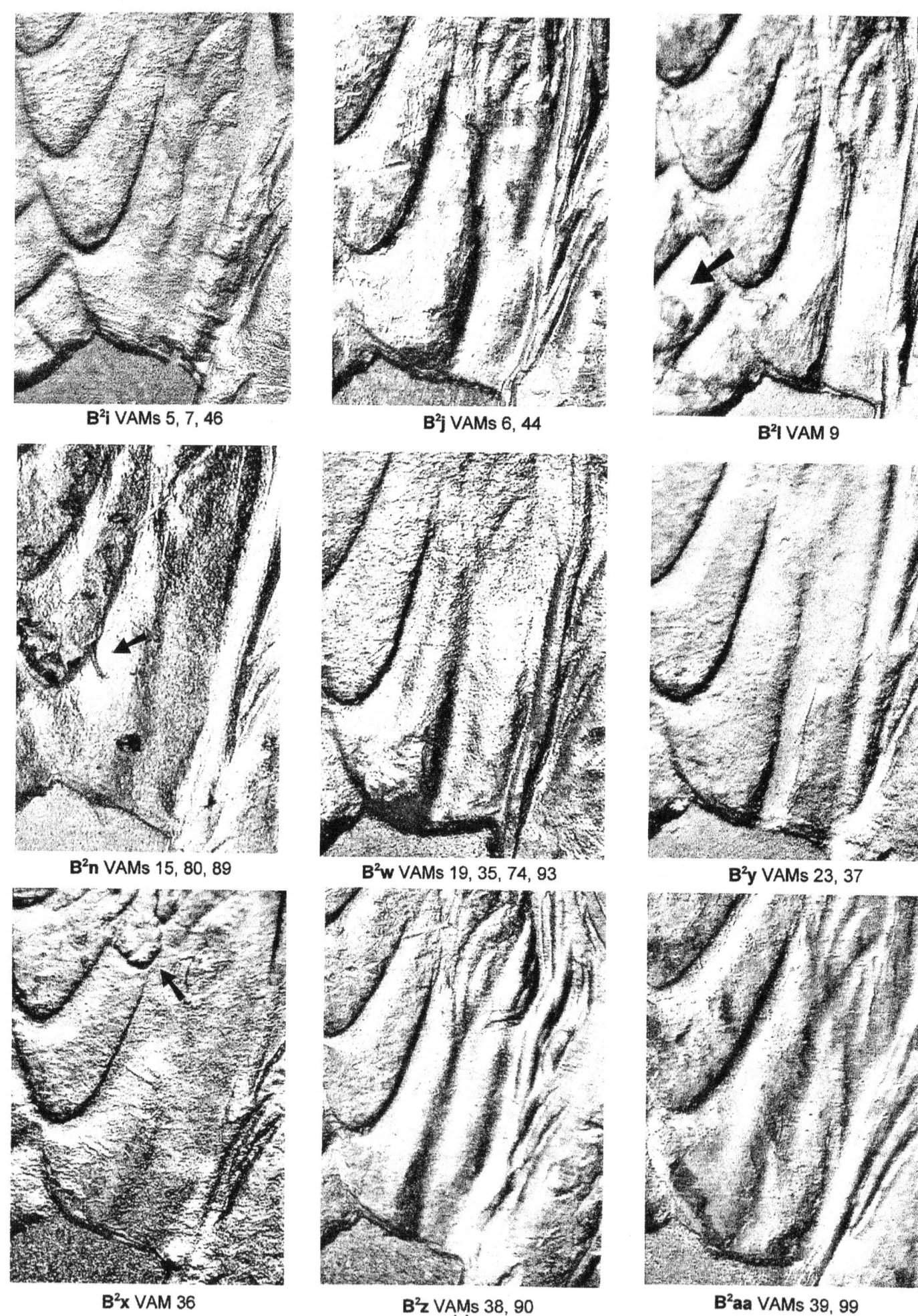

B²i VAMs 5, 7, 46

B²j VAMs 6, 44

B²l VAM 9

B²n VAMs 15, 80, 89

B²w VAMs 19, 35, 74, 93

B²y VAMs 23, 37

B²x VAM 36

B²z VAMs 38, 90

B²aa VAMs 39, 99

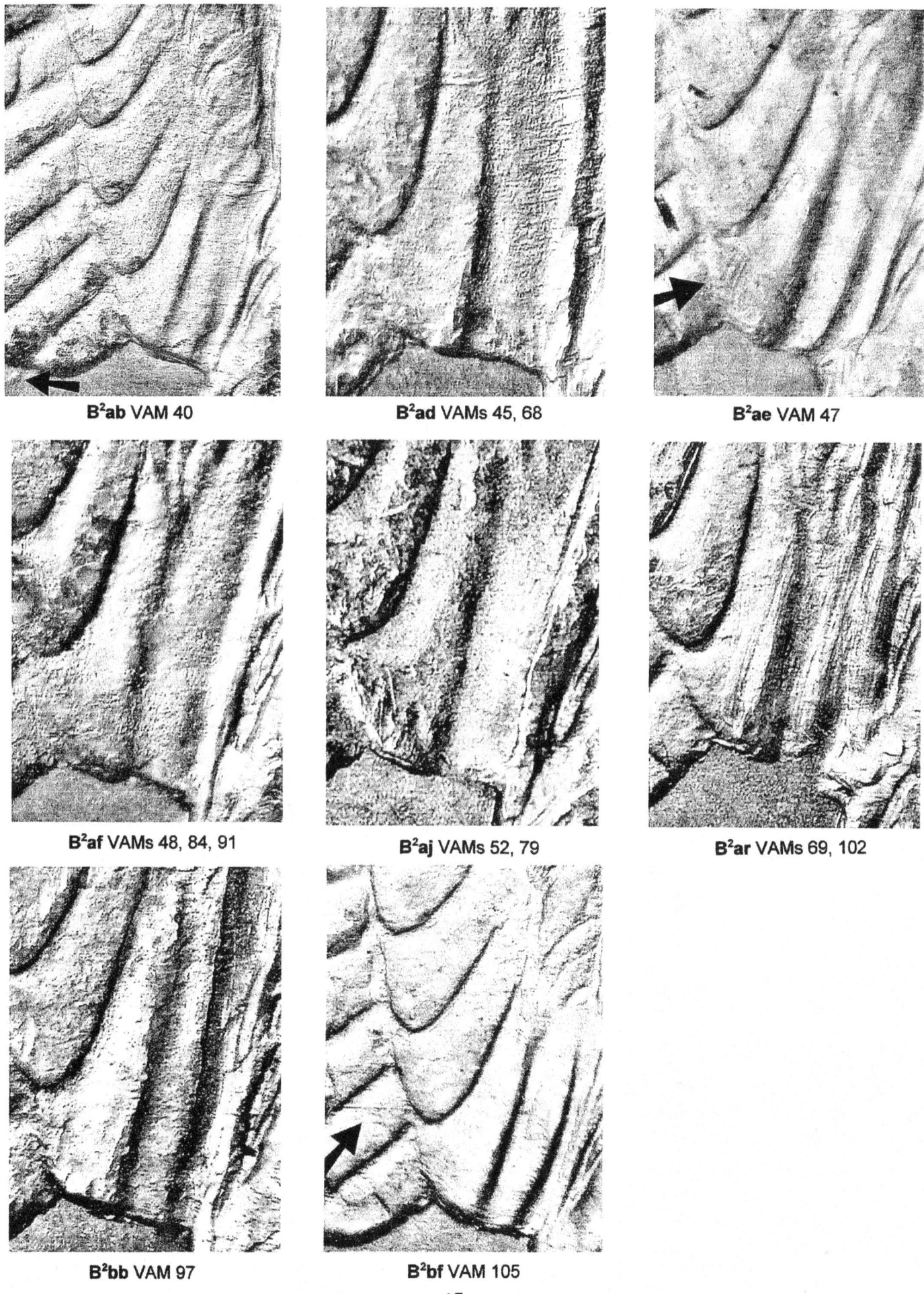

B²ab VAM 40

B²ad VAMs 45, 68

B²ae VAM 47

B²af VAMs 48, 84, 91

B²aj VAMs 52, 79

B²ar VAMs 69, 102

B²bb VAM 97

B²bf VAM 105

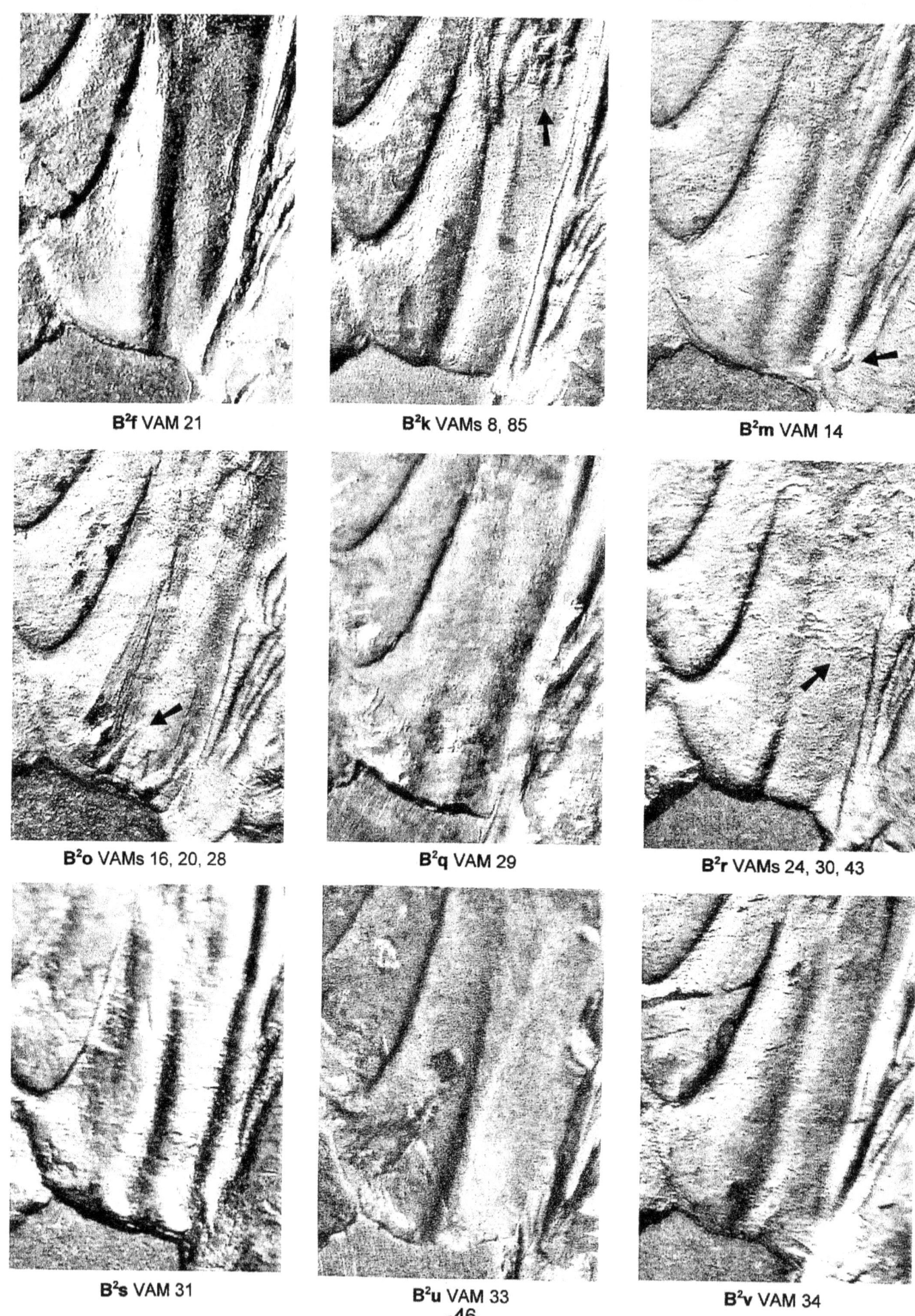

B²f VAM 21

B²k VAMs 8, 85

B²m VAM 14

B²o VAMs 16, 20, 28

B²q VAM 29

B²r VAMs 24, 30, 43

B²s VAM 31

B²u VAM 33

B²v VAM 34

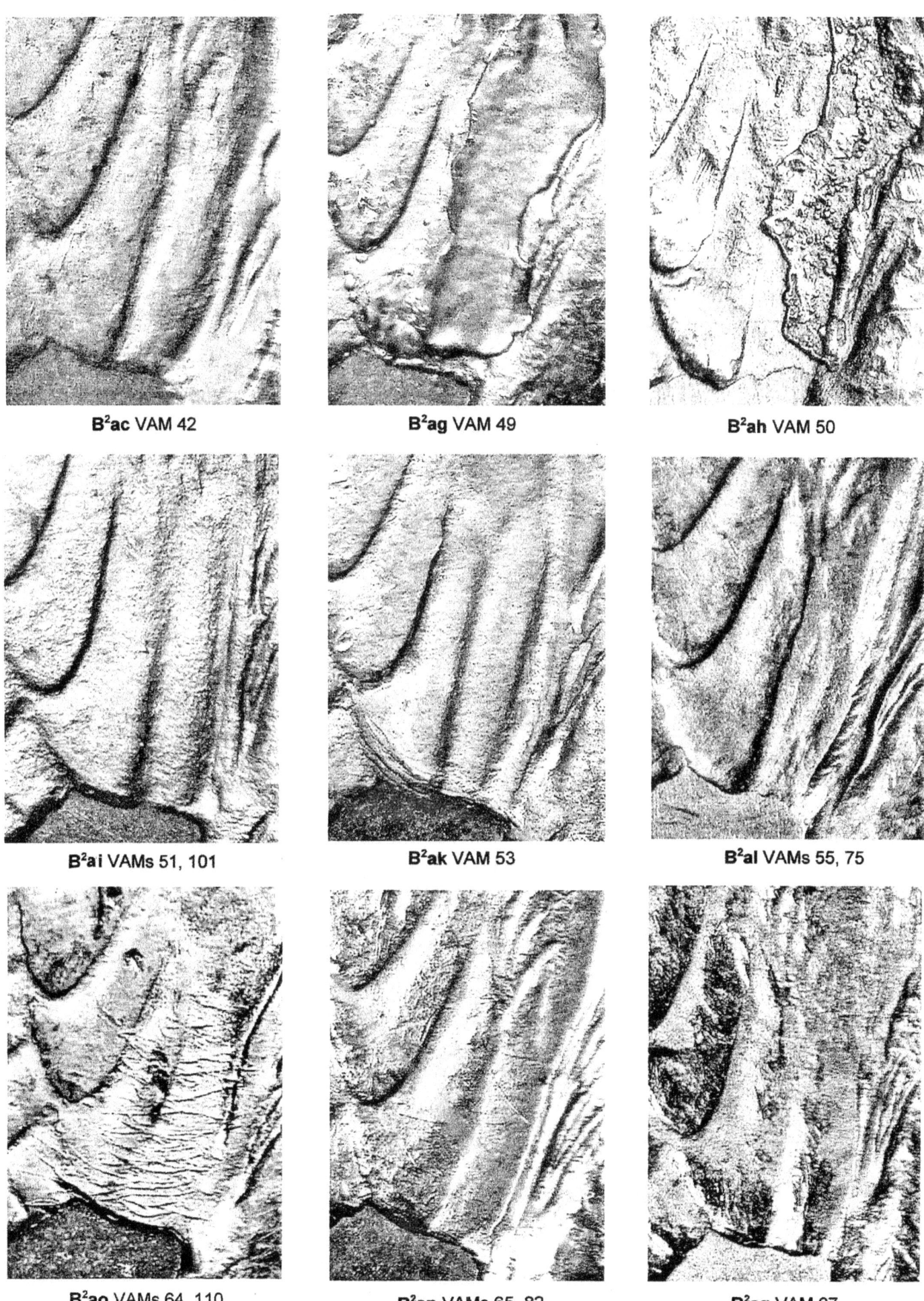

B²ac VAM 42

B²ag VAM 49

B²ah VAM 50

B²ai VAMs 51, 101

B²ak VAM 53

B²al VAMs 55, 75

B²ao VAMs 64, 110

B²ap VAMs 65, 82

B²aq VAM 67

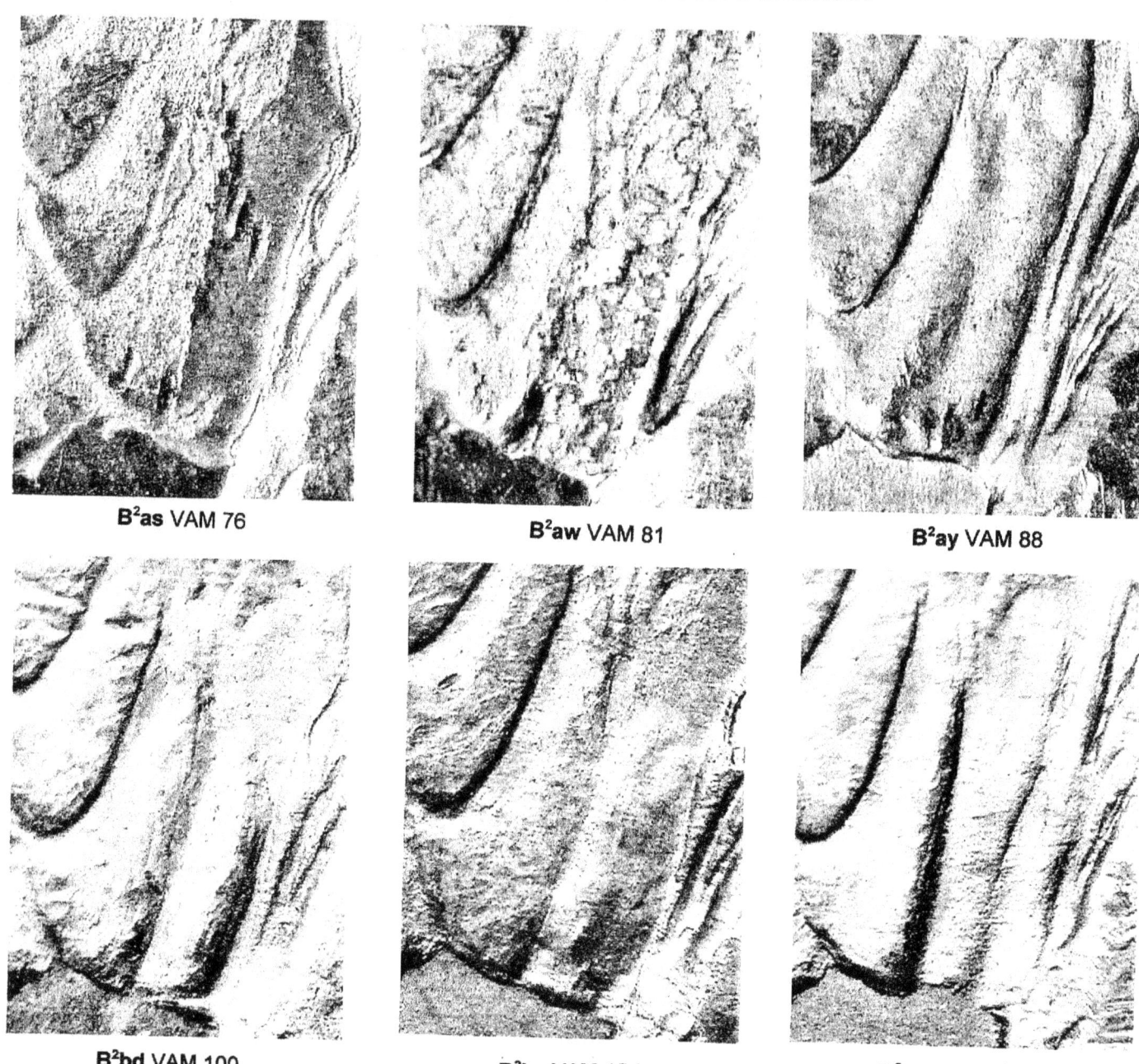

B²as VAM 76

B²aw VAM 81

B²ay VAM 88

B²bd VAM 100

B²be VAM 104

B²a VAM 1C/95

1878 S SHARED & MULTIPLE OBVERSE DIE VARIETIES

An ongoing study by Craig Lickenbrock and Jeff Seawell

Shared Obverse Die Varieties

II 1	1D & 106	Progression 106, 1D
II 1	1G die 1 & 96 *[1]	
II 1	1G die 2 & 78 die 1	Progression 78-1, 1G-2
II 1	8 die 1 & 28	Progression 28, 8-1
II 1	8 die 2 & 8A & 47 die 1	Progression 8-2, 8A, 47-1
II 1	40 & 45 & 64	Progression 64, 40, 45
II 1	46 & 46A & 52	Progression 46, 46A, 52
II 1	47 die 3 & 69	Progression 47-3, 69
II 6	7 & 24	Progression 24, 7
II 7	9 & 21 & 53 & 79	Progression 79, 9, 53, 21
II 8	10 & 65 & 100 & 109 *[1]	
II 9	11 & 22 & 77 & 111 *[1]	
II 11	14 & 15 & 44	Progression 15, 44, 14 (by Clayton Christiansen)
II 15	20 & 49 & 83 & 101 & 103	Progression 103 (die combo 1, 2, 3), 49, 103 (combo 4), 83, 101, 20 *[2]
II 17	29 & 31	Progression 29, 31
II 20	33 & 42	Progression 42, 33
II 21	50 & 76	Progression 50, 76
II 23	26 & 57 & 60 *[1]	
II 24	56 & 62 *[1]	
II 26	35 & 55	Progression 55, 35
II 27	66 & 92 *[1]	
II 30	73 & 107	
II 32	38 & 84 & 89	Progression 89, 38, 84
II 38	80 & 90	Progression 80, 90
II 40	94 & 95 *[1]	
II 43	23 & 34	Progression 34, 23
II 44	99 & 102	Progression 102, 99

*[1] Match not confirmed by authors.

*[2] II 15 obverse paired with seven reverse dies. Longest string in 1878 S series. Reverse of VAM 103-3 & 49 are same die. Engraved wing feather added to 103-3 die while out of press for polishing to remove die clash. Only known case of a used die having engraved wing feather added.

Multiple Obverse Varieties

II 1	1G	2 obverse dies
II 1	8	2 obverse dies
II 1	36	3 obverse dies
II 1	47	3 obverse dies
II 1	78	4 obverse dies

Multiple Reverse Varieties

B²a	86	2 reverse dies
B²a	103	4 reverse dies

Aug 2012

1878 S OBVERSE DIE DESIGNATIONS TO VAM NUMBER

Die	VAMs	Die	VAMs
II 1	1, 1B, 1C, 1D, 1E, 1G, 1I, 2, 8, 8A, 18, 18A, 25, 27, 28, 36, 36A, 36B, 39, 40, 43, 45, 46, 46A, 47, 48, 51, 52, 59, 61, 63, 64, 67, 69, 71, 72, 74, 74A, 78, 81, 82, 88, 96, 97, 104, 105, 106, 108	II 22	54
		II 23	26, 57, 60
		II 24	56, 62
		II 25	58
II 2	unused (was VAM 3)	II 26	35, 55
II 3	unused (was VAM 4)	II 27	66, 92
II 4	5	II 28	68
II 5	6	II 29	unused (was VAM 31)
II 6	7, 24	II 30	73, 107
II 7	9, 21, 53, 79	II 31	75, 75A
II 8	10, 65, 100, 109	II 32	38, 84, 89
II 9	11, 22, 77, 111, (11 may not exist)	II 33	unused (was VAM 48)
II 10	12 (may be same as 93)	II 34	91, 91A
II 11	14, 15, 44	II 35	85
II 12	16	II 36	86
II 13	17, 17A, 17B, 17C	II 37	87
II 14	19, 19A	II 38	80, 90
II 15	20, 49, 83, 101, 103	II 39	93
II 16	unused (was VAM 21)	II 40	94, 95
II 17	29, 31	II 41	37, 37A
II 18	30, 30A	II 42	98
II 19	41	II 43	23, 34
II 20	33, 33A, 42, 42A	II 44	99, 102
II 21	50, 76	II 45	110

1878 S B² REVERSE BROKEN r VARIETIES DIE DESIGNATION TO VAM NUMBER

Die	VAMs	Die	VAMs
★ B^2b	2, 10, 11, 12	B^2bf	105
B^2h	unused (was VAM 23)		
B^2i	5, 7, 46, 46A		
B^2j	6, 44		
B^2l	9		
B^2n	15, 80, 89		
B^2w	19, 19A, 35, 74, 74A, 93		
B^2x	36, 36A		
B^2y	23, 37		
B^2z	38, 90		
B^2aa	39, 99		
B^2ab	40		
B^2ad	45, 68		
B^2ae	47		
B^2af	48, 84, 91, 91A		
B^2aj	52, 79		
★ B^2am	61		
B^2ar	69, 102		
B^2bb	97 (r almost completely broken)		

★ no engraved wing feather   Aug 2012

1878 S B² REVERSE r NOT BROKEN VARIETIES DIE DESIGNATION TO VAM NUMBER

Die	VAMs
★ B²a	1, 1B, 1C, 1D, 1E, 1G, 1I, 41, 54, 73 (1D die), 86, 87, 94, 95, (1C die), 103, 109, 111
★ B²c	25 (may not exist)
★ B²d	17, 17A, 66
★ B²e	18
B²f	21
★ B²g	22
B²k	8, 8A, 85
B²m	14
B²o	16, 20, 28
B²q	29
B²r	24, 30, 43
B²s	31
B²t	unused (was VAM 32)
B²u	33
B²v	34
B²ac	42
B²ag	49
B²ah	50

Die	VAMs
B²ai	51, 101
B²ak	53
B²al	55, 75, 75A
★ B²an	63
B²ao	64, 110
B²ap	65, 82
B²aq	67
B²as	76
★ B²at	77
★ B²au	78, 98
B²av	unused (was old VAM 79)
B²aw	81
★ B²ax	83
B²ay	88
★ B²az	92
★ B²ba	96
★ B²bc	71
B²bd	100
B²be	104
★ B²bg	106
★ B²bh	107
★ B²bi	108

1878 S B¹ REVERSE VARIETIES DIE DESIGNATION TO VAM NUMBER
(All B¹ reverse varieties have r in Trust not broken)

Die	VAMs	Reeds
★ B¹a	26	(186)
★ B¹b	27	(185)
★ B¹c	56, 58	(184) (?)
★ B¹d	57	(186)
★ B¹e	59	(?)
★ B¹f	60	(186)
★ B¹g	62	(185)
★ B¹h	72	(186)

★ no engraved wing feather

Aug 2012

Reported/revised in: (no mark 1999 & earlier), • 2000, ★ 2001, □ 2002, ○ 2003, ▽ 2004, § 2005, # 2006, ¶ 2007, ▸ 2008, ✓ 2009, ✚ 2010, ◊ 2011, ✗ 2012

1   **II 1 • B²a (Normal Die)**   (184)   I-1   R-2

    Obverse II 1– Normal die of 1878 P type II with broken left point on number 4 star on right and 7 in date doubled slightly on right side (a hub defect).

    Reverse B²a– Normal die of 1878 P type B² with small III S mint mark.

1A (Eliminated, same as VAMs 16 or 28)

§1B(revised) **II 1 • B²a (Pitted Tail Feathers, Lines in Hair & Eagle's Talons)**   (184, 186)   I-2   R-4

    Obverse II 1– Heavy die polishing lines in hair at back of neck. Over polished nostril. Fourth right star broken.

    Reverse B²a– Two heavy diagonal die gouge lines in space above eagle's right talons and a heavy diagonal line in space between eagle's right wing and leg. Later die state shows raised dots from die rust pits at upper right in tail feathers and lower right wreath. Two die chips in lower part of eagle's right wing. Early die gouge die state has 186 reeds and later rusted die state has 184 reeds. R in Trust not broken.

◊1C (Same dies as VAM 95, but 1C designation still used.)

#1D(revised) **II 1 • B²a (Doubled D, Scratches in Tail Feathers)**   (185)   I-3   R-5

    Obverse II 1– *Die markers–* Heavy diagonal polishing lines in LIBER and two vertical lines in front of eye. Die later polished which weakened lines in front of eye and some of lines in LIBER and open nostril. Point of fourth right star broken. (Same as VAM 106.)

    Reverse B²a– Slightly doubled D in DOLLAR on left side and at bottom. Diagonal die scratches in lower part of eagle's tail feathers, thru lower top berry in left wreath, middle of eagle's right wing and long vertical line in lower part of eagle's right wing next to feather ends. (Same as VAM 73.) (Formerly VAM 1)

□1E   **II 1• B²a (Die Gouges in Right Wreath)**   (181)   I-3   R-6

    Reverse B²a– Heavy, broad die gouges in outer leaves of second and third leaf clusters from bottom of right wreath plus die gouge on left side of M in AMERICA.

▽1F (Eliminated, same as VAM 63)

✗1G(revised) **II 1 • B²a (Lines in LIB & Eagle's Left Wing Tip, Acid Treated Obverse Die 2)**   (185)   I-3   R-4

    Obverse II 1– Die 1– Heavy polishing lines thru LIB in LIBERTY. (Also VAM 96.) Die 2-- Missing nostril from over polished die. Light acid treated lower hair edge gaps with smooth areas and sharp edges. Short gouge right side of cotton boll. (Also VAM 78 Die 1.)

    Reverse B²a– Heavy horizontal polishing lines at top of eagle's left wing.

1H (Eliminated, same as VAM 1B)

✚1I   **II 1 • B²a (Gouges Bottom of Eagle's Left Wing)**   (184)   I-3   R-6

    Obverse II 1– Over polished nostril. Fourth right star left point slightly shallow. *Die marker–* Diagonal die scratch at back of nostril.

    Reverse B²a– Three long diagonal die gouges at bottom left of eagle's left wing. R in Trust not broken. III S mint mark set slightly to left at normal height.

§2(revised) **II 1 • B²b (Broken R in Trust)**   (184)   I-2   R-2

    Reverse B²b– Same as B²a, but with die fill on arm of r in Trust which can be partial or completely missing. (A hub break since it also appears on some 1878 P 7 TF & 1879 S.) May always exist in combination with engraved wing feather.

3 (Eliminated) II 2 • B²a (Doubled LIBERTY Right) (Same obverse as VAM 29/31, listed before engraved wing feather known)

4 (Eliminated) II 3 • B²a (Doubled Date) (Same obverse as VAM 29/31, listed before engraved wing feather known)

▸5(revised) **II 4 • B²i (Doubled 878, Tripled Eyelid, Engraved Wing Feather)**   (184)   I-4   R-4

    Obverse II 4– Both 8's doubled on right inside of upper loop opening. Cross bar of the 7 is doubled at top and right side. S of PLURIBUS and UNU of UNUM slightly doubled on right side. LUR-BUS doubled on left side. All letters of LIBERTY doubled with shift down. Lower hair slightly doubled. Nostril, lips, chin and neck doubled. Cotton leaves doubled at top. Wheat leaves slightly doubled on right side. Eyelid slightly tripled. Point of fourth right star not broken. Die chip in middle of cheek and two at lower right cotton leaves. Thread-like impression below ear next to hair front.

    Reverse B²i– Feather engraved between eagle's right wing and leg. Center of wings over polished. R in Trust broken. Very slight doubling of TED STATES AMER.

¶6(revised) **II 5 • B²j (Doubled Motto, Engraved Wing Feather)**   (184)   I-5   R-4

    Obverse II 5– Motto letters doubled on top surface. Doubled 6 and 7 left stars, 4, 5 and 6 right stars and right outside of ear. Doubled LIBERTY shifted left and up and left wheat leaves and kernels. Point on fourth right star not broken.

    Reverse B²j– Feather engraved between eagle's right wing and leg. Engraving lines between eagle's right wing and body and in middle of both wings. R in Trust broken. III S mint mark set slightly right. Very slight doubling of UNITED STATES OF AMERICA bottom of letters towards rim.

§7(revised) **II 6 • B²i (Doubled LIBERTY & Wheat Leaves, Engraved Wing Feather)**   (184)   I-3   R-4

    Obverse II 6– Doubled top left of Liberty head including LIBERTY with shift down, hair below LIBERTY, wheat leaves and kernels on right side and top two cotton leaves on right side. Heavy polishing lines in front of LIBERTY head profile on some specimens. Fourth right star broken. Horizontal line left of ear with dot inside ear. (Also VAM 24.)

◊8(revised) **II 1 • B²k (Engraved Wing Feather)**   (184)   I-4   R-3

    Obverse II 1– Die 1– Curved die scratch in front of forehead and horizontal die scratch between ends of lower two cotton leaves. Fourth right star broken. Same die as VAM 28. Die 2– Tiny die chip below Phrygian cap fold. Fourth right star broken. Die chip on E of PLURIBUS. Same die as some VAM 47 Die 1.

Reverse B²k– Feather engraved between eagle's right wing and leg. Engraved bars between eagle's right wing and body plus engraved patch in middle of eagle's right wing on earlier die states. R in Trust not broken. Die chip on lower right serif of E in UNITED on later obverse Die 2 die states. Both wings over polished in center with obverse Die 2.

✗8A(revised) II 1 • B²k (Engraved Wing Feather, Rusted Die Wings)　　　　　(184)　　　I-4　　　R-5

Obverse II 1– Has Obverse Die 2. Some fine polishing lines around Liberty head.

Reverse B²k– Raised dots from rusted die on eagle's wings with some splotches on eagle's left wing from possible acid treatment. Fine polishing lines in fields.

#9(revised) II 7 • B²l (Doubled and Broken B, Engraved Wing Feather)　　　　(184)　　　I-2　　　R-4

Obverse II 7– Die flakes at top of E-P with R slightly doubled at left and B at top right inside of lower loop and bottom crossbar broken. Fourth right star broken. *Die marker:* Polishing lines on bottom of Phrygian cap.

Reverse B²l– Feather engraved between eagle's right wing and leg. Fine engraving lines between eagle's right wing and body. R in Trust broken. Tiny die chip on second outer bottom feather of eagle's right wing.

10　　II 8 • B²b (Doubled Motto) (Likely doesn't exist, is VAM 65 or 100.)

11　　II 9 • B²b (Doubled Motto) (Likely doesn't exist, is VAM 22 or 77.)

12　　II 10 • B²b (Doubled Motto) (Possibly same as VAM 93.)　　　　　　(?)　　　I-2　　　R-4

Obverse II 10– Motto letters doubled slightly on lower portion of top surface. Fourth right star broken.

13 (Eliminated, same as VAM 33)

14　　II 11 • B²m (Doubled LIBERTY Left, Engraved Wing Feather)　　　　(184)　　　I-2　　　R-3

Obverse II 11– LIBERTY slightly doubled left. P in PLURIBUS has bulge at top right outside. L & R slightly doubled on left side and bottom of B crossbar is thin. Fourth right star broken. *Die marker–* Horizontal lines and raised dots in hair at jaw-neck junction.

Reverse B²m– Portions of eagle's wings over polished in middle. Feather engraved between eagle's right wing and leg. R in Trust not broken.

▽15(revised) II 11 • B²n (Lines in Eagle, Engraved Wing Feather, Doubled LIBERTY Left)　　(184)　　I-3　　R-5

Reverse B²n– Two vertical gouges in lower part of both wings, heavy die polishing lines in middle of both wings and two diagonal lines between eagle's legs. Feather engraved between eagle's right wing and leg. R in Trust partially broken.

16　　II 12 • B²o (Die Scratch on Wing, Engraved Wing Feather)　　　　(184)　　　I-3　　　R-4

Obverse II 12– E PLURIB letters doubled on right side and some on bottom. 1 in date doubled slightly on bottom. Number 3 stars on right and left doubled. LIBERTY slightly doubled/quadrupled to left. Ear doubled at top right outside. Hair strands doubled behind ear. Point of fourth right star only slightly broken.

Reverse B²o– Vertical die scratch through lower part of eagle's right wing. Some specimens show a die chip in middle of eagle's breast. Feather engraved between eagle's right wing and leg. Die chip lower right serif of E in UNITED. R in Trust not broken.

◇17(revised) II 13 • B²d (Doubled D, Over Polished Lower Obverse)　　　　(184)　　　I-2　　　R-4

Obverse II 13– Bottom of die over polished with shallow date and missing portions of lower hair line on later die state. First 8 has small die chip on right side between loops. Part of fourth right star left point completely missing on over polished die state. Eyelid doubled below front with short spike from front of eye below doubling. (Possibly same as II 30 obverse of VAMs 73 & 107.)

Reverse B²d– D in DOLLAR doubled at left top outside and at left and right bottom outside. Small III S mint mark set slightly to left. R in Trust not broken. Earliest die state has horizontal polishing lines below middle tail feathers. *Die marker–* Die gouge on right ribbon.

✓17A(revised) II 13 • B²d (Doubled D, Denticle Impressions Reverse)　　　　(184)　　　I-5　　　R-6

Obverse II 13– 7 has raised slanted dash at very bottom. Shallow raised dots at left inside of lower loop of both 8's. Point of fourth right star completely missing. Late die state with most denticle impressions polished and worn away.

Reverse B²d– Slightly raised denticle impressions band thru O, a band between LL and a double band below OL and four slanted impressions below left tail feathers. Late die state with denticle impressions at UN & STAT weak from die wear.

✓17B　　II 13 • B²d (Doubled D, Denticle Impressions Obverse & Reverse)　　(184)　　　I-5　　　R-6

Obverse II 13– Five small raised dots of denticle impressions next to Liberty head neck in field. Six raised dots in band across lower part of date from left inside of left and right 8s and two raised arcs at bottom of 7. Lateral spacing between dots is same as denticle spacing. First reported case of denticle impressions on obverse. VAM 17A doesn't show obverse denticle impressions and VAM 17C doesn't show denticle impressions at date, except for dot inside lower loop of 8 because of die polishing/wear.

Reverse B²d– Four raised denticle inside end impressions in a band at O, four in band at LL, five in double band below OL and four in slanted band below left tail feathers as in VAM 17A. Four curved raised lines between UN and four above N in UNITED that resemble denticle inside ends. Seven similar curved raised lines above A in STATES and one above right T and five vertical lines above ST with spacing of denticles. Initial denticle impressions die state.

✓17C　　II 13 • B²d (Doubled D, Denticle Impressions Obverse Neck & Reverse)　(184)　　I-5　　R-6

Obverse II 13– Later die state of VAM 17B with slightly polished die that has removed denticle impressions at date except for one at left inside of both 8s lower loop. Denticle impressions show at Liberty head neck edge.

Reverse B²d– Die wear has weakened denticle impressions at UN & STAT but ones at OLL and below tail feathers still show. Middle denticle impressions die state.

◇18(revised) II 1 • B²e (Extra Engraved Wing Feathers)　　　　　　(184)　　　I-4　　　R-5

Obverse II 1– Point of fourth right star only partially broken. Diagonal die clash line extending to left from eyelid tip. (Also VAMs 59 & 72.)

Reverse B²e– Fine engraving lines in middle of both eagle's wings where die was over polished due to incorrect basining. R in Trust not broken.

◇18A　　II 1 • B²e (Extra Wing Feathers, Break Right Star)　　　　　(184)　　　I-4　　　R-6

Obverse II 1– Radial die crack at left side of first right star with displaced field break.

□19(revised) II 14 • B²w (Doubled Motto, Die Gouge Cap, Engraved Wing Feather) (181) I-5 R-4
    Obverse II 14– LIBERTY slightly doubled with shift up. Nostril and eyelid doubled as are E PL-R-BUS U of motto. Thick broad horizontal die gouge across wheat leaves and top cotton leaf. Field is slightly concave. Doubled profile from hair down to chin. Broken fourth right star.
    Reverse B²w– Feather engraved between eagle's right wing and leg. Some engraved bars between eagle's right wing and body. R in Trust broken. D in DOLLAR doubled at top left and bottom outside. Several stages of over polishing.

□19A   II 14 • B²w (Doubled Motto, Die Gouge Cap, Engraved Wing Feather) (181) I-5 R-6
    Reverse B²w– Arm of R completely missing in Trust with open G in God. Die extremely over polished after die clashed with letters of UNITED STATES very shallow and a number of leaves disconnected in wreath. Small dots of metal all over eagle from rusted die.

20   II 15 • B²o (Concave Obverse, Engraved Wing Feather) (184) I-3 R-3
    Obverse II 15– Field slightly concave, especially near the rim. Fourth right star broken. Die chips on surface of E.
    Reverse B²o– No die scratch on eagle's right wing or die chip on eagle's breast. R in Trust not broken.

§21(revised) II 7 • B²f (Doubled LIBERTY Left, Broken B, Concave Obverse, Engraved Wing Feather) (184) I-3 R-4
    Obverse II 7– Same die as for VAM 9 but further polished with slightly concave fields near rim, especially at top right.
    Reverse B²f– Left wreath, lower part of right wreath, UNITED STATES, ONE DOLLAR and left star doubled towards rim. Doubled o in God at bottom. Slanted die gouge between eagle's right wing and body. Feather engraved between eagle's right wing and leg. Engraving lines between eagle's right wing and body. R in Trust not broken.

✦22(revised) II 9 • B²g (Doubled Motto, S Set Left) (185) I-5 R-6
    Obverse II 9– All motto letters strongly doubled. All left stars doubled on left side with 6 and 7 also doubled on right. Doubled 1, 2, 4, 5 and 6 right stars. 1 and 7 in date doubled at top right. First 8 doubled on lower left outside of upper loop and top inside of both loops. Second 8 tripled at left inside of upper loop. Fourth right star doubled but not broken. Some die states shown vertical fine die polishing lines in fields.
    Reverse B²g– Small III S mint mark set left and slightly high. R in Trust not broken. Some die states shown vertical fine die polishing lines in fields and over polished tail feathers and lower part of eagle's right wing.

§23(revised) II 43 • B²y (Doubled Profile, Engraved Wing Feather, S/S Left) (184) I-3 R-4
    Obverse II 43– Liberty head profile slightly doubled from front of LIBERTY band, front edge of hair, nose, lips and chin. Slight doubling on PLU-BUS UNUM towards rim, top of Phrygian cap, right wheat leaf and LIBERTY on right side. *Die marker:* Rough flaked surface of hair above second right star. Fourth right star broken.
    Reverse B²y– Feather engraved between eagle's right wing and leg. III S mint mark re-punched with short diagonal line at top middle inside of upper loop and curved line within lower loop. Engraved bars between eagle's right wing and body. R in Trust partially broken. Eagle's left wing slightly over polished in center.

✗24(revised) II 6 • B²r (Doubled LIBERTY & Wheat Leaves, Engraved Wing Feather) (185) I-2 R-5
    Obverse II 6– No polishing lines in front of Liberty head profile. (Also VAM 7.)
    Reverse B²r– Feather engraved between eagle's right wing and leg with possible acid treatment at top.. R in Trust not broken. Portions of eagle's left wing over polished in middle and shallow UNITED. Die chip back of top arrow head. (Also VAMs 30 & 43.)

§25   II 1 • B²c (S Set High and Right) (May not exist) (184) I-2 R-4
    Reverse B²c– Small III S mint mark set slightly high and to right. (Photo not available)

26(revised) II 23 • B¹a (Long Nock, Center Arrow Feather, S Tilted Left) (186) I-5 R-7
    Obverse II 23– Eyelid doubled at bottom front and short spikes at eye bottom front and lower part of eye socket.
    Reverse B¹a– Normal die of 1878 P B¹ type with long center arrow shaft. Small III S mint mark set slightly to right with slight tilt to left. *Die marker* of small dot in incuse line next to eagle's left leg.

□27(revised) II 1 • B¹b (Long Nock, Center Arrow Shaft) (185) I-5 R-7
    Obverse II 1– Three faint spikes below eyelid front, short vertical line in eyelid top corner and short vertical line at top of eye socket above eyelid.
    Reverse B¹b– Small III S mint mark centered and upright. *Die marker* of medium-sized die chip above top arrow feather. No diagonal polishing lines on tail feathers next to eagle's right leg. Denticle above second S in STATES broken.

¶28(revised) II 1 • B²o (Die Scratch on Wing, Engraved Wing Feather) (184) I-3 R-4
    Obverse II 1– Same die as Die 1 of VAM 8 with die scratch in front of forehead and one between lower cotton leaf ends. Some LDS specimens show faint vertical die crack in back of scratch on forehead of VAM 8. Die chip on E of PLURIBUS.

✦29(revised) II 17 • B²q (Tripled LIBERTY, Dbld Nostril & Eyelid, Sagging Jaw, Eng Wing Feather) (184) I-5 R-4
    Obverse II 17– LIBERTY tripled to left and right. Doubled eyelid, nostril, hair above date top cotton leaves and US UNUM. Tripled front and bottom of chin. 18-8 slightly doubled at bottom outside. Both 8's doubled at top left inside of upper loop, possibly from die polishing. Bottom of jaw has more rounded appearance from engraving lines to eliminate doubled profile. Only known case of engraving on Morgan dollar obverse die. Diagonal die gouge at top left of first U in PLURIBUS. Fourth right star broken.
    Reverse B²q– Feather engraved between eagle's right wing and leg. Engraved bars between eagle's right wing and body. Fully struck specimens show raised dots of rusted die on UNITED letters and leaves at top of left wreath. R in Trust not broken. Hub doubling on lower arrow head and tops of ONE DO towards coin center.

§30(revised) II 18 • B²r (Quadrupled LIBERTY, Doubled Nostril, Eyelid, Engraved Wing Feather) (185) I-2 R-4
    Obverse II 18– LIBERTY quadrupled with doubling to left, right and bottom. Doubled wheat kernels, nostril and eyelid, with ends of eyelid slightly tripled. Fourth right star broken.

✦30A   II 18 • B²r (Quadrupled LIBERTY, Doubled Nostril, Eyelid, Engraved Wing Feather, Die Break U) (181) I-2 R-5
    Obverse II 18– Radial die crack from rim thru right side of left U in PLURIBUS down to hair with displaced field die break.

♯31(revised) II 17 • B²s (Tripled LIBERTY, Dbld Nostril & Eyelid, Sagging Jaw, Engraved Wing Feather) (184) I-5 R-4
    Obverse II 17– Later die state further polished removing date doubling. Latest die state has large die chip between right 8 loops on left side.

Reverse B²s– Feather engraved between eagle's right wing and leg. R in Trust not broken. *Die marker:* Short diagonal polishing line in vee between neck and wing.

♯**32** (Eliminated, same as VAM 48)

♯**32A** (Eliminated, became VAM 91A)

○**33**(revised) **II 20 • B²u (Engraved Wing Feather, Doubled L-R-BU, S/S Notches)** (184) I-2 R-4

    Obverse II 20– Doubled L-R-BU in motto. Fourth right star broken. Spike above eyelid.

    Reverse B²u– Feather engraved between eagle's right wing and leg. R in Trust not broken, Slightly doubled D in DOLLAR at top left. Small III S mint mark set slightly high and to right and slightly doubled as notches on top and bottom serifs.

✗**33A** **II 20 • B²u (Engraved Wing Feather, Doubled L-R-BU, S/S Notches, Clashed Obverse st)** (184) I-2 R-5

    Obverse II 20– Clashed die with faint partial incuse st of Trust from reverse showing in right hair vee of lower hair edge. Fine vertical polishing lines in field at neck and back of cap ribbon. (Same as VAM 42A.)

    Reverse B²u– Couple fine die chips at lower part of eagle's right wing.

§**34**(revised) **II 43 • B²v (Doubled Profile & Reverse Legend, Engraved Wing Feather)** (184) I-2 R-4

    Reverse B²v– Feather engraved between eagle's right wing and leg. UNITED STATES OF and left wreath outer leaves slightly doubled towards rim. Fine engraving lines between eagle's right wing and body. R in Trust not broken.

▢**35**(revised) **II 26 • B²w (Sextupled Left Stars, Doubled Profile, Engraved Wing Feather)** (181) I-3 R-3

    Obverse II 26– LIBERTY slightly doubled on left side. Doubled LIBERTY band edge, hair above forehead, forehead, nose, lips and chin. All left stars very slightly tripled to sextupled towards rim with 4-7 most prominent. Right stars faintly doubled towards rim. PLURIBUS UNUM doubled to sextupled at top of letters towards rim. Top of Phrygian cap and right wheat leaf doubled. Later die states show die polishing. Fourth right star broken. *Die marker:* Triangular die chip at back of jaw-neck junction adjacent to hair curl.

✗**36**(revised) **II 1 • B²x (Engraved Wing Feather, Acid Treated Feathers)** (184) I-5 R-5

    Obverse II 1– Die 1. Two raised dots inside ear. Fourth right star broken. Slight doubling of lower serif of B in PLURIBUS and front of Liberty band. Die 3. Fourth right star broken. Doubled B lower loop on right inside and bottom. P has bulge at top right outside. Long polishing line at jaw-neck junction.

    Reverse B²x– Feather engraved between eagle's right wing and leg. Portions of feathers acid treated with raised areas in center of both wings, next to body on eagle's left wing and on upper tail feathers. R in Trust broken. Most extensive touch-up engraving and strong acid treatment on any Morgan dollar working die.

✗**36A**(revised) **II 1 • B²x (Engraved Wing Feather, Acid Treated Feathers, Die Gouge Wheat Leaf)** (184) I-5 R-6

    Obverse II 1– Small diagonal die gouge from top of left wheat leaf thru left wheat grain stalk. Slight doubling of front of LIBERTY band and slight tripling of LIBERTY. Different Die 2 than normal VAM 36 Dies 1 & 3.

✗**36B**(revised) **II 1 • B²x (Engraved Wing Feather, Acid Treated Feathers, Die Break E)** (184) I-5 R-7

    Obverse II 1– Die crack from denticles in radial direction on left side of E in E PLURIBUS with displaced field below E. First obverse Die 1 with break that likely caused a change to second obverse die of VAM 36A.

§**37**(revised) **II 41 • B²y (Doubled UNUM, Engraved Wing Feather, S/S Left)** (184) I-2 R-4

    Obverse II 41– Slightly doubled US UNUM towards rim, Phrygian cap top, right wheat leaf, front edge of hair and front of LIBERTY band. Fourth right star broken. Some specimens show polishing lines in front of Liberty head face. *Die marker:* Small curved gouge line at lower left side of lower cotton leaf.

✗**37A** **II 41 • B²y (Doubled UNUM, Engraved Wing Feather, S/S Left, Beveled Dies)** (184) I-3 R-5

    Obverse II 41– Beveled field at denticles at 1-2 right stars from possible feed finger damage on one side between both dies.

    Reverse B²y– Beveled field at denticles at S-OF from possible feed finger damage on one side.

▽**38**(revised) **II 32 • B²z (Engraved Wing Feather, Die Gouge Right Wing, Doubled Lower Hair & 8-8)** (184) I-3 R-5

    Obverse II 32– Slightly doubled L in PLURIBUS on left and bottom, R of left side and B at bottom. US UNUM slightly tripled towards rim. Doubled profile from front of LIBERTY band down to jaw. Lower hair slightly doubled towards rim. Both 8's slightly doubled at top inside of upper loop. Fourth right star broken. *Die marker:* Dot die chip in hair behind eye.

    Reverse B²z– Feather engraved between eagle's right wing and leg. Engraved bars between eagle's right wing and body. R in Trust broken. Wide diagonal die gouge at top inside and lower middle of eagle's right wing. Some specimens show die chip on F in OF.

♯**39**(revised) **II 1 • B²aa (Engraved Wing Feather)** (181) I-2 R-5

    Obverse II 1– Some tiny die chips in front of ear and dot at back of nose. Both 8's have raised metal in loops from die polishing. Fourth right star broken.

    Reverse B²aa– Feather engraved between eagle's right wing and leg. Fine engraving lines between eagle's right wing and body. R in Trust broken. Die chip back of top arrow head. Some light polishing lines on left field with long polishing line from bottom of eagle's right wing down to olive branch and diagonal die gouge on outside of eagle's left leg. Later die state than VAM 99.

40 **II 1 • B²ab (Engraved Wing Feather, Acne Die Chips)** (184) I-2 R-3

    Obverse II 1– Several tiny die chips on cheek, nose and behind eye. Fine vertical line at rear of eye and diagonal line thru LI. (Same die as VAM 45 & 64.)

    Reverse B²ab– Feather engraved between eagle's right wing and leg. Engraved bar between eagle's right wing and body. R in Trust broken.

41 **II 19 • B²a (Doubled LIBERTY Up, Nostril, Cap Fold Front)** (184) I-4 R-4

    Obverse II 19– LIBERTY slightly doubled up. Strongly doubled front of Phrygian cap fold. Doubled nostril, eyelid, lips, chin, lower hair and wheat grains. Fourth right star broken.

    Reverse B²a– Heavy vertical gouges in eagle's right wing. Heavy horizontal polishing lines in middle of eagle's left wing. Rotated reverse of 11° CCW.

✚**42**(revised) **II 20 • B²ac (Doubled L-R-BU, Engraved Wing Feather)** (184) I-2 R-3

    Reverse B²ac– Feather engraved between eagle's right wing and leg. R in Trust not broken. Hub doubling on lower arrow head and tops of ONE DO towards coin center.

+42A II 20 • B²ac (Doubled L-R-BU, Engraved Wing Feather, Clashed Obverse st)   (184)   I-2   R-5
  Obverse II 20– Clashed die with faint partial incuse st of Trust from reverse showing in right hair vee of lower hair edge. Fine vertical polishing lines in field at neck and back of cap ribbon.
  Reverse B²ac– Fine vertical polishing lines at left and right and top fields to erase die clash marks.

+43(revised) II 1 • B²r (Engraved Wing Feather)   (185)   I-2   R-3
  Obverse II 1– Raised polished areas inside loops of first 8 and wheat stalks. Die Chip on E of E PLURIBUS. Fourth right star broken.

∇44(revised) II 11 • B²j (Engraved Wing Feather, Doubled LIBERTY Left)   (184)   I-2   R-4

+45(revised) II 1 • B²ad (Engraved Wing Feather, 9 Upper Tail Feathers, Reverse Die used in 1879) (184)   I-5   R-4
  Obverse II 1– Small die chips below eyelid, on nose, behind eye and on cheek with vertical die gouge at rear of eye. (Same die as VAM 40 & 64.)
  Reverse B²ad– Feather engraved between eagle's right wing and leg. R in Trust slightly broken. Slightly doubled UNITED STATES towards rim. Two small vertical tail feathers engraved at very left side of upper tail feathers that engraver mistakenly added to normal blank area to create 9 upper tail feathers. Normal upper tail feather next to two added ones slightly strengthened on right side as added ridge. Middle over polished outer feathers of eagle's left wing have been strengthened by engraving. Die later used on 1879 S VAM 9 & 77. (Same die as VAM 68.)

§46(revised) II 1 • B²i (Engraved Wing Feather, Worm-Eye Die Scratch)   (184)   I-2   R-4
  Obverse II 1– Thin worm-like die scratch behind eye and couple small die chips on cheek in front of ear. Fourth right star broken. (Same die as VAM 52.)

□46A II 1 • B²i (Engraved Wing Feather, Extra Wreath Berry Die Break)   (184)   I-3   R-6
  Obverse II 1– Couple small die chips on cheek.
  Reverse B²i– Die break on left side of second berry cluster from top of left wreath to form extra looking berry or leaf. Later die state has small die chip on left star and in wreath opposite left star.

♯47(revised) II 1 • B²ae (Engraved Wing Feather)   (184)   I-2   R-3
  Obverse II 1– Die 1-- Tiny die chip below Phrygian cap fold. Same die as VAM 8 Die 2. Fourth right star broken. Die 2– Polishing scratch in top of ER in LIBERTY and polished loops of first 8. Fourth right star broken. Die 3– Long horizontal die scratch between hair locks in back of neck. Fourth right star broken. Same die as VAM 69.
  Reverse B²ae– Feather engraved between eagle's right wing and leg. R in Trust broken. Slightly doubled bottom inside of ITED STATES F and tops of In God We. Later die states show polishing lines in fields. *Die marker:* Tiny die dig at end of third tail feather from right.

✗48(revised) II 1 • B²af (Engraved Wing Feather, Acid Treated Eagle, S Tilted Right)   (184)   I-4   R-4
  Obverse II 1– Slight doubling of B in PLURIBUS at bottom, edge of forehead, front of hair and top of Phrygian cap. Shallow over polished ear. Fourth right star broken.
  Reverse B²af– Feather engraved between eagle's right wing and leg. R in Trust partially broken with triangle on arm. III S mint mark set slightly high with slight tilt to right. Diagonal die scratch right of wreath bow. Acid treated areas at eagle's left and right wing-body junction, middle of eagle's right wing, upper and lower tail feathers and upper arrow feather. (Also VAMs 84 & 91.)

✗49(revised) II 15 • B²ag (Acid Treated Wing Feather)   (189)   I-5   R-5
  Obverse II 15– Polished concave obverse with diagonal clash lines at neck.
  Reverse B²ag– Acid treated feather between eagle's right wing and leg extending up between wing and body with smooth top and rough sides. A long continuous acid treated area. R in Trust not broken. Same die as VAM 103 Die Combo 3 with same die markers but polished and engraved after dies clashed. *Die markers:* Raised dot on fourth feather from bottom of eagle's left wing with line above and two lines below it, gouge in eagle's mouth and diagonal line at left side of tail feathers between eagle's legs.

✗50(revised) II 21 • B²ah (Tripled Eyelid, Acid Treated Wing Feather, S Tilted Left)   (184)   I-5   R-6
  Obverse II 21– Eyelid slightly tripled in front of eye just below front of eyelid. Point of fourth right star broken. Die chip at mouth corner.
  Reverse B²ah– Acid treated feather between eagle's right wing and leg extending up between wing and body to top of wing with dots on surface and two layers at bottom. A long continuous acid treated area. Heavy polishing lines in fields. Small III S mint mark centered and tilted left. R in Trust not broken.

▶51(revised) II 1 • B²ai (Engraved Wing Feather, Over Polished Ear, Weak STAT)   (184)   I-3   R-4
  Obverse II 1– Over polished ear and faint spike below eyelid front. Fourth right star broken.
  Reverse B²ai– Feather engraved between eagle's right wing and leg. R in Trust not broken. Slight notch at top of top serif of small S mint mark. Center of eagle's right and left wings over polished and STAT is very shallow. Slightly doubled tops of ONE DOL towards coin center. (Also VAM 101.) *Die marker:* Two horizontal polishing lines in upper tail feathers.

○52(revised) II 1 • B²aj (Engraved Wing Feather, Worm-Eye Die Scratch)   (184)   I-2   R-4
  Obverse II 1– Thin worm-like die scratch behind eye and two tiny die chips in hair bun. Broken fourth right star. (Same die as VAM 46/46A.)
  Reverse B²aj– Feather engraved between eagle's right wing and leg. Engraved ridge between eagle's right wing and body. R in Trust broken. *Die marker:* Long vertical polishing line in lower part of eagle's right wing.

§53(revised) II 7 • B²ak (Dbld LIBERTY, Broken B, Concave Obv., Dbld Left Wreath, Eng. Feather) (184)   I-3   R-4
  Obverse II 7– Same concave die as VAM 21.
  Reverse B²ak– Outside leaves on left wreath and UNITED STATES OF slightly doubled towards rim. Feather engraved between eagle's right wing and leg. Engraved bars between eagle's right wing and body. R in Trust not broken. Diagonal die scratch just above engraved wing feather. Die chip on first T in STATES on some specimens.

54 II 22 • B²a (Doubled Profile)   (181)   I-2   R-3
  Obverse II 22– Liberty head profile doubled on nose, lips and chin. First four stars on left doubled towards rim. LIBERTY doubled slightly on left.

✗55(revised) II 26 • B²al (Sextupled Left Stars, Doubled Profile, Engraved Wing Feather, Acid Treated Wings) (181) I-3   R-5

    Reverse B²al– Shallow feather engraved between eagle's right wing and leg. Slightly doubled UNITED STAT and top leaf cluster of left wreath towards rim. R in Trust not broken. Raised dots, lines and splotches in center of both wings from acid treated die, but later die state than VAM 75A and die polished again. *Die markers:* Tiny raised dot on right side of upper tail feathers between eagle's legs and curved depressed area on lowermost outside feather of eagle's right wing.

▸56(revised) II 24 • B¹c (Long Nock, Center Arrow Feather, S Set High)   (184)   I-5   R-7

    Obverse II 24– Two horizontal bars out from front of eye. L of LIBERTY slightly doubled on lower left serif. Small die chip at top of Phrygian cap.

    Reverse B¹c– Small III S mint mark set high, slightly to left and upright. *Die marker* of lower part of tail feathers between eagle's legs missing due to curved raised metal.

57(revised) II 23 • B¹d (Long Nock, Center Arrow Feather, S Set Left)   (186)   I-5   R-7

    Reverse B¹d– Small III S mint mark set slightly left well below wreath, with slight tilt to left. *Die marker* of small die chip at lower right outside of S mint mark and small die chips in field below S mint mark.

58   II 25 • B¹c (Long Nock, Center Arrow Feather, S Set High)   (?)   I-5   R-7

    Obverse 25– Thick spike just below eyelid in front of eye. Slight doubling inside inner ear.

59(revised) II 1 • B¹e (Long Nock, Center Arrow Feather, S Set Slightly Left)   (?)   I-5   R-7

    Obverse II 1– Diagonal die clash line extending to left from eyelid tip. (Also VAMs 18 & 72.)

    Reverse B¹e– Small III S mint mark set very slightly left of center, but not as far left or as high as VAM 57. *Die markers* of vertical polishing line between eagle's right leg and tail feathers and diagonal polishing line on middle tail feather below olive branch.

60(revised) II 23• B¹f (Long Nock, Center Arrow Feather, S Set High & Left)   (186)   I-5   R-7

    Reverse B¹f– Small III S mint mark set high and to left, but further left than VAM 56. *Die markers* of diagonal polishing lines on lower part of tail feathers next to eagle's right leg.

61   II 1 • B²am (Doubled Reverse Motto)   (?)   I-2   R-4

    Reverse B²am– Slight doubling towards rim on bottom inside of UNITED STAT letters and top outside of left wreath leaves. R in Trust broken.

62   II 24 • B¹g (Long Nock, Center Arrow Feather, S Set Far Left)   (185)   I-5   R-7

    Reverse B¹g– Small III S mint mark set far to left and slightly high. *Die marker* of large raised metal area at junction of olive branch and top arrow feather.

✓63(revised) II 1 • B²an (S/S Right)   (185)   I-3   R-6

    Obverse II 1– Diagonal die scratch in front of eye. Beveled insides of 8's loops. Later die state has polished die with shortened scratch in front of eye and removed beveling in loops of both 8's. *Die marker*– Long diagonal polishing line in hair below cap rear.

    Reverse B²an– III S mint mark doubled as curved diagonal line in middle of upper loop opening. Long horizontal die scratch thru neck and eagle's right wing. R in Trust not broken. No engraved wing feather.

◇64(revised) II 1 • B²ao (Engraved Wing Feather With Lines, 8 Upper Tail Feathers)   (184)   I-5   R-5

    Obverse II 1– (Same die as VAMs 40 & 45.)

    Reverse B²ao– Same die as VAM 110 but later die state with feather engraved between eagle's right wing and leg with fine horizontal engraving lines across it. Smooth engraved feathers in middle of eagle's left wing and engraved lines in middle of eagle's right wing. Engraved vertical bar on very left side of upper tail feathers to make 8 upper tail feathers. Similar to 1878 S VAMs 45/68 and 1879 S Rev 78 VAMs 9/77 that share a reverse with 9 upper tail feathers. R in Trust not broken

▸65(revised) II 8 • B²ap (Doubled Motto, Double Spikes Eye, Engraved Wing Feather)   (185)   I-3   R-5

    Obverse II 8– PLURIB doubled with LU doubled at top and RIB doubled at bottom. UN doubled at bottom and right U in UNUM doubled at top left. Upper wheat leaves doubled on right side. Two short spikes below eyelid. Ear slightly doubled at right outside. Point of fourth right star not broken.

    Reverse B²ap– Feather engraved between eagle's right wing and leg. R in Trust not broken.

§66(revised) II 27 • B²d (Doubled Ear & Eyelid, Doubled D)   (185)   I-2   R-6

    Obverse II 27– Slightly doubled ear on right inside and eyelid below front. Fine line thru top of IB in LIBERTY to left wheat leaf. Fourth right star broken.

    Reverse B²d– Horizontal polishing lines below middle tail feathers, same as VAM 17 EDS.

▫67   II 1 • B²aq (Engraved Wing Feather, S Set Left)   (184)   I-2   R-5

    Reverse B²aq– Feather engraved between eagle's right wing and leg. R in Trust not broken. Small III S mint mark set to left and upright.

✚68   II 28 • B²ad (Doubled LIBERTY, Engraved Wing Feather, 9 Upper TF, Reverse Die Used in 1879) (184) I-5   R-5

    Obverse II 28– LIBERTY doubled on left side. LIBERTY band edge, front of hair, bottom front of eye and chin slightly doubled.

    Reverse B²ad– Die later used on 1879 S VAM 9 & 77. (Same die as VAM 45.)

◇69(revised) II 1 • B²ar (Engraved Wing Feather, Die Chips R & Wing)   (184)   I-2   R-5

    Obverse II 1– *Die marker*- Horizontal die scratch in hair behind neck.

    Reverse B²ar– Feather engraved between eagle's right wing and leg with vertical engraving lines in that area possibly with acid treatment. R in Trust broken. Small III S mint mark in normal position with slight tilt to right. Slightly doubled UNITED S-TE towards rim. Die chip on lower right of R in DOLLAR and in middle of eagle's right wing inner feathers.

§70 (Eliminated, same as VAM 31)

▫71 (Old 71 same as VAM 35)

§71   II 1 • B²bc (S Set High)   (185)   I-2   R-4

    Reverse B²bc– Small III S mint mark set high but not as high as VAM 77. Some horizontal lines on partial feather between eagle's right wing and leg. R in Trust not broken.

▫72   II 1 • B¹h (Long Nock, Center Arrow Shaft, S Tilted Left)   (186)   I-5   R-7

    Obverse II 1– Diagonal die chips below eyelid front. Point of fourth right star not broken. (Also VAMs 18 & 59.)

Reverse B¹h– Small III S mint mark centered and tilted slightly to left. *Die markers* of diagonal polishing line to left and right of eagle's right leg above claws.

□73   **II 30 • B²a (Doubled Eyelid with Spike, Lines in Tail Feathers)**   (185)   I-3   R-5
    Obverse II 30– Eyelid doubled below front with short spike from front of eye below doubling. Fourth right star broken.
    Reverse B²a– Diagonal die polishing lines in eagle's tail feathers. (Same die as VAM 1D.)

§74(revised) **II 1 • B²w (Engraved Wing Feather, Broken R)**   (181)   I-3   R-3
    Obverse II 1– *Die marker:* Diagonal die polishing line at back of eye socket. Fourth right star broken.
    Reverse B²w– R arm completely broken to form Tiust. Latest die state with very over polished reverse.

§74A   **II 1 • B²w (Engraved Wing Feather, Broken R, Die Chip Left Wreath)**   (181)   I-3   R-6
    Reverse B²w– Small die chip on left wreath outside leaf opposite NI.

#75(revised) **II 31 • B²al (Doubled E L-BUS, UNUM, Engraved Wing Feather)**   (181)   I-2   R-4
    Obverse II 31– E L-BUS & UNUM letters slightly doubled at bottom inside towards rim. Left stars very slight sextupled towards rim. Chin slightly doubled. Fourth right star broken. *Die markers:* Comma die chip at top inside of ear and large die chip at top of Phrygian cap.
    Reverse B²al– Earlier die state than VAM 55. Initial die state not over polished. After dies clashed, center of both wings slightly over polished.

✗75A(revised) **II 31 • B²al (Doubled E L-BUS, UNUM, Engraved Wing Feather, Acid Treated Wings)** (181)   I-2   R-5
    Reverse B²al– Raised dots, lines and splotches in center of both wings from light acid treatment. Heavy die file and polishing lines in fields in attempt to remove rusted die pits. Die later polished again after clashing.

✗76(revised) **II 21 • B²as (Tripled Eyelid, Acid Treated Wing Feathers)**   (184)   I-5   R-5
    Reverse B²as– Smooth acid treated feather between eagle's right wing and leg with some smooth acid treated bars in middle of eagle's left wing and smooth patches between eagle's right wing and body, in eagle's right wing and to left and right of eagle's right leg. R in Trust not broken. Unusual acid treated smooth patches in wings and at eagle's leg.

□77   **II 9 • B²at (Doubled Motto, S Set Very High)**   (?)   I-5   R-6
    Reverse B²at– Small III S mint mark centered and set very high. R in Trust not broken and wing feather next to eagle's right leg not engraved.

✗78(revised) **II 1 • B²au (Lines on Partial Inside Wing Feather, S Set Left, Tilted Left, Acid Treated Obv. Die 1)** (181, 185) I-2 R-4
    Obverse II 1– Die 1– Slightly over polished lower hair with smooth raised areas with sharp edges in hair gaps from acid treatment6 to fill in missing hair. Short gouge at right side of right cotton boll. (Same obverse as VAM 1G Die 2.) (185 reeds) Die 2– Faint die doubling line below eyelid front. (185 reeds) Die 3– Die over polished with cap ribbon divided into separated pieces with tiny die chip near forward piece. Die gouge at top inside and right inside of ear. (181 reeds) Die 4– Two tiny die chips at end of cap ribbon. (181 reeds)
    Reverse B²au– Small III S mint mark set slightly left with slight tilt to left. R in Trust not broken. *Die markers:* Short horizontal lines on partial lower feather between eagle's right wing and leg with some fine vertical polishing lines on left side. (Same reverse die as VAM 98.)

79 (Old 79 eliminated, same as VAM 53)

§79   **II 7 • B²aj (Doubled LIBERTY, Broken B, Engraved Wing Feather)**   (184)   I-2   R-4
    Obverse II 7– Same die as for VAM 9 but not concave.

✗80(revised) **II 38 • B²n (Engraved Wing Feather, Lines in Eagle, Doubled E-PL-R-B)**   (184)   I-3   R-5
    Obverse II 38– Slightly doubled E at bottom and right side of vertical bar, P at bottom, L at top left and bottom, R at left and B at bottom and right inside of both loops. LIBERTY slightly doubled to left. *Die marker*– Fine diagonal polishing line at eye front and double horizontal line at back of nostril. Fourth right star broken.

✗81   **II 1 • B²aw (Acid Treated Wing Feather)**   (184)   I-5   R-5
    Reverse B²aw– Acid treated feather between eagle's right wing and leg and body with raised dots on acid treated area. A long touch-up acid treated area. Small III S mint mark set slightly to left with slight tilt to left. Small raised dot in middle of eagle's left wing. R in Trust not broken.

✗82(revised) **II 1 • B²ap (Engraved Wing Feather, Die Chips Lip)**   (185)   I-2   R-5
    Obverse II 1– *Die marker*- Small die chips on lower lip.

#83   **II 15 • B²ax (Doubled Eagle's Left Wing)**   (184)   I-2   R-5
    Obverse II 15– Polished concave obverse.
    Reverse B²ax– Doubled eagle's left wing upper feathers, D in DOLLAR and top edge of eagle's right wing. Slight doubling of In God We Trust letters to right. R in Trust not broken.

✗84(revised) **II 32 • B²af (Engraved Wing Feather, S Tilted Right, Doubled Lower Hair & 8-8, Acid Treated Eagle)** (184) I-4 R-4
    Obverse II 32– Polished down with slightly concave obverse.

○85   **II 35 • B²k (Doubled Eyelid, Engraved Wing Feather)**   (?)   I-4   R-5
    Obverse II 35– Doubling below eyelid and top part of eye socket.

✓86(revised) **II 36 • B²a (Doubled Ear Lower Inside)**   (186)   I-2   R-4
    Obverse II 36– Ear doubled at lower right inside. Fourth right star broken. *Die marker*– Several short diagonal die scratches at base of cotton bolls.
    Reverse B²a– Die 1– Small III S mint mark set slightly to left and filled. *Die markers*– Four short diagonal die scratches between eagle's left leg and tail feathers. Diagonal polishing lines on lower feather between eagle's right wing and leg. R in Trust not broken. (Often found in Redfield collection holders.) Die 2– Small S mint mark set slightly to left. *Die markers*– Small die chips on upper tail feathers in middle and lower left on some specimens. Die 3– Small III S mint mark centered and not filled. Heavy die polishing lines in middle of both wings and on upper tail feathers. Two horizontal polishing spikes at wing edge below In.

▽87   **II 37 • B²a (Spiked Eye, Doubled Motto)**   (185)   I-3   R-6
    Obverse II 37– Two spikes below eyelid front with one very thick and a short one at bottom of eye front. Doubled motto letters towards coin center.
    Reverse B²a– Fine raised dots all over eagle from rusted die.

∇88　II 1 • B²ay (S/S Top Left Inside, Engraved Wing Feather)　　　　(184)　　I-3　R-5
　　　Obverse II 1– Touch of doubling on ear at left inside and right outside plus top right of right wheat leaf.
　　　Reverse B²ay– III S mint mark set slightly left and doubled as slightly curved vertical line at left side of upper loop opening.
　　　　　Feather engraved between eagle's right wing and leg. R in Trust not broken.

✗89(revised) II 32 • B²n (Engraved Wing Feather, Lines in Eagle, Doubled Lower Hair & 8-8) (184)　I-3　R-4

∇90　II 38 • B²z (Engraved Wing Feather, Die Gouge Right Wing, Doubled E-PL-R-B)　(184)　　I-2　R-5

✗91　II 34 • B²af (Engraved Wing Feather, S Tilted Right, Doubled US UNUM & LIBERTY, Acid Treated Eagle) (184) I-4 R-6
　　　Obverse II 34– Slight surface doubling at bottom and top inside of lower loop of B in PLURIBUS. Small raised dot between LI.
　　　　　LIBERTY doubled on left side. Slight doubling of front of LIBERTY band, hair above forehead, top of Phrygian cap and
　　　　　US UNUM towards rim. Fourth right star broken.

✗91A　II 34 • B²af (Engraved Wing Feather, S Tilted Rt., Doubled US UNUM, Acid Treated Eagle, Die Gouge Cap) (184) I-4 R-5
　　　Obverse II 34– Horizontal die gouge at back of Phrygian cap.

∇92　II 27 • B²az (Doubled Ear & Eyelid, Doubled D, Vertical Polishing Lines Wing)　(185)　　I-2　R-6
　　　Reverse B²az– D in DOLLAR doubled at left top outside and at left and right bottom outside. R in Trust not broken. Similar to
　　　　　VAM 17 but different die. Heavy vertical polishing lines in eagle's right wing next to leg with wide gouge in lower part
　　　　　of wing and between two left tail feathers. Later die state polishing removed upper lines.

∇93　II 39 • B²w (Engraved Wing Feather, Doubled L)　　　　　　　(181)　　I-2　R-4
　　　Obverse II 39– Slightly doubled P at top, L at top left, R at left and right and B at bottom in PLURIBUS. Slightly doubled front of
　　　　　LIBERTY band and hair edge above forehead. Left stars slightly doubled to quadrupled towards rim. Fourth right star
　　　　　broken. *Die markers:* Single polishing line lower left of R in LIBERTY. Short horizontal polishing line at right edge of
　　　　　Phrygian cap ribbon.

◇94(revised) II 40 • B²a (Doubled PLURIBUS UNUM, Die Chip R)　　　　　(184)　　I-2　R-5
　　　Obverse II 40– PLURIBUS UNUM doubled towards rim with L doubled on left and right sides. Slightly doubled LIBERTY on
　　　　　left side, front of LIBERTY band, top of Phrygian cap, lower hair edge above date, right wheat leaf on right side. Light
　　　　　polishing lines in fields. Fourth right star broken. Die chip at top right of E in PLURIBUS. *Die marker–* Wavy raised line
　　　　　between tops of BE in LIBERTY. (Die also used for VAM 95.)

95 (Old 95 eliminated, same as VAM 46)

◇95(revised) II 40 • B²a (Doubled PLURIBUS UNUM, Die Chip R, Reverse Die Used in 1879) (184)　I-4　R-5
　　　Reverse B²a– Lightly engraved shallow feathers between eagle's right wing and leg. Slightly doubled D in DOLLAR at bottom.
　　　　　Die chip on upper right of top loop of R in AMERICA. R in Trust not broken. (Same die as VAM 1C.) Die later used on
　　　　　1879 S VAMs 4, 23 and 25.

§96　II 1 • B²ba (S/S Triangles, Lines in LIB)　　　　　　　　(185)　　I-3　R-4
　　　Obverse II 1– Heavy die polishing lines thru LIB in LIBERTY. (Same as VAM 1G Die 1.)
　　　Reverse B²ba– Centered III S mint mark doubled with curved line on left inside of upper loop with raised triangle above it and
　　　　　vertical raised triangle in lower loop. R in Trust not broken. Feather not engraved between eagle's right wing and leg.

§97　II 1 • B²bb (Engraved Wing Feather, Die Gouge Eagle's Left Wing)　　　(184)　　I-3　R-5
　　　Reverse B²bb– Feather engraved between eagle's right wing and leg. Slanted die gouge on lower inside of eagle's left wing.
　　　　　Slightly doubled UNITED and upper left wreath towards rim. Small III S mint mark centered. R in Trust almost
　　　　　completely broken.

§98　II 42 • B²au (Doubled 878 and Nostril)　　　　　　　　　(185)　　I-3　R-5
　　　Obverse II 42– Both 8's doubled at top left inside of upper loop. 7 doubled at top right of vertical shaft. (Doubling on date
　　　　　different than VAM 4 which has minor doubling at bottom of digits, top of 7 & less at top inside of 8's upper loops.)
　　　　　Nostril strongly doubled. Eyelid slightly doubled as is lower hair on right side. LIBERTY slightly doubled at top ,
　　　　　bottom, left and right. Point of fourth right star completely broken off. Ear slightly doubled at left inside and right
　　　　　outside. Doubled left side of top cotton leaf. *Die marker:* Die chip at back of lower Phrygian cap below ribbon.

§99　II 44 • B²aa (Engraved Wing Feather, Doubled Motto)　　　　　(181)　　I-2　R-4
　　　Obverse II 44– Slightly doubled L-BUS UNUM at bottom inside of letters. R doubled slightly on left side and E at top right.
　　　　　Phrygian cap top and right wheat leaf very slightly doubled. Fourth right star broken. *Die marker:* Two short lines below
　　　　　hair below designer's initial M before die was polished after clashing.

§100　II 8 • B²bd (Doubled Motto & Ear, Double Spikes Eye, Engraved Wing Feather)　(186)　I-3　R-5
　　　Reverse B²bd– Feather engraved between eagle's right wing and leg. R in Trust not broken.

#101　II 15 • B²ai (Concave Obverse, Die Chips on E, Shallow STAT, Engraved Wing Feather) (184)　I-2　R-5
#102　II 44 • B²ar (Doubled Motto, Engraved Wing Feather)　　　　　(184)　　I-2　R-5
#103　II 15 • B²a (Die Chip E)　　　　　　　　　　　(181, 184, 185)　I-2　R-5-6
　　　Die Combo 1– Obverse not concave, earliest die state, die scratch end of Phrygian cap ribbon. Fourth right star broken. Reverse–
　　　　　Die marker: Double vertical polishing lines in middle of eagle's left wing. Reeding 185. R in Trust not broken.
　　　Die Combo 2– Obverse not concave, die scratch end of cap ribbon. Fourth right star broken. Reverse– *Die marker:* Strong die
　　　　　polishing line in top middle of eagle's left wing. Reeding 181. R in Trust not broken.
　　　Die Combo 3– Obverse not concave, die scratch end of cap ribbon. Fourth right star broken. Reverse–*Die markers:* Raised dot on
　　　　　fourth feather from bottom of eagle's left wing with line above and two lines below it, gouge in eagle's mouth and
　　　　　diagonal line at left side on tail feathers between eagle's legs. Earlier die state than VAM 49 without acid treated wing
　　　　　feather. Interest Factor 3 because of VAM 49 association. Other die combos I-2. Reeding 181. R in Trust not broken.
　　　Die Combo 4– Obverse polished and slightly concave with die scratch at end of cap ribbon removed. Some have diagonal die clash
　　　　　line at neck. Fourth right star broken. Reverse– *Die marker:* Short double horizontal polishing lines at top inside of
　　　　　eagle's right leg. Slight doubling of bottom inside of ITED. Reeding 184. R in Trust not broken.

#104　II 1 • B²be (Die Gouges Lower Hair & Wing, Engraved Wing Feather)　　(184)　　I-2　R-5
　　　Obverse II 1– Short die gouge in hair space above 7 and two short die gouges in space above lower hair right vee. Fourth right star
　　　　　broken.

Reverse B²be– Feather engraved between eagle's right wing and leg. Small III S mint mark set slightly left. Long vertical die gouge in upper part of eagle's left wing and some fine short die scratches in eagle's left wing. R in Trust not broken. Some specimens show fine vertical polishing lines in fields to remove die clash marks.

#105   **II 1 • B²bf (Engraved Wing Feather, Triangle on r, Over Polished Reverse)**   (181)   I-2   R-5

Obverse II 1– Diagonal die scratch on nose bridge in front of eye. Small die chip at bottom of Phrygian cap below ribbon. Broken fourth right star. Slightly doubled left inside and right outside of ear from defect in one of hubs.

Reverse B²bf– Feather engraved between eagle's right wing and leg. Short feather engraved between eagle's right wing and body. R in Trust partially broken with triangle on arm. Shallow UNITED STAT with over polished tail feathers. Thin vertical polishing lines in middle of eagle's right wing. Engraving in middle of both wings to strengthen over polished feathers. *Die marker:* Tiny triangular die gouge at top of wreath leaf below arrow feathers on some specimens.

#106   **II 1 • B²bg (High S Tilted Slightly Left)**   (185)   I-2   R-5

Obverse II 1– Same die as VAM 1D, but earlier die state.

Reverse B²bg– Small III S mint mark set high with slight tilt to left. R in Trust not broken. Over polished die with shallow TED STAT and top left denticles. Heavy polishing lines in fields. *Die marker*– Diagonal die scratch in tail feathers below arrow shafts.

#107   **II 30 • B²bh (Doubled Eyelid with Spike, Doubled D)**   (185)   I-3   R-6

Reverse B²bh– D in DOLLAR doubled at left top outside and slightly at lower right outside. Small III S mint mark set slightly to left. R in Trust not broken. *Die marker*– Double vertical die scratches on 7-9 feathers from bottom of eagle's right wing near inner feathers.

¶108   **II 1 • B²bi (S/S Lines)**   (184)   I-2   R-6

Obverse II 1– Small die chip right of next to bottom cotton leaf.

Reverse B²bi– Centered III S mint mark re-punched with vertical line in center of lower loop, spike in center of upper loop and split top and bottom serifs. Feather not engraved between eagle's right wing and leg. R in Trust not broken. Series of short vertical die scratches in middle of eagle's right outer wing feathers, near inner feathers. Single horizontal die scratch thru eagle's right leg, mostly on right side.

¶109   **II 8 • B²a (Doubled Motto, Double Spikes Eye)**   (185)   I-3   R-6

◊110   **II 45 • B²ao (Engraved Wing Feather, 8 Upper TF, Doubled Cap Top, US UNUM & Wheat Leaf)** (184) I-5   R-6

Obverse II 45– Slightly doubled top of Phrygian cap, right side of right wheat leaf, front of LIBERTY band, LIBERTY to right, top of upper right cotton leaf and tops of US UNUM towards rim. *Die marker*– Short vertical die scratch at top of forehead near hair line.

Reverse B²ao– Same die as VAM 64 but earlier die state with feather engraved between eagle's right wing and leg with fine horizontal engraving lines across it. Smooth engraved feathers in middle of eagle's left wing and engraved lines in middle of eagle's right wing. Engraved vertical bar on very left side of upper tail feathers to make 8 upper tail feathers. Similar to 1878 S VAMs 45/68 and 1879 S Rev 78 VAMs 9/77 that share a reverse with 9 upper tail feathers. R in Trust not broken.

◊111   **II 9 • B²a (Doubled Motto)**   (185)   I-5   R-6

Reverse B²a– R in Trust not broken. S mint mark in normal position and very slightly high. *Die markers*– Horizontal polishing line on 4 & 5 tail feathers, vertical polishing line between feathers left of eagle's right leg and two die chips to right of lower part of eagle's right leg.

VAM 26 Doubled Eyelid & Spike

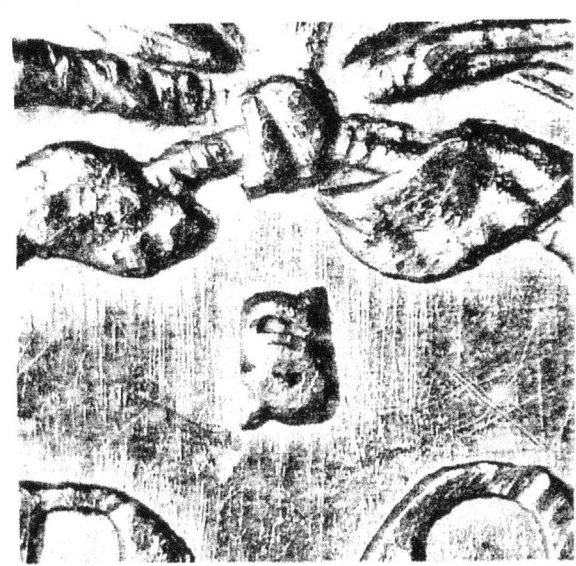

VAM 26 S Tilted Slightly Left

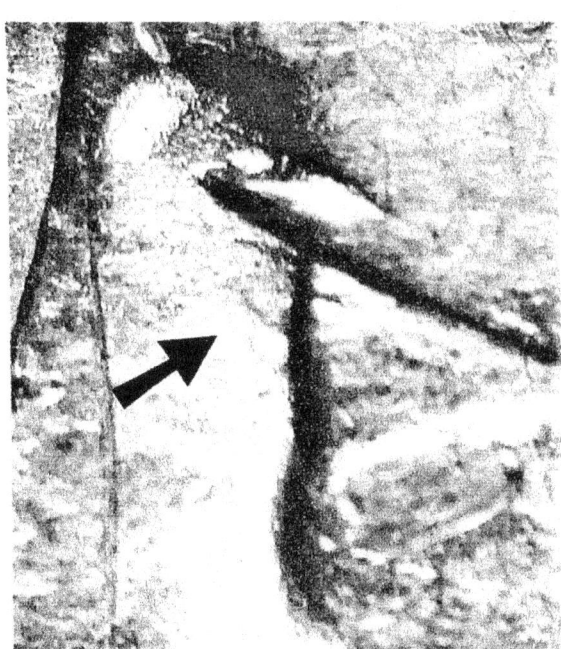

VAM 27 Spikes Below Eyelid

VAM 26 Dot in Tail Feathers

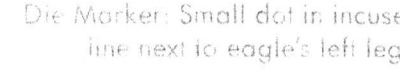 Die Marker: Small dot in incuse
line next to eagle's left leg.

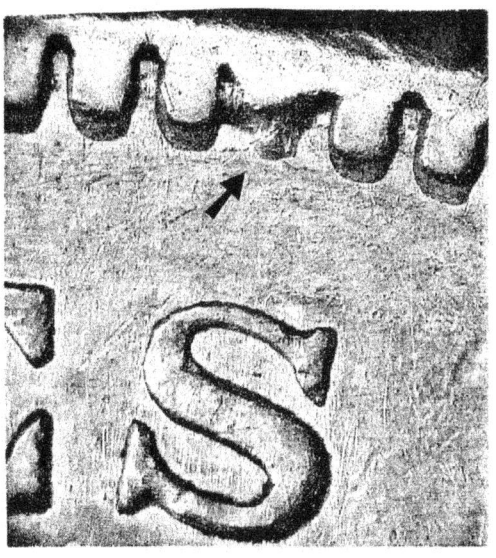

VAM 27 Broken Denticle

VAM 27 Lines in Eye Socket

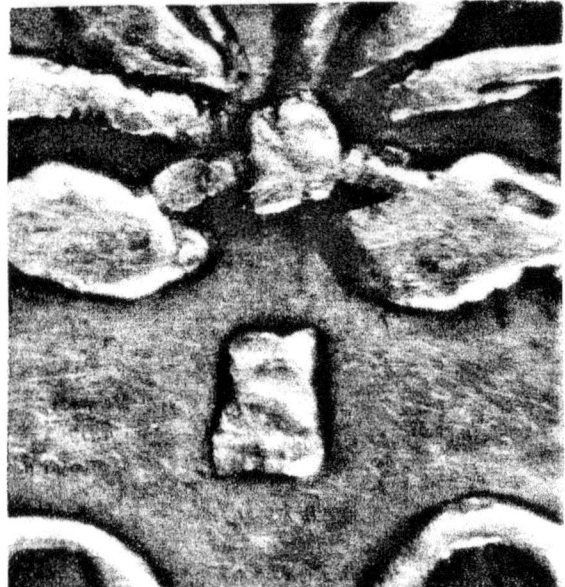

VAM 27 Centered S Mint Mark

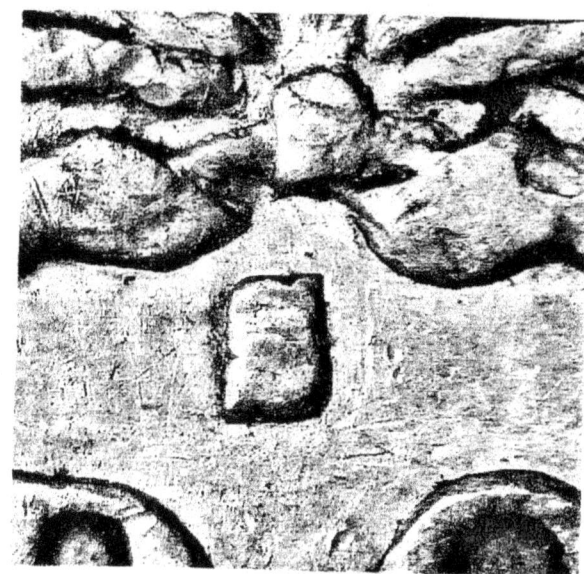

VAM 56 S Set High & Left

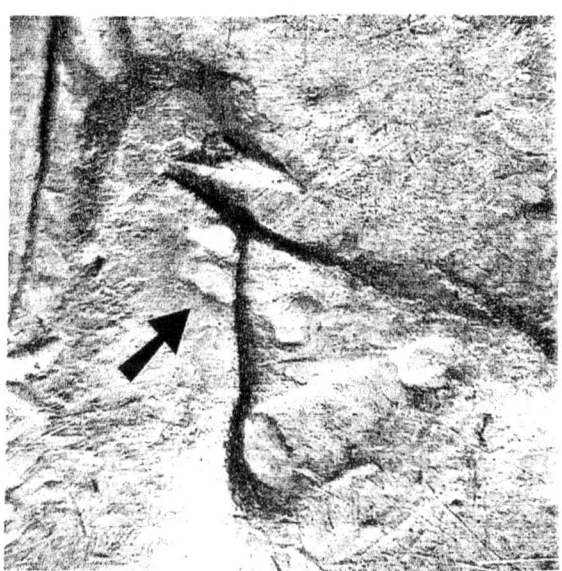

VAM 56 Bars Eye Front

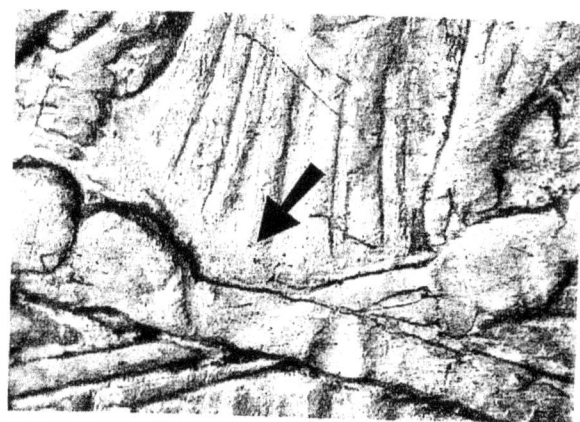

VAM 56 Missing Tail Feathers

Die Marker: Lower part of tail feathers between eagle's legs missing due to curved raised metal.

VAM 58 Spiked Eye

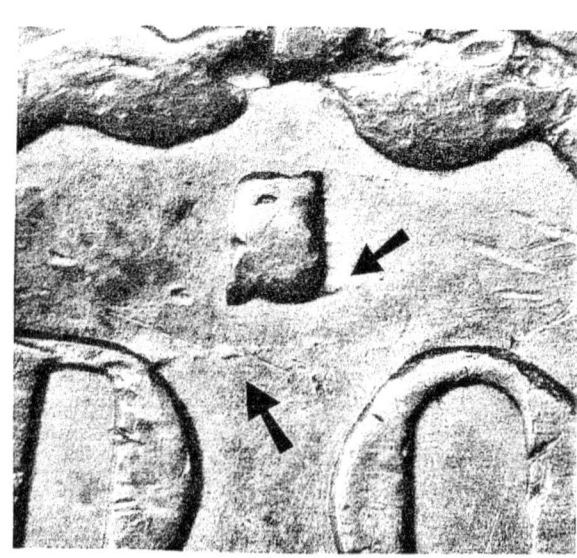

VAM 57 S Set Left & Tilted Left

Die Marker: Small die chip lower right outside of S mint mark. Small die chips below S mint mark

VAM 59 Die Clash Line Eye

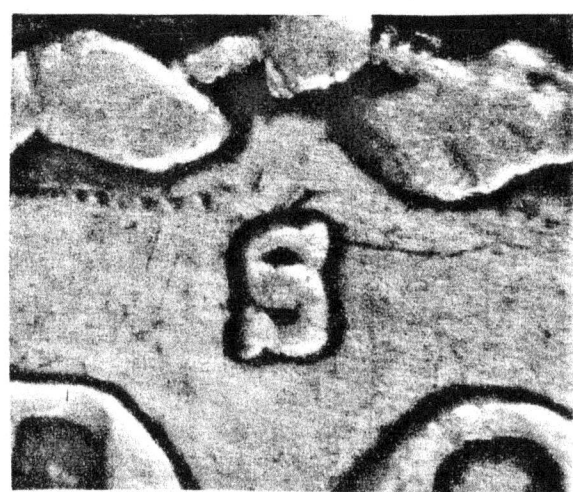

VAM 59 S Set Slightly Left

Die Marker: Vertical polishing line between eagle's right leg & tail feathers. Diagonal polishing line on middle tail feather below olive branch.

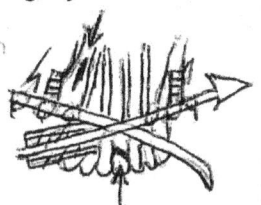

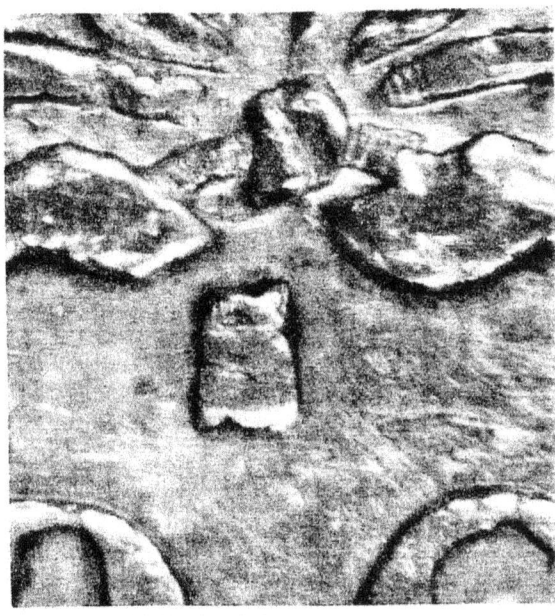

VAM 60 S Set High & Left

Die Marker: Diagonal polishing lines on lower part of tail feathers next to eagle's right leg.

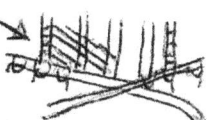

VAM 62 Bars Eye Front

VAM 62 Die Chip Cap

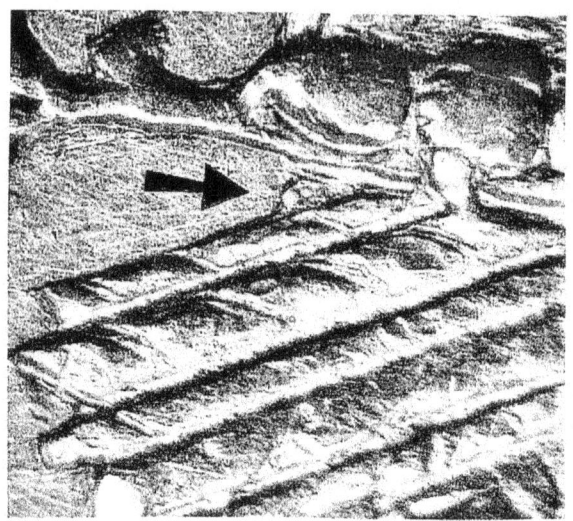

VAM 62 Raised Metal Area

Die Marker: Large raised metal area at junction of olive branch & top arrow feather.

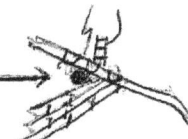

VAM 72 Die Chips Below Eyelid

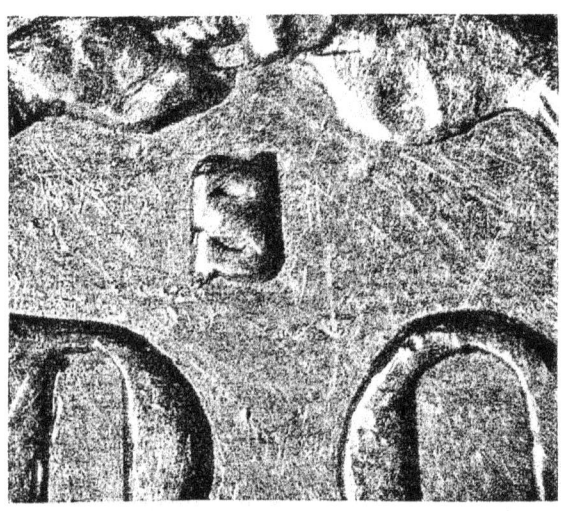

VAM 62 S Set Far Left

VAM 59/72 Polishing Lines I

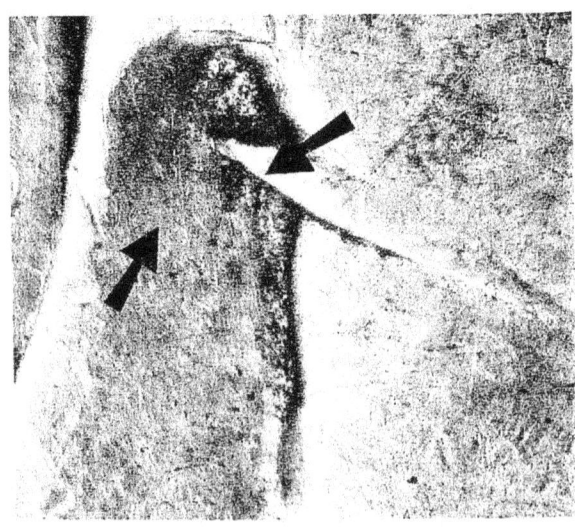

VAM 59/72 Die Chip & Polishing Lines Eye

VAM 59/72 Polishing Line Cotton Leaf

VAM 72 Diagonal Polishing Lines Leg

Die Marker: Diagonal polishing line to
left & right of eagle's right leg
above claws.

VAM 72 Die Scratches Upper Tail Feathers

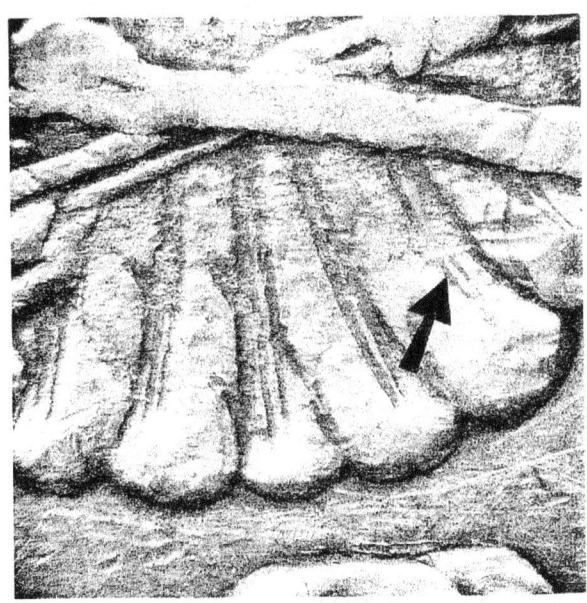

VAM 72 Die Scratch Line Tail Feathers

VAM 72 S Tilted Left

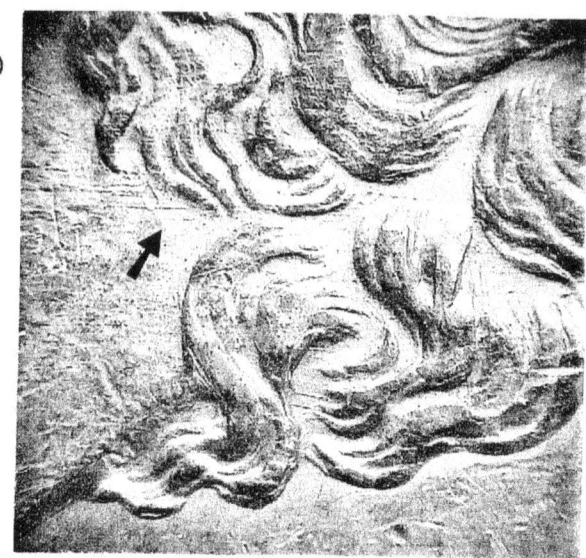

VAM 1B Lines in Hair

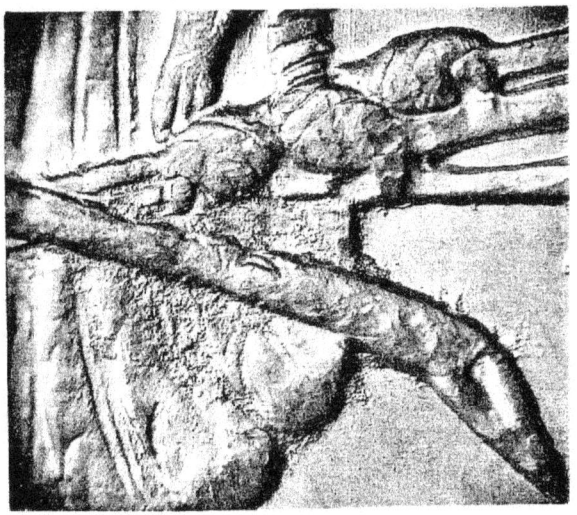

VAM 1B Rust Spots (Possible Acid Treated)

VAM 1B Rusted Die Wreath (Possible Acid Treated)

VAM 1B Lines Eagle's Talons

VAM 1C/95 Doubled PL

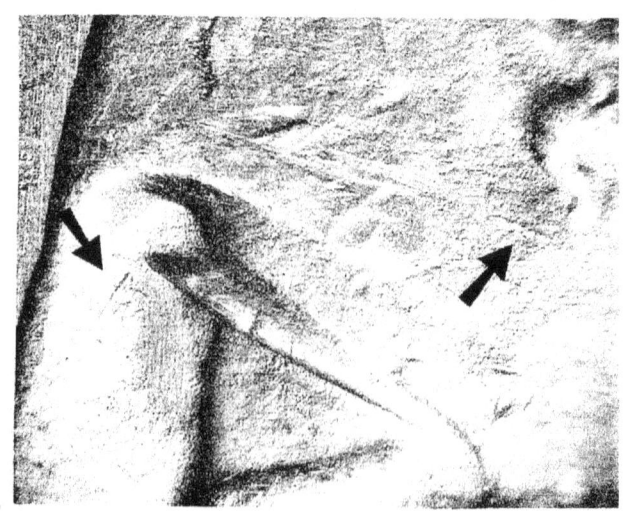

VAM 1C/95 Die Scratches Eyelid & Curl

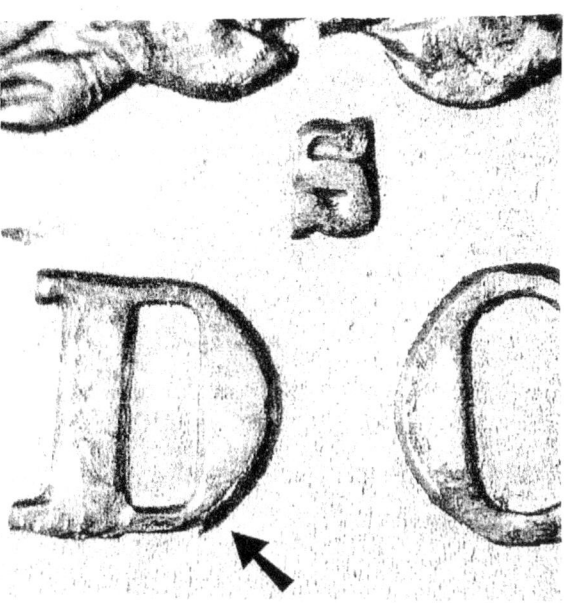

VAM 1C/95 Doubled D

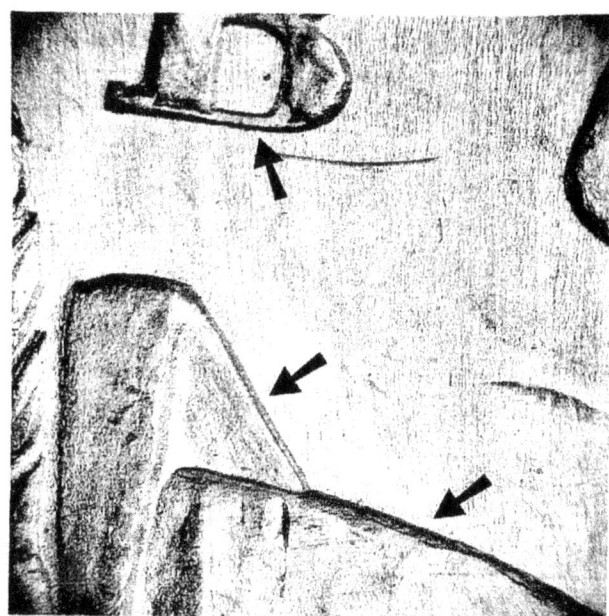

VAM 1C/95 Doubled B, Wheat Leaf & Cap

VAM 1C/95 Die Chip R

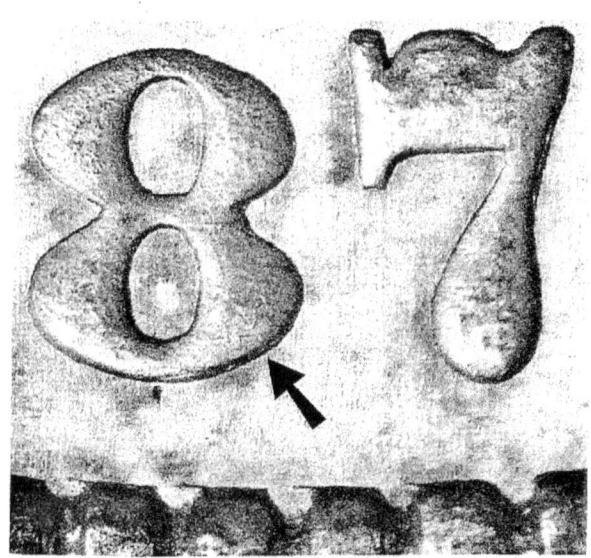

VAM 1C/95 Doubled 8

VAM 1C/95 Engraved Wing Feather

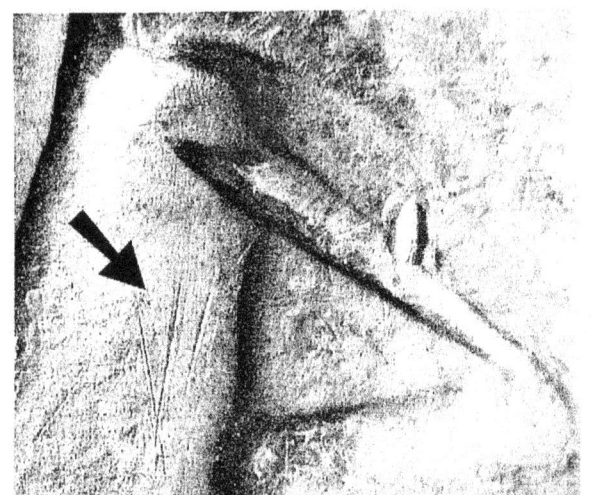

VAM 1D Double Lines Eye Front

VAM 1D Lines in LIBER

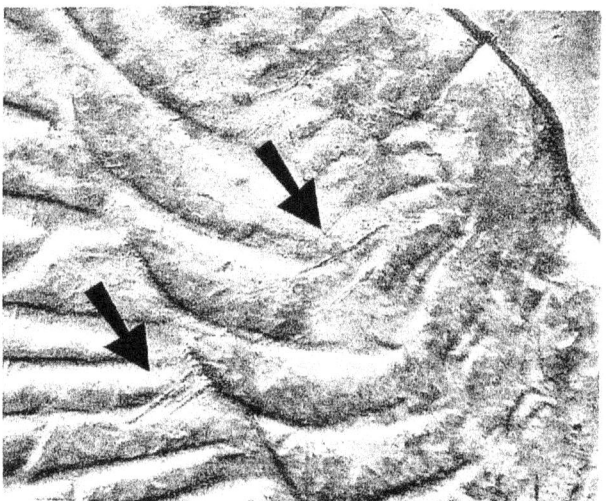

VAM 1D Scratches in Wing

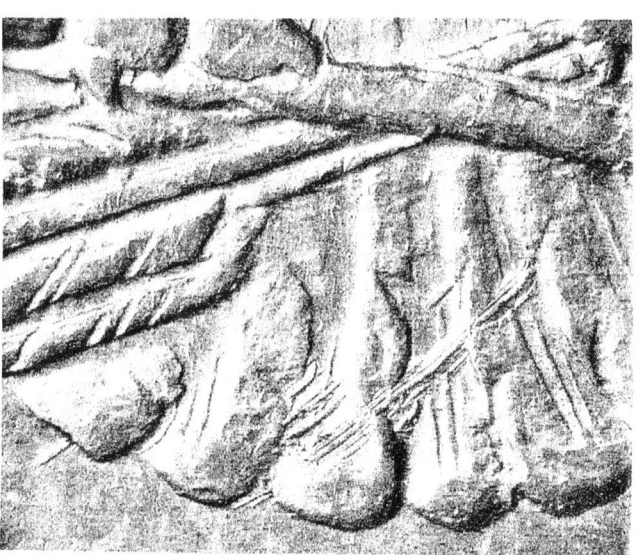

VAM 1D Gouges in Tail Feathers

VAM 1D Vertical Line Wing

VAM 1D Doubled D

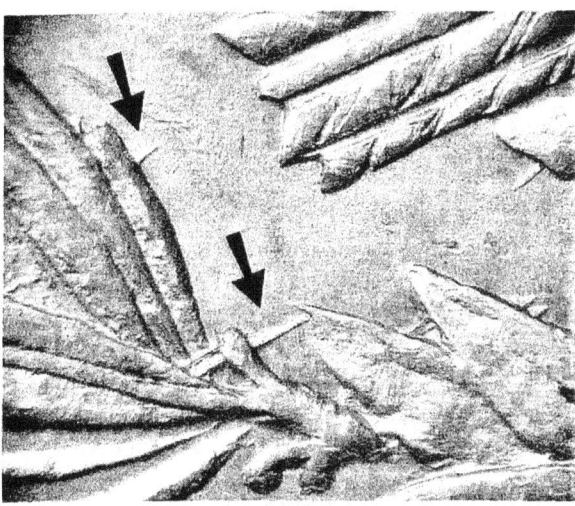

VAM 1D Scratches in Wreath

VAM 1E Die Gouges Rt. Wreath

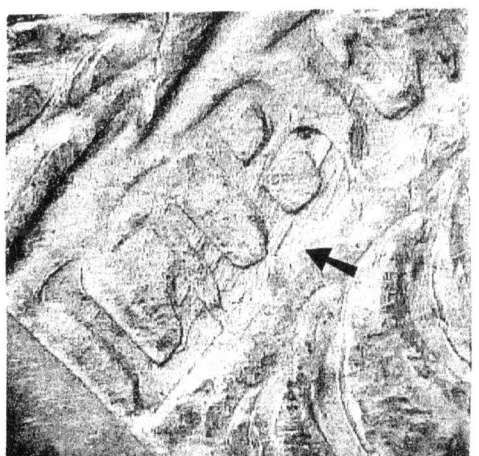

VAM 1G Die 1 Lines in LIB

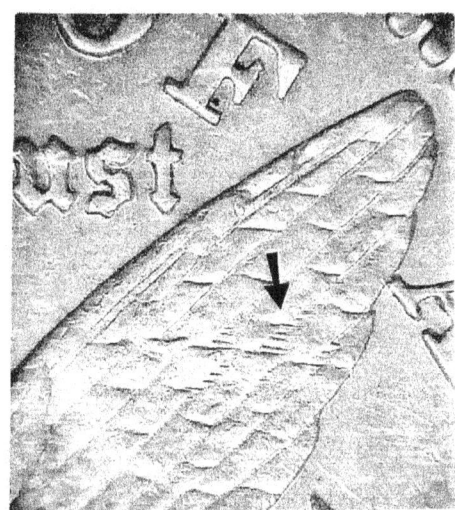

VAM 1G Lines in Wing

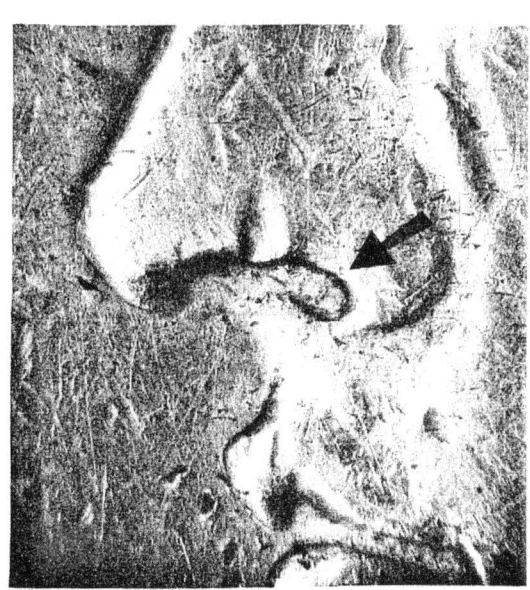

VAM 1I Scratches in Nostril

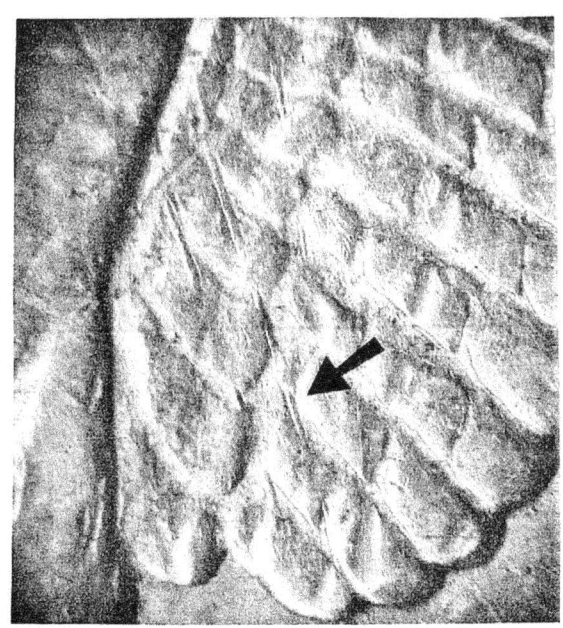

VAM 1I Gouges in Wing

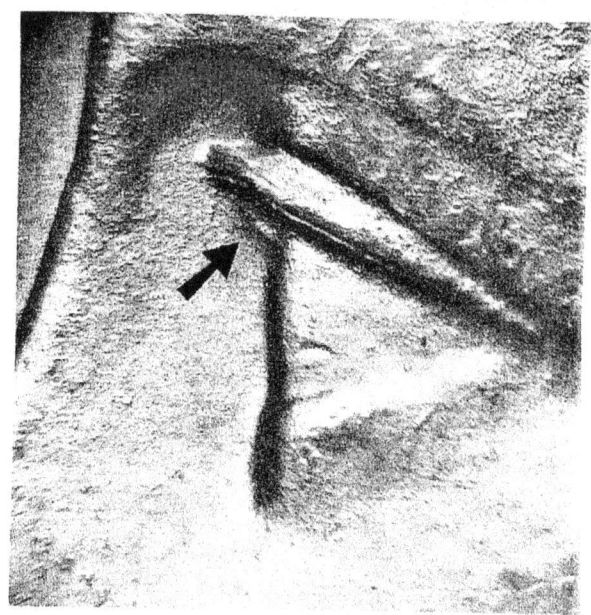

VAM 5 Tripled Eyelid

VAM 5 Doubled BU

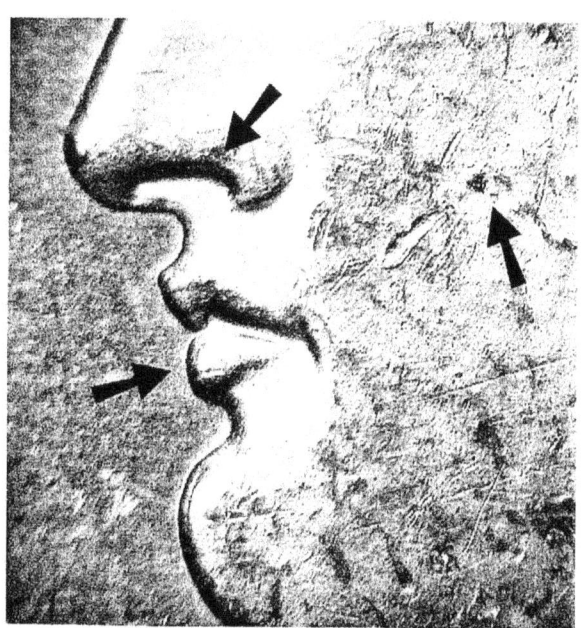

VAM 5 Doubled Nose & Lips

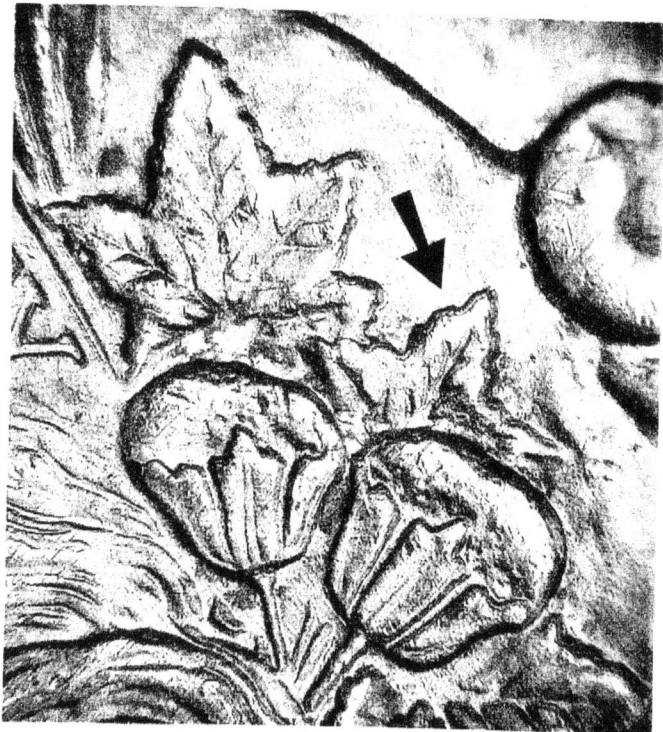

VAM 5 Doubled Cotton Leaves

VAM 5 Doubled Date

VAM 5 Engraved Wing Feather

VAM 5 Die Chips & Scratch

VAM 5 Doubled Legend

VAM 6 Engraving on Feathers

VAM 6 Engraving on Feathers

VAM 6 S Set Right

VAM 6 Doubled Motto

VAM 6 Engraving Lines

VAM 7 Doubled LIBERTY

VAM 6 Engraved Wing Feather

VAM 7 Doubled Cotton & Wheat Leaves

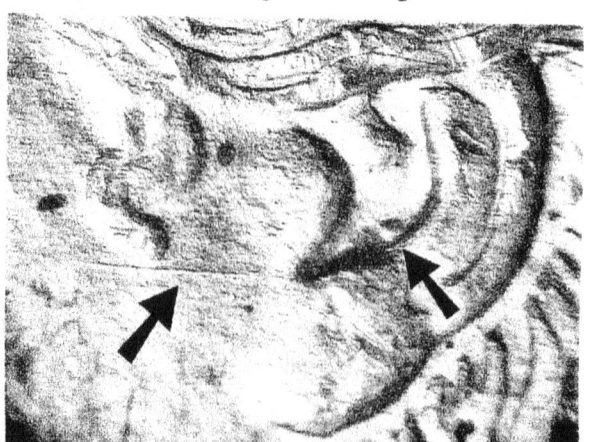

VAM 7 Dot in Ear with Line

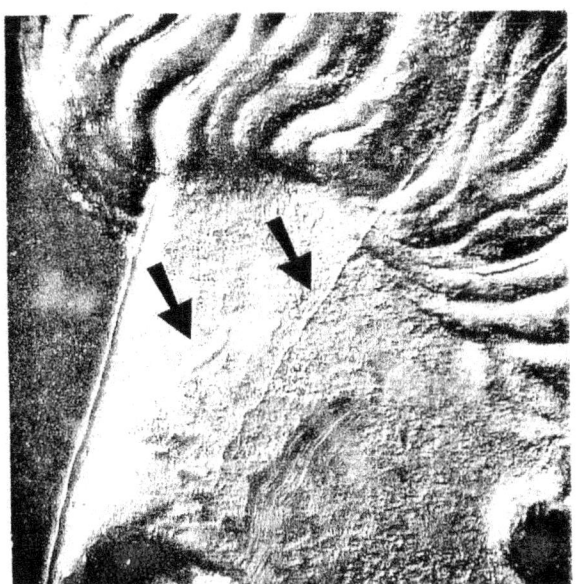

VAM 8 Die 1 Scratch & Crack Forehead

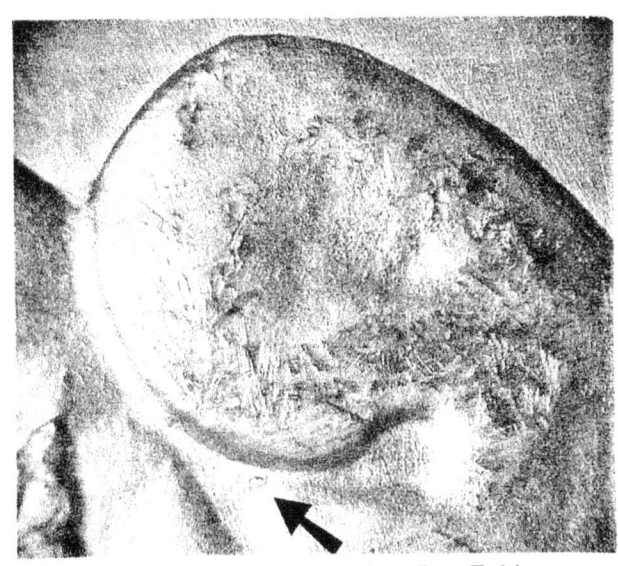

VAM 8 Die 2 Chip Below Cap Fold

VAM 8 Die 1 Line Impression

VAM 8 Engraving
Wing-Body

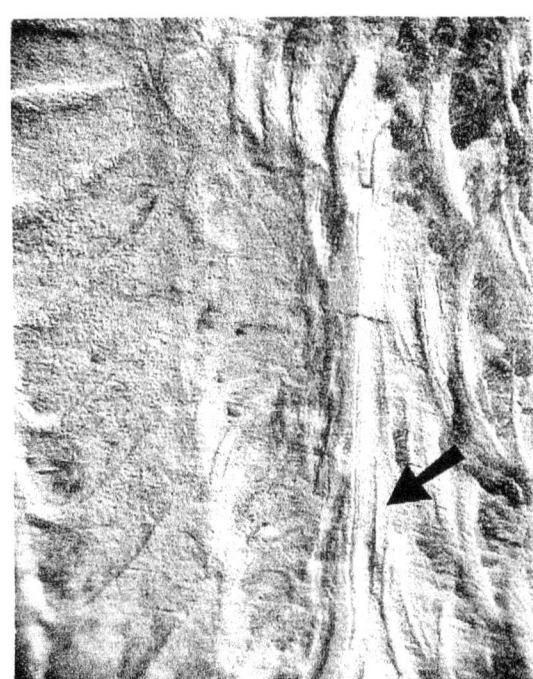

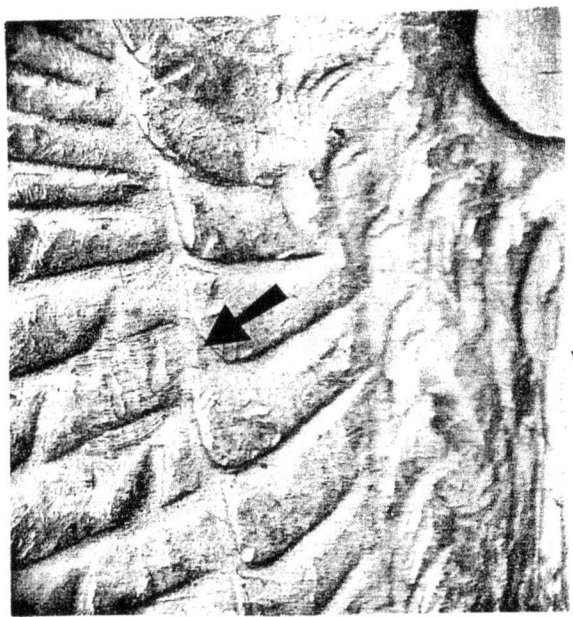

VAM 8 Engraved Patch

VAM 8 Engraved
Wing Feather

VAM 8A Die Chip
On E

VAM 8A Rusted Die Wing

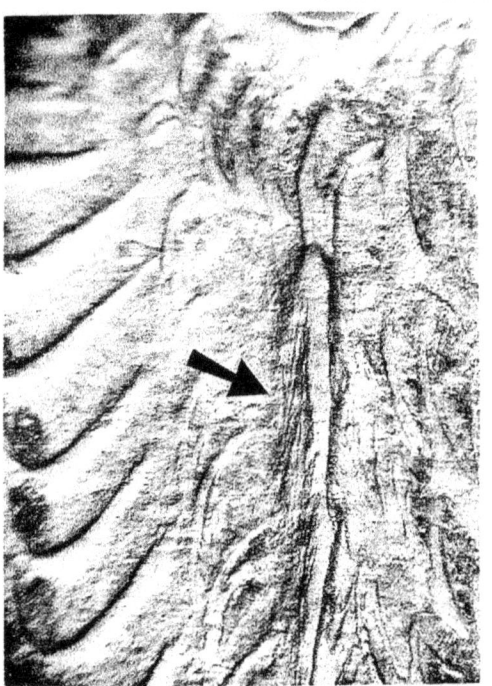

VAM 9 Engraving Wing-Body

VAM 9 Doubled B

VAM 9 Engraved Wing Feather

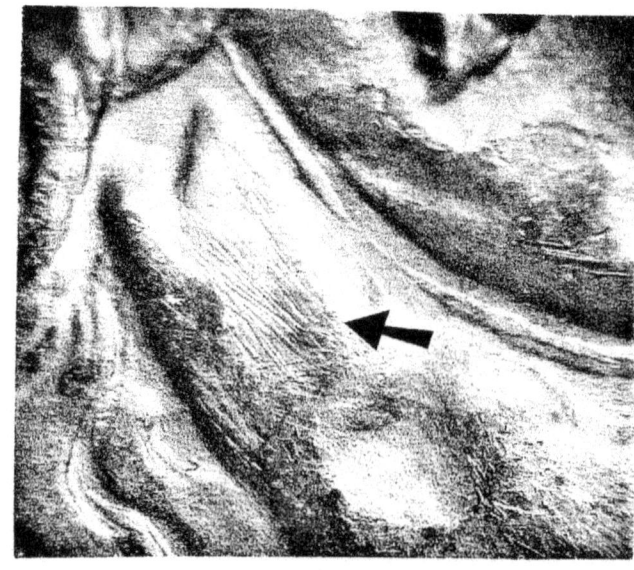

VAM 9 Lines Below Cap Bottom

VAM 12 Doubled Motto

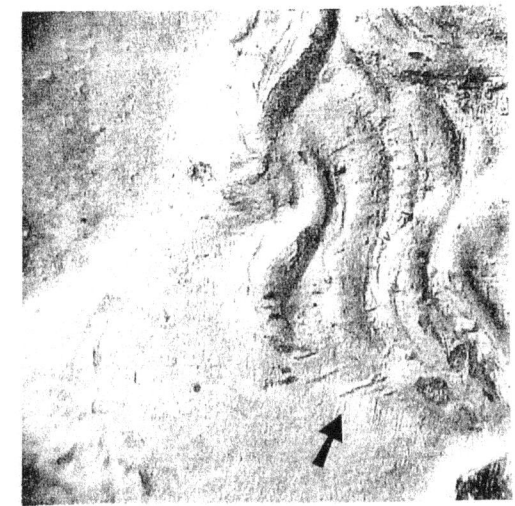

VAM 14 Lines in Hair

VAM 14 Doubled B

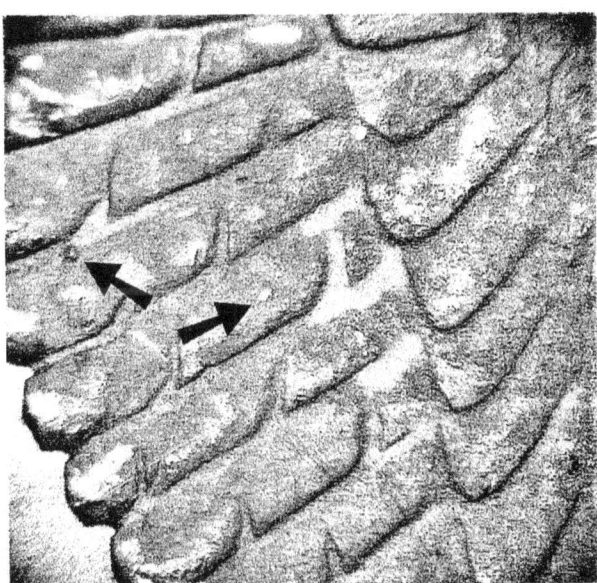

VAM 14 Over Polished & 2 Dots

VAM 15 Bulge on P

VAM 14 Engraved Wing Feather

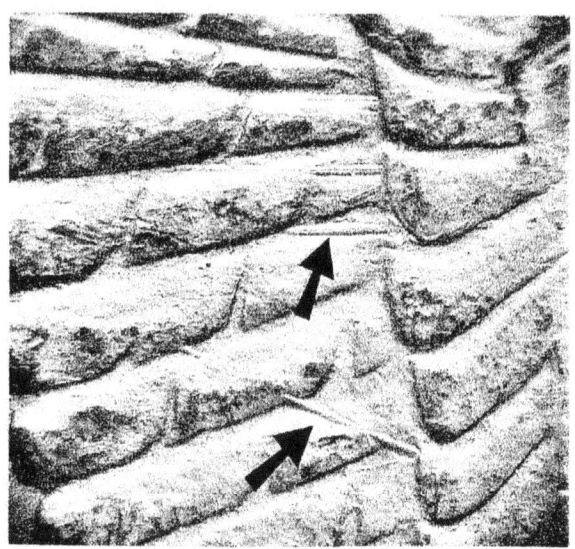

VAM 15 Polishing Lines

VAM 15 Lines in Wing

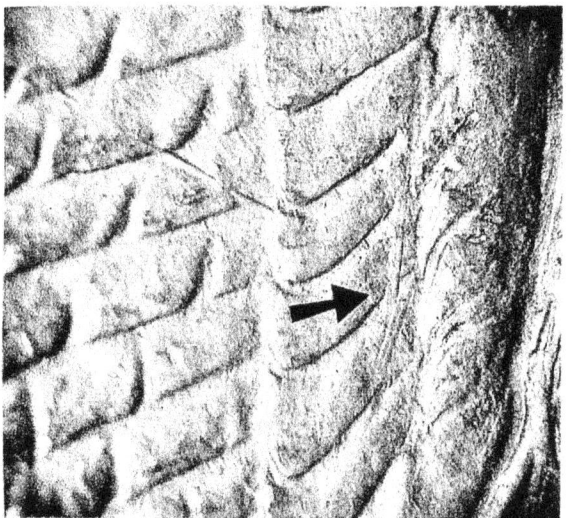

VAM 15 Gouges in Wing

VAM 15 Gouges in Wing

VAM 15 Engraved Wing Feather

VAM 15 Double Lines in Tail Feathers

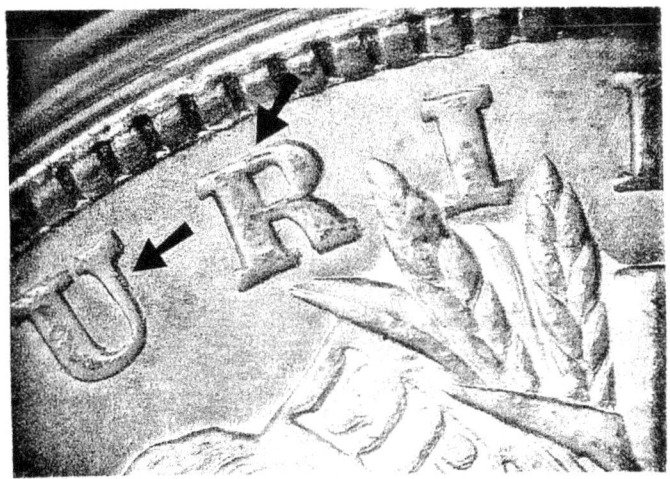

VAM 16 Doubled Motto

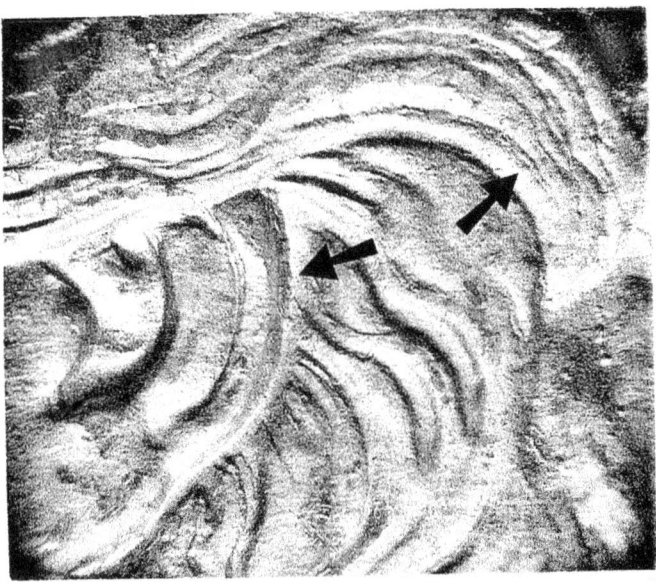

VAM 16 Doubled Ear & Hair

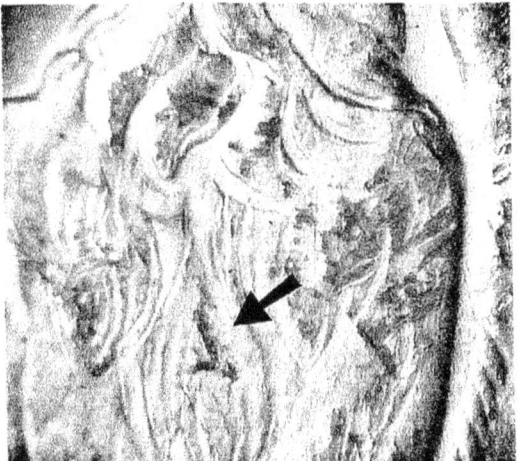

VAM 16 Die Chip

VAM 17
Doubled D

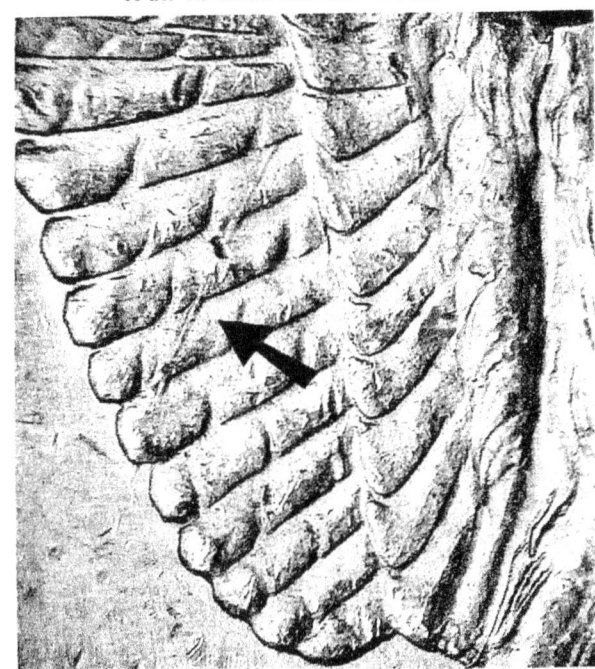

VAM 16 Line in Wing

VAM 17 Polishing Lines Below Tail Feathers, EDS

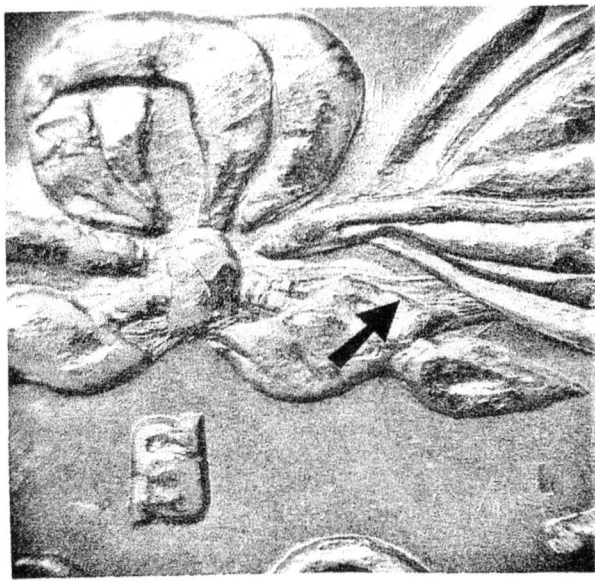

VAM 17 Die Gouge Ribbon

VAM 17A Over Polished Hair

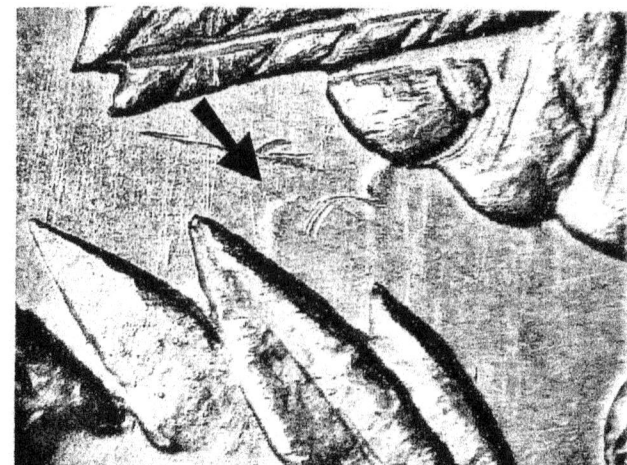

VAM 17A Denticle Impressions Below Tail Feathers

VAM 17A Lengthened Denticle Spaces

VAM 17A Denticle Impressions OLL

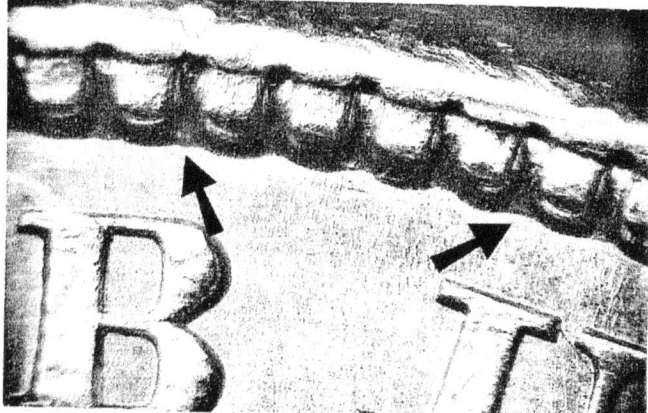

VAM 17A Lengthened Denticle Spaces

VAM 17 Doubled Eyelid Front

VAM 17B Denticle Impressions Date

VAM 17B Denticle Impressions Neck

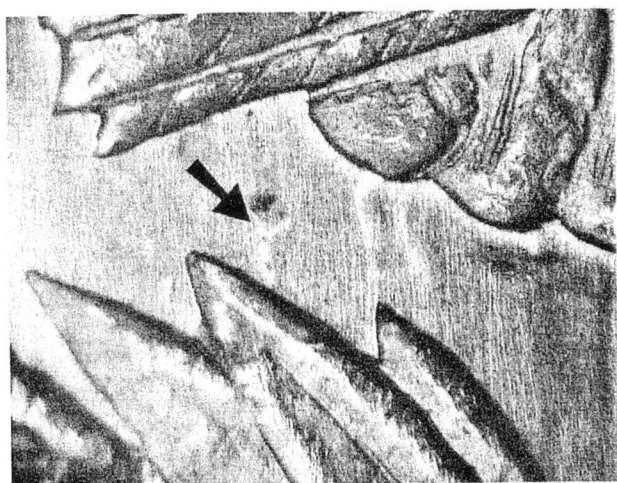

VAM 17B Denticle Impressions Below TF

VAM 17B Denticle Lines Above ST

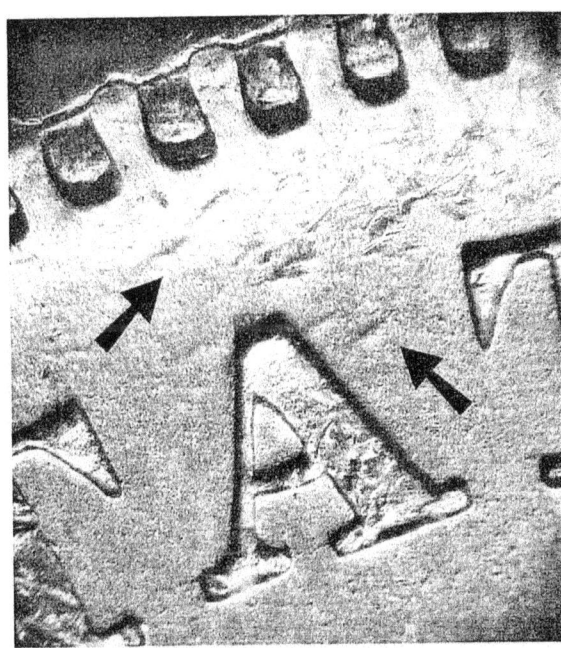

VAM 17C Denticle Impressions AT

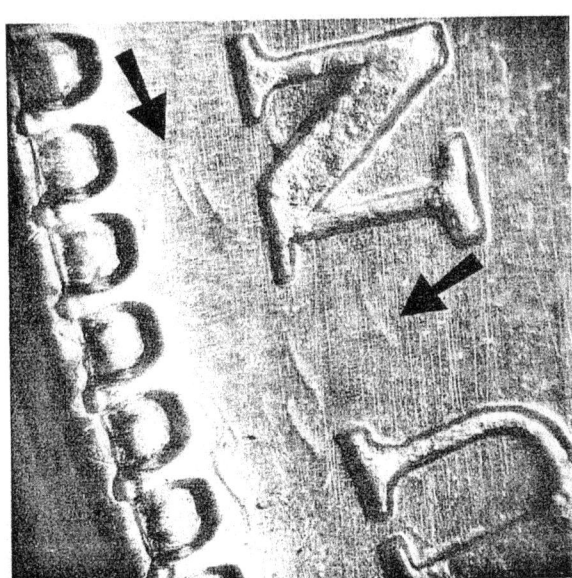

VAM 17B Denticle Impressions UN

VAM 17B Denticle Impressions OLL

VAM 18 Lines in Wing

VAM 18 Lines in Wing

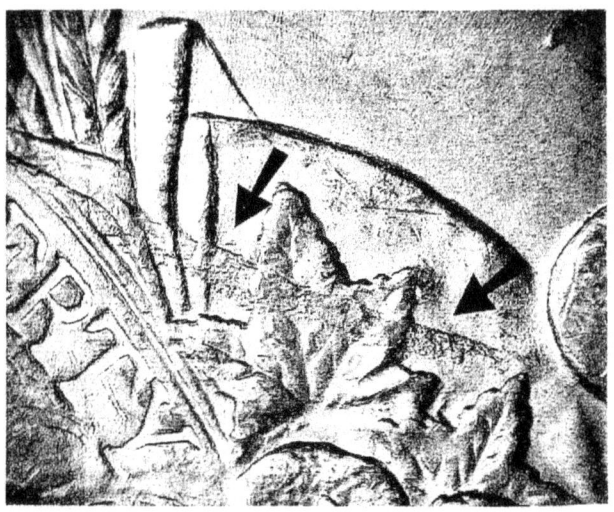

VAM 19 Cap Band Gouge

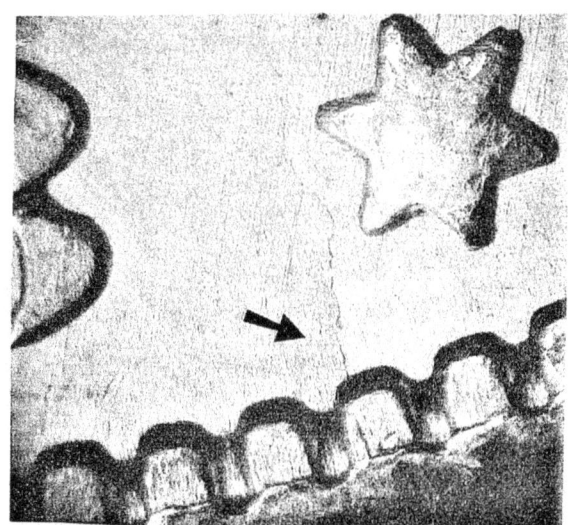

VAM 18 A Die Break First Right Star

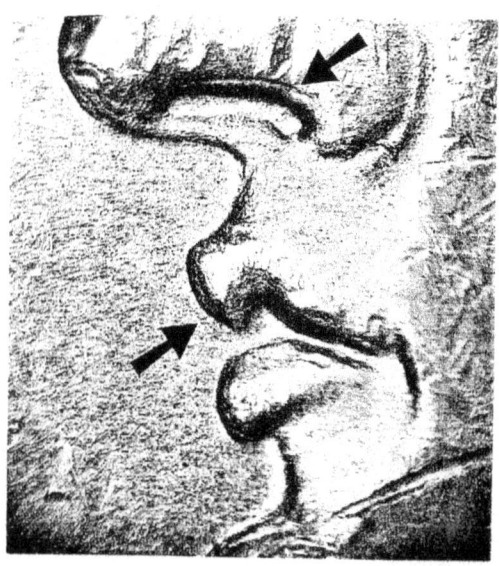

VAM 19 Doubled Nostril & Lips

VAM 19 Doubled PL

VAM 19A Shallow
STATES

VAM 19A Disconnected Leaves

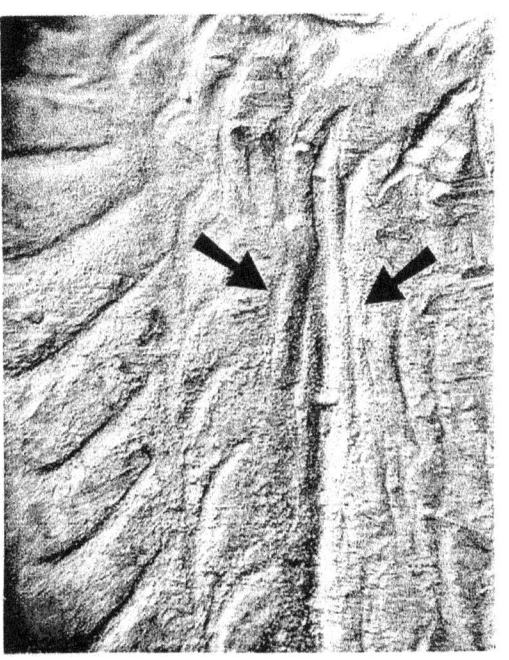

VAM 19A Engraving Wing-Body

VAM 19A Rusted Die

VAM 19 Engraved Wing Feather

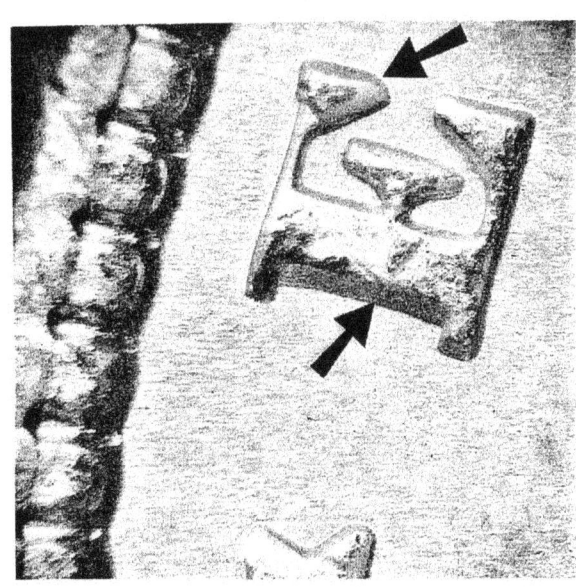

VAM 20 Die Chips E

VAM 20 Engraved Wing Feather

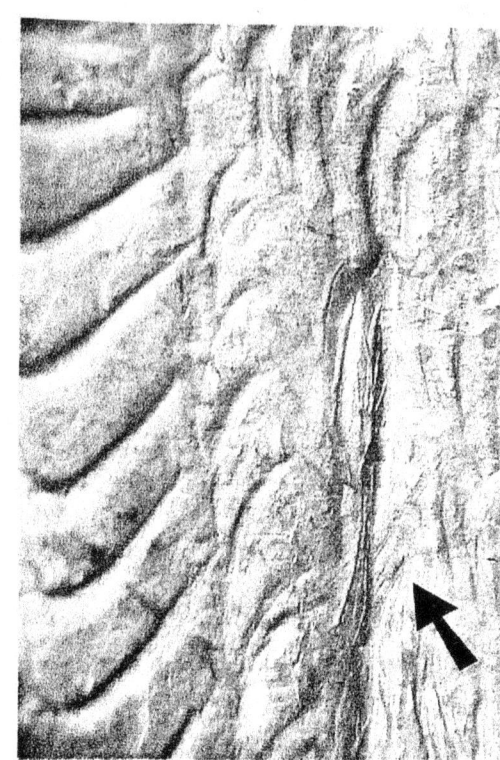

VAM 21 Engraving Wing-Body, Gouge

VAM 21 Doubled Legend

VAM 21 Engraved Wing Feather

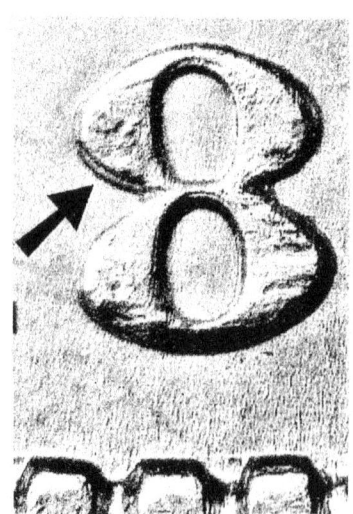

VAM 22 Doubled 8

VAM 22 Polished Obverse

VAM 22 Polished Reverse

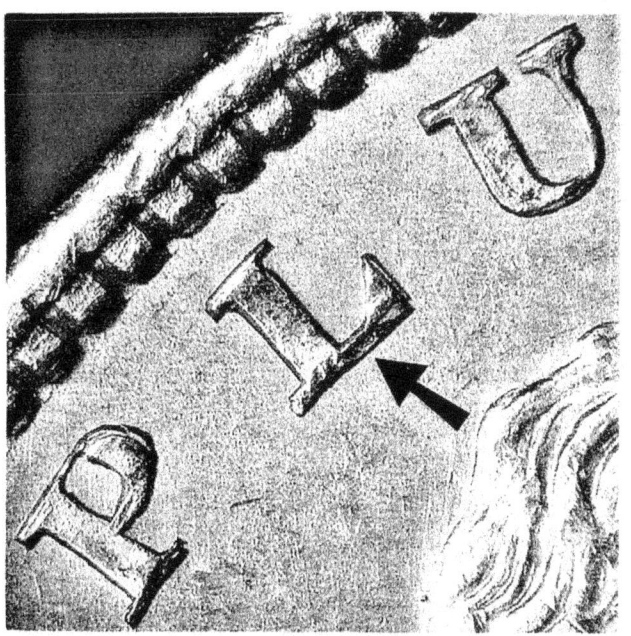

VAM 22 Doubled Motto PLU

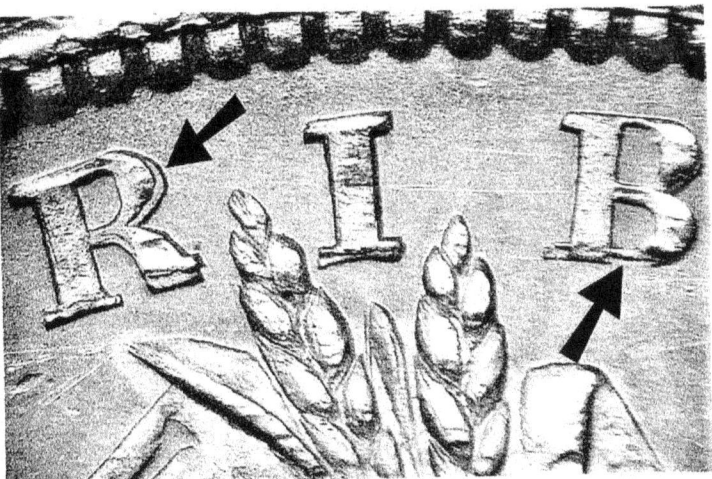

VAM 22 Doubled Motto RIB

VAM 22 Doubled Star & E

VAM 22 Over Polished Wing-Body

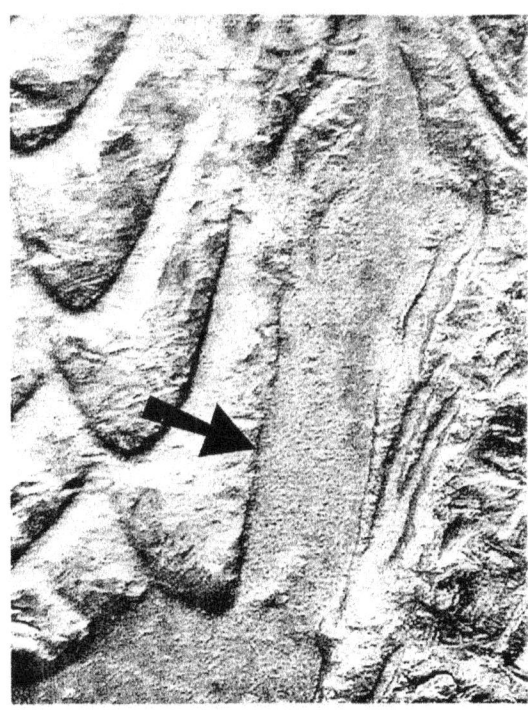

VAM 22 Over Polished Wing-Leg

VAM 22
S Set Left

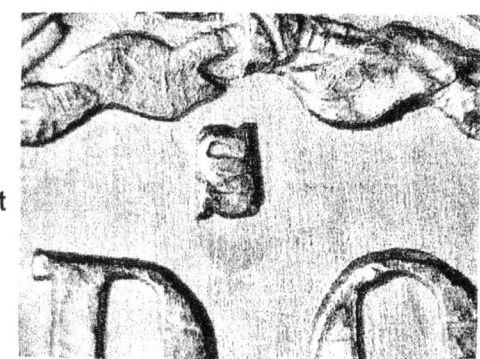

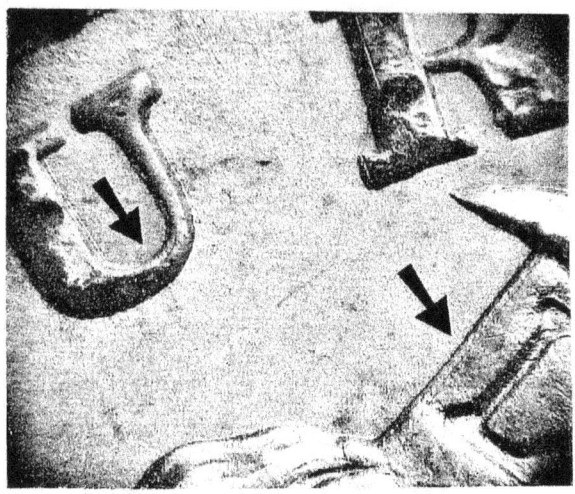

VAM 23 Doubled Motto

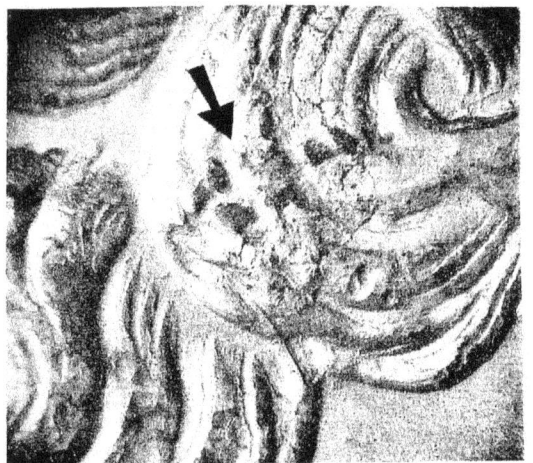

VAM 23 Die Flakes Hair

VAM 23 S/S Left

VAM 28
Die Chip E

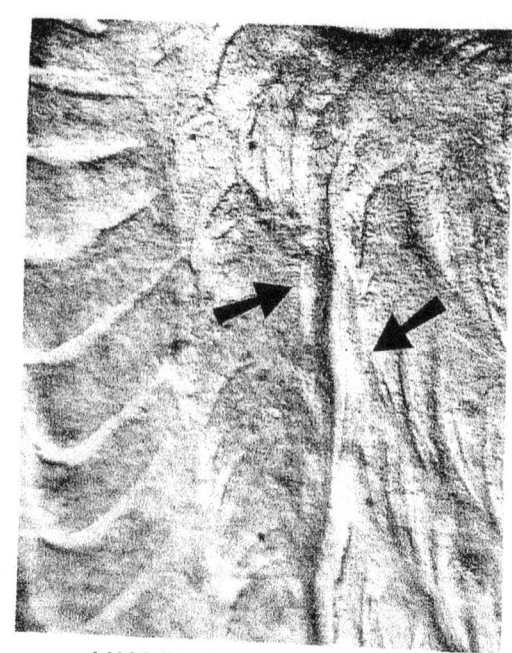

VAM 23 Engraving Wing-Body

VAM 23 Engraved Wing Feather

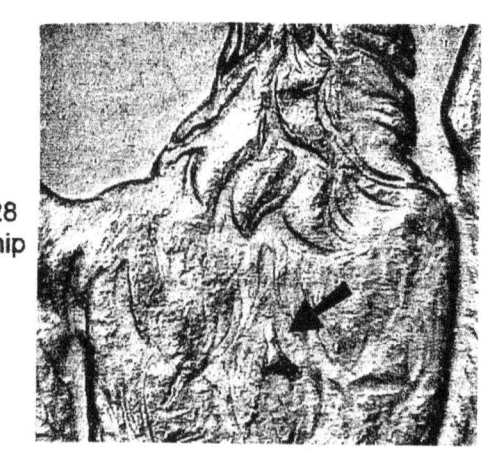

VAM 28
Die Chip

VAM 29 Doubled Eyelid

VAM 29 Gouge Above U

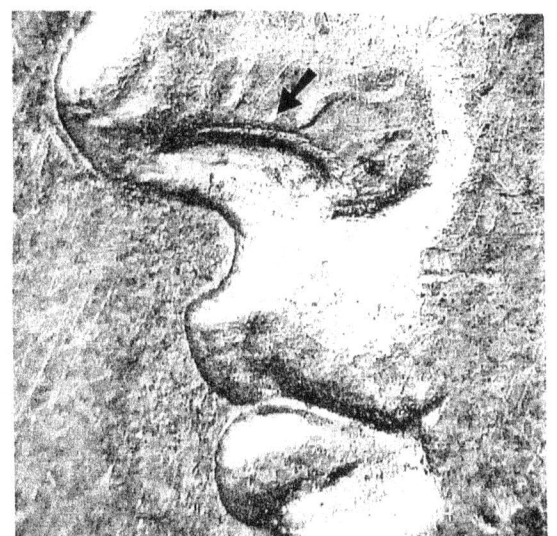

VAM 29 Doubled Nostril

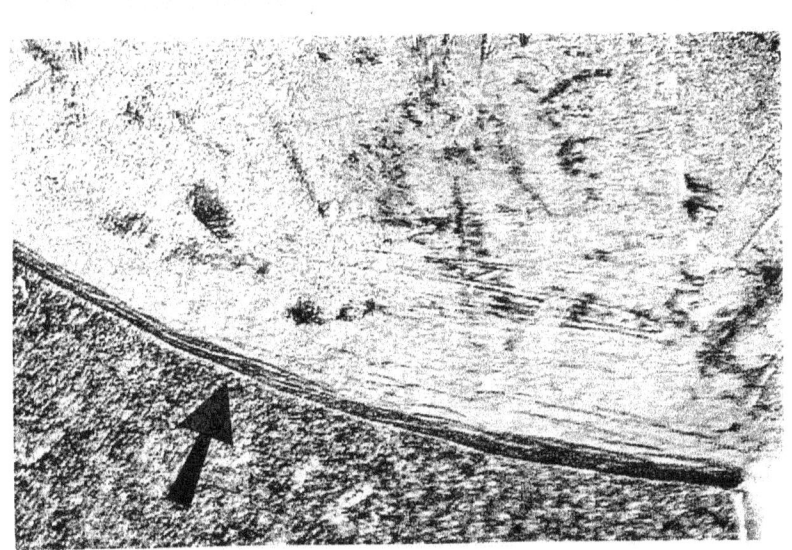

VAM 29 Engraving Lines Jaw Edge

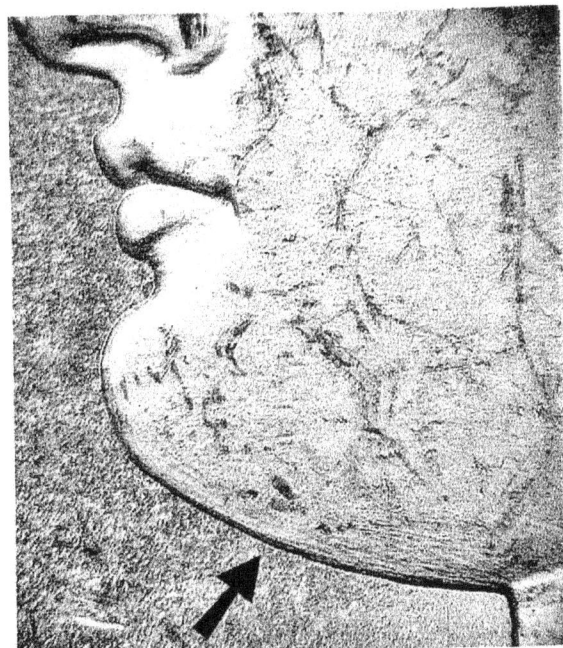

VAM 29 Engraved Sagging Jaw

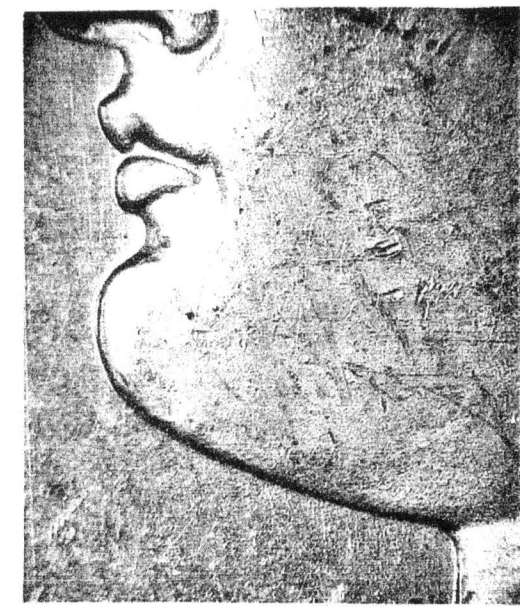

VAM 51 Normal Jaw

-85-

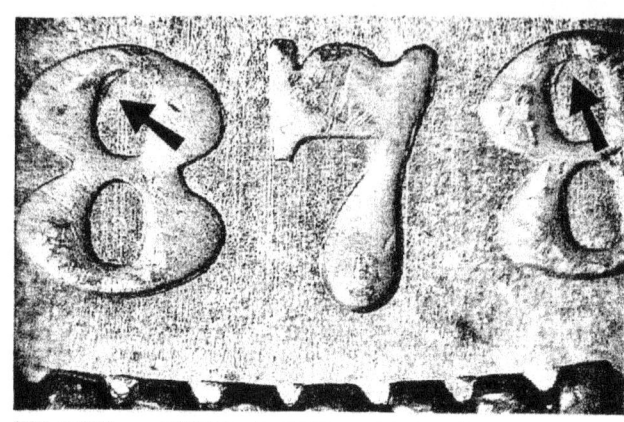

VAM 29
Doubled Date

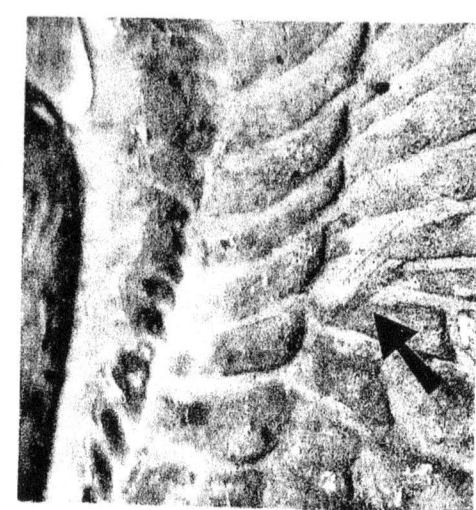

VAM 29 Polishing Lines

VAM 29
Rust Pits UNITED

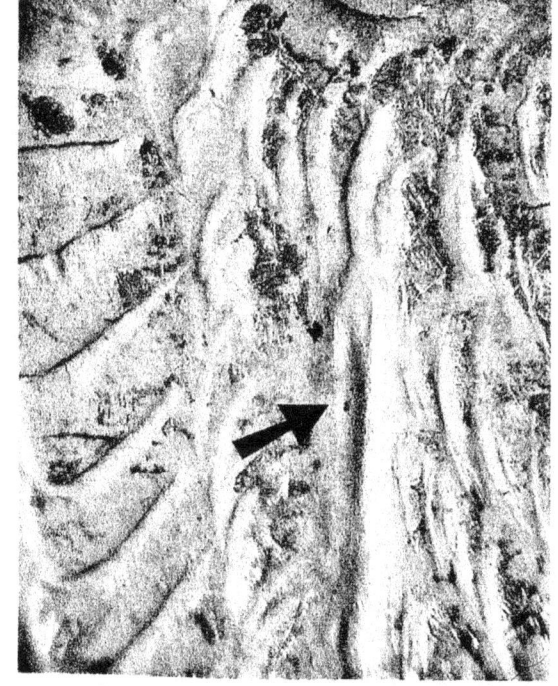

VAM 29 Engraving Wing-Body

VAM 30
Quadrupled LIBERTY

VAM 30
Doubled Eyelid

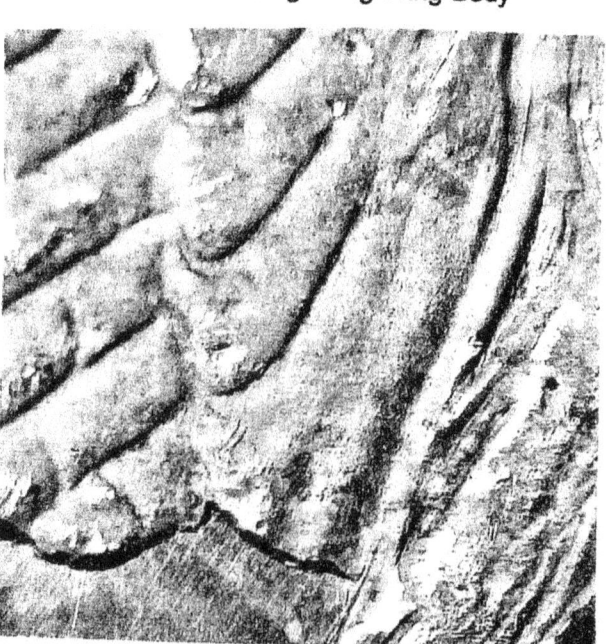

VAM 29 Engraved Wing Feather

VAM 30 Die Chip Arrow Head

VAM 30 Engraved Wing Feather (Possible Acid Treated)

Vam 31 Engraving Wing-Body

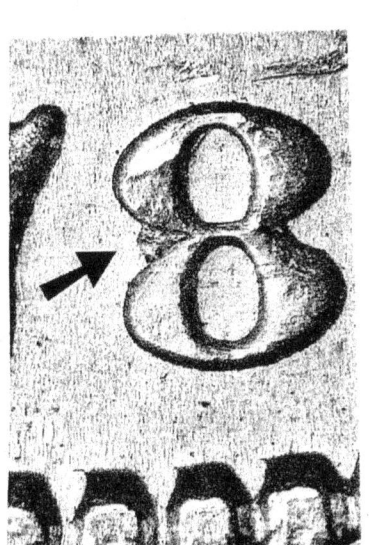

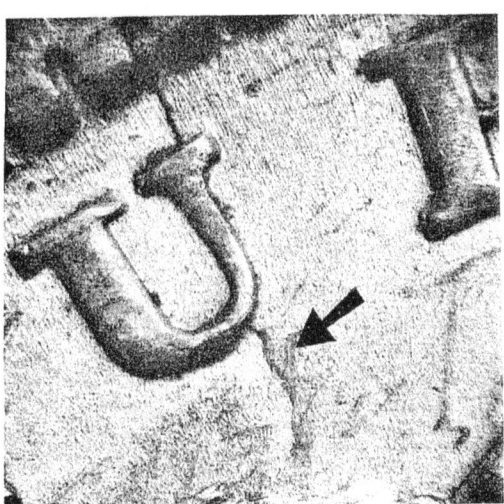

VAM 30A Die Break U

VAM 31 Die Chip 8

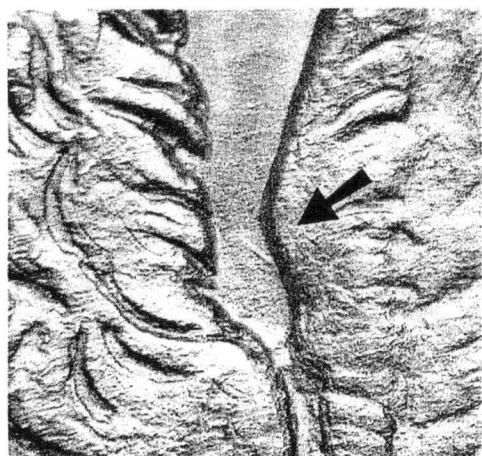

VAM 31 Die Scratch

VAM 31 Engraved Wing Feather

VAM 33 Spike Above Eye

VAM 33 Die Chips

VAM 33 Engraved Wing Feather

VAM 33 Doubled B

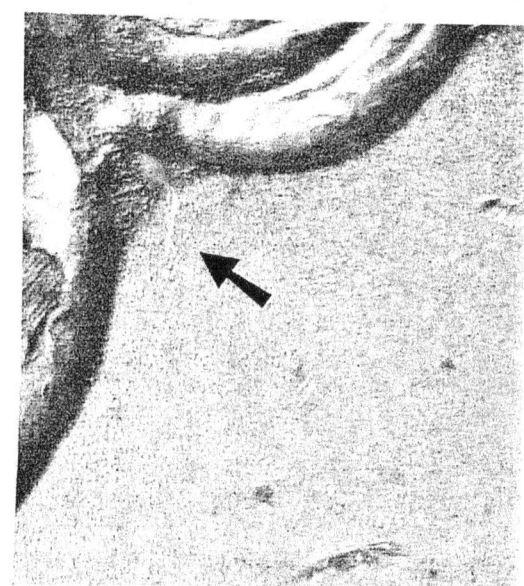

VAM 33A Clashed st

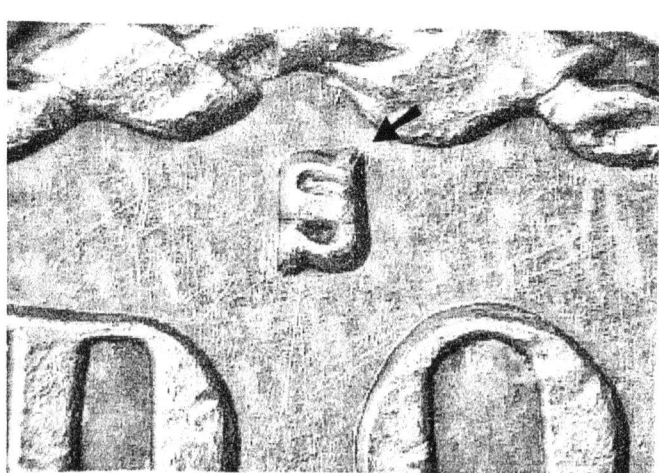

VAM 33 S/S Notches

VAM 34 Doubled Legend

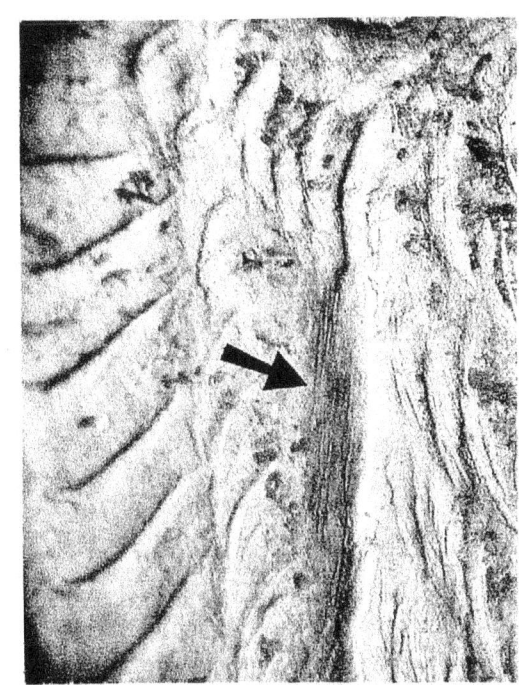

VAM 34 Engraving Wing-Body

VAM 35 Doubled Motto & Hair

VAM 34 Engraved Wing Feather

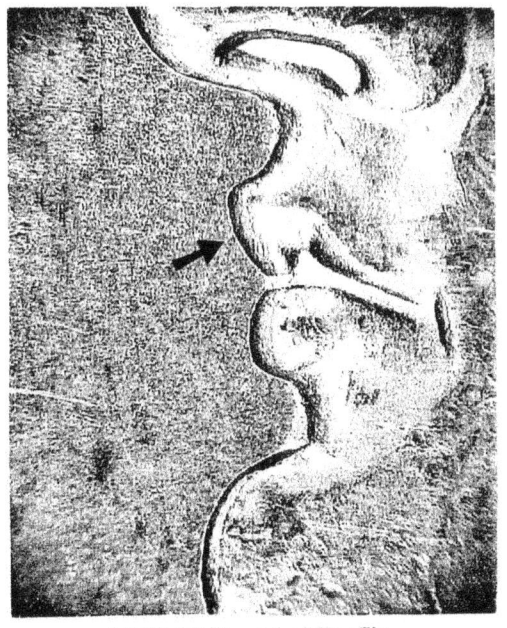

VAM 35 Doubled Profile

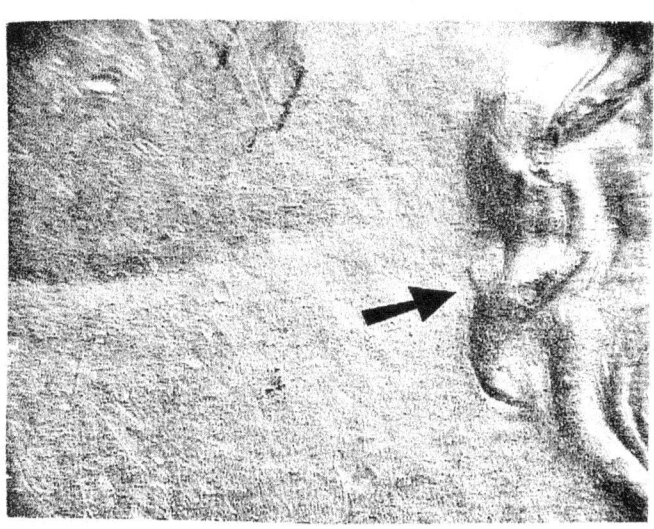

VAM 35 Die Chip

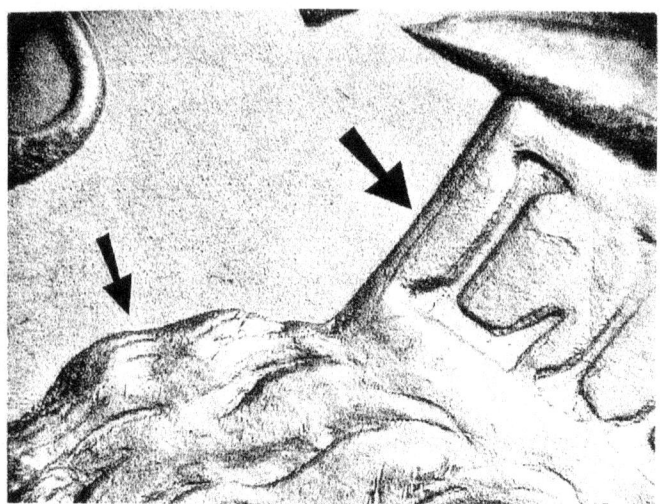

VAM 35 Doubled Front of Hair

VAM 35 Polished Doubled Front of Hair

VAM 36 Engraving Wing-Body

VAM 35 Engraving Lines

VAM 36 Engraved Wing Feather

VAM 35 Engraved Wing Feather

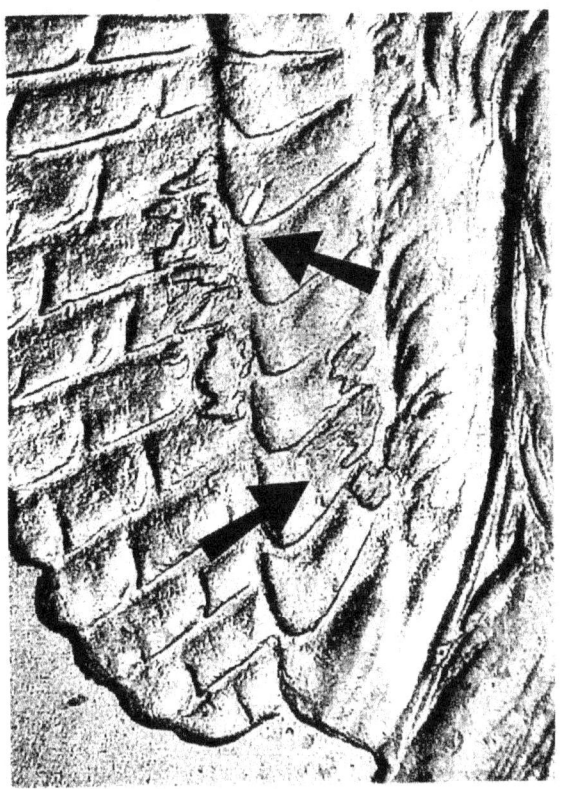

VAM 36 Acid Treated Wing

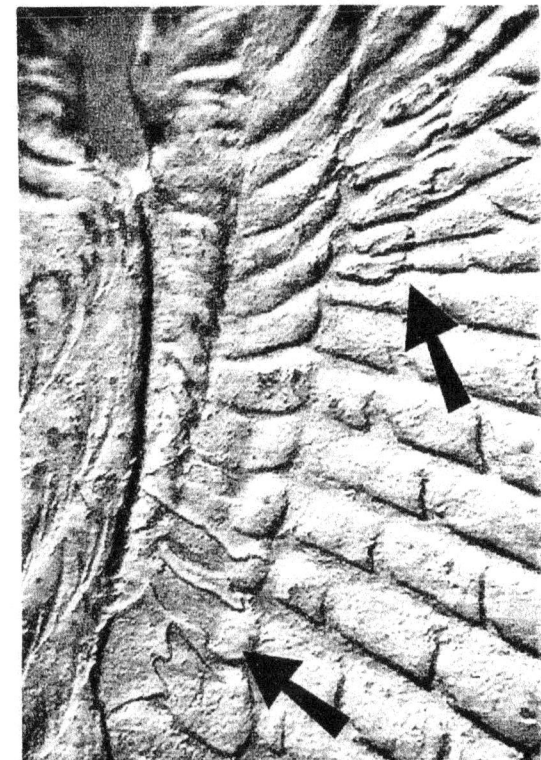

VAM 36 Acid Treated Wing

VAM 36 Dots Inside Ear

VAM 36 Acid Treated Tail Feathers

VAM 36A Gouge Wheat Leaf

VAM 36 Doubled B Serif

VAM 36 Die 3 Bulge & Surface Roughness P

VAM 36 Die 3 Doubled B

VAM 36 Die 3 Jaw-Neck Scratch

VAM 36B Die Break E

VAM 37A Beveled Field S-OF

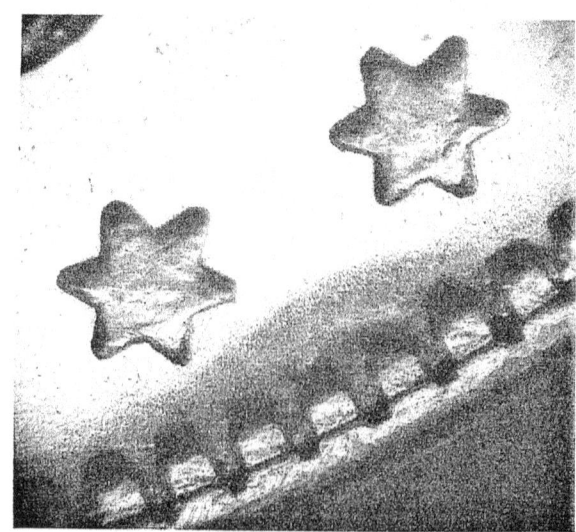

VAM 37A Beveled Field 1-2 Rt. Stars

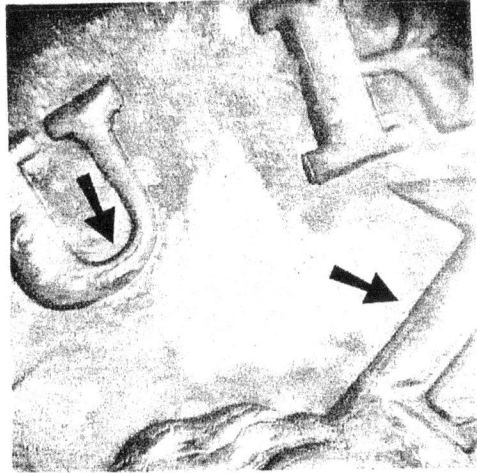

VAM 37 Doubled Motto

VAM 37 Doubled Motto

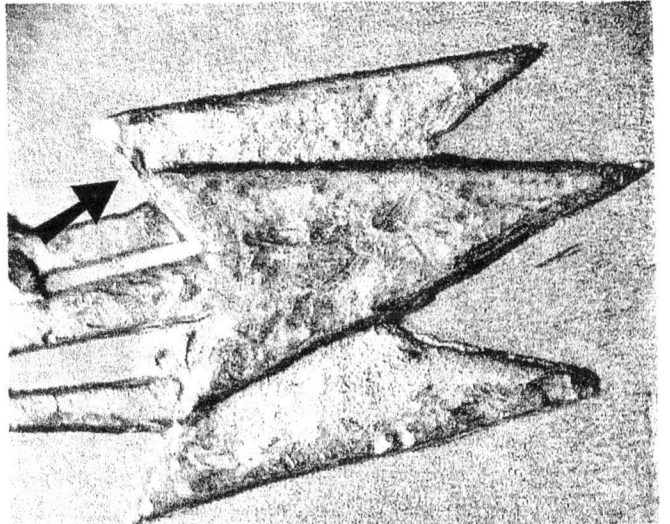

VAM 37 Die Chip Arrow Head

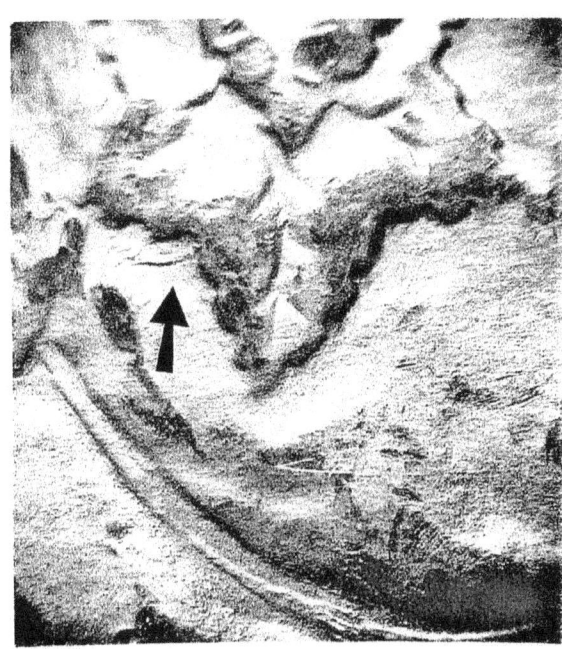

VAM 37 Curved Die Gouge

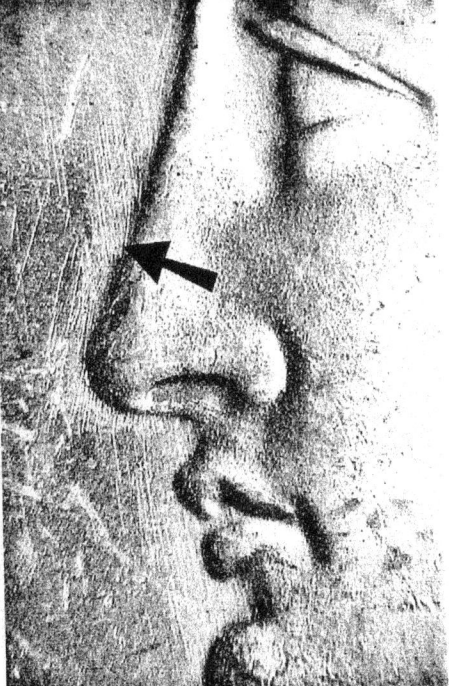

VAM 37 Polishing Lines

VAM 38 Die Chip F

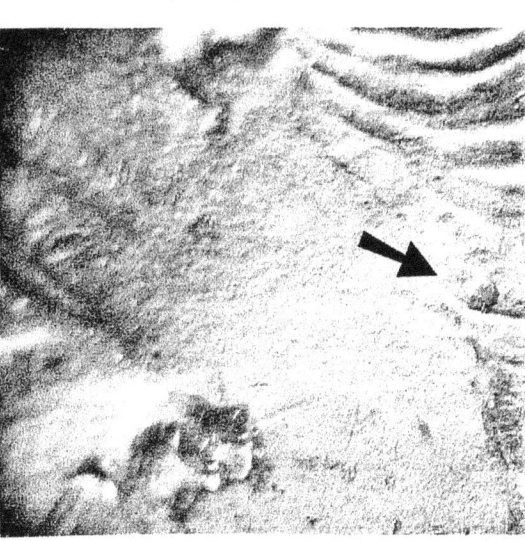

VAM 38 Dot Die Chip Behind Eye

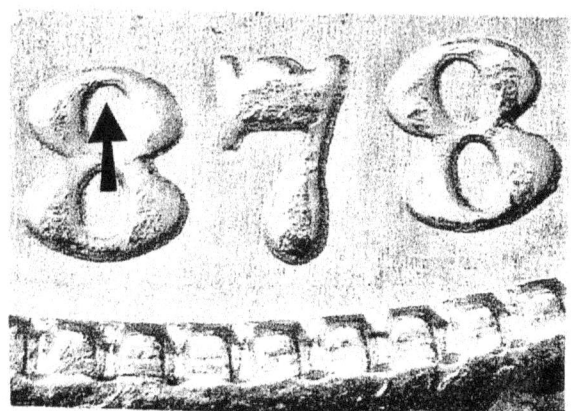

VAM 38 Doubled 8-8

VAM 38 Doubled L

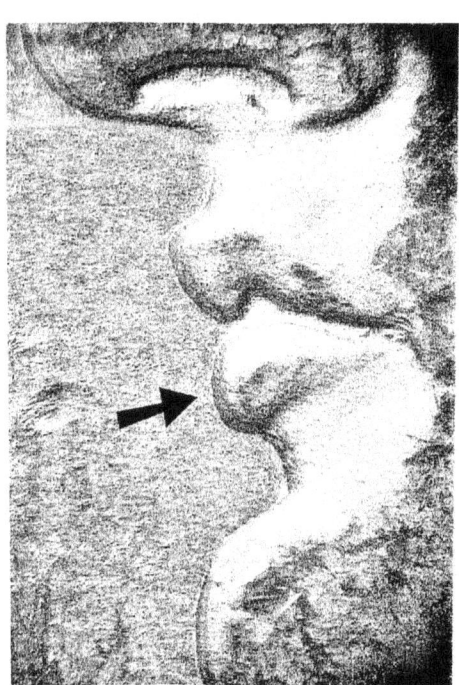

VAM 38 Doubled Profile

VAM 38 Tripled UNUM

VAM 38 Engraving Wing-Body

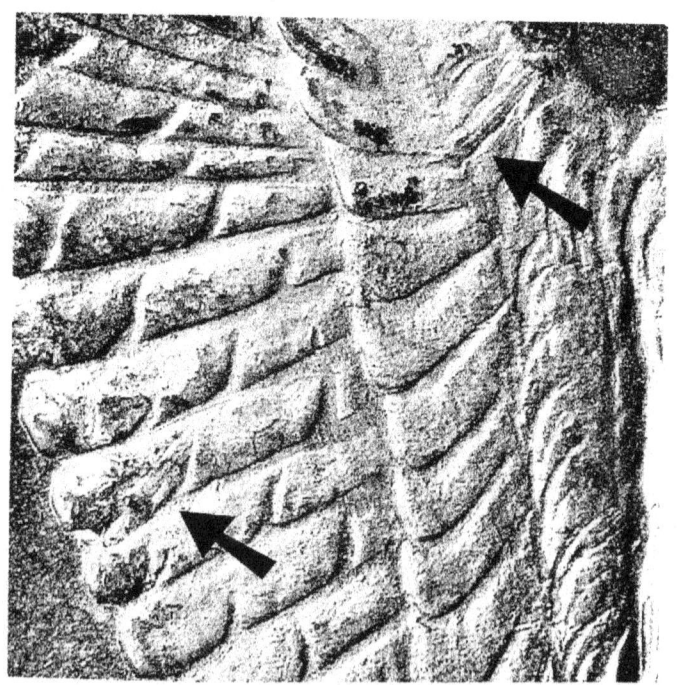

VAM 38 Die Gouges Wing

VAM 38 Engraved Wing Feather

VAM 39 Dot Behind Nose

VAM 39 Polishing in 8's

VAM 39 Die Chips

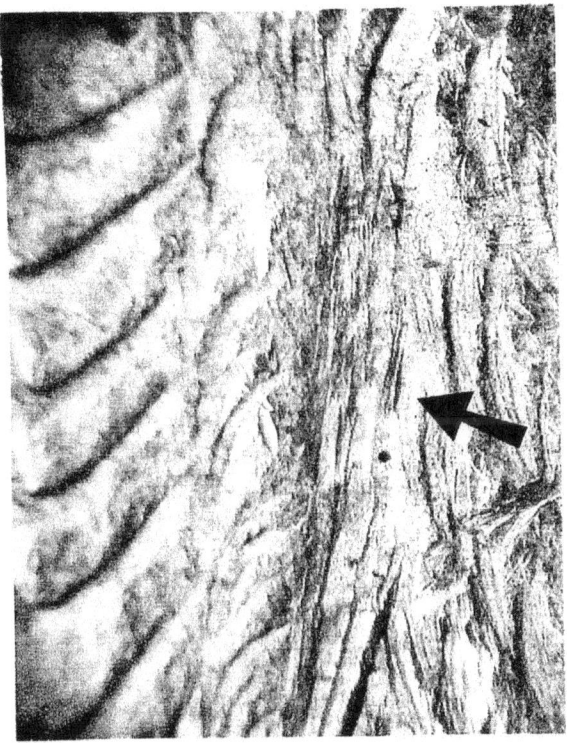

VAM 39 Engraving Lines Wing-Body

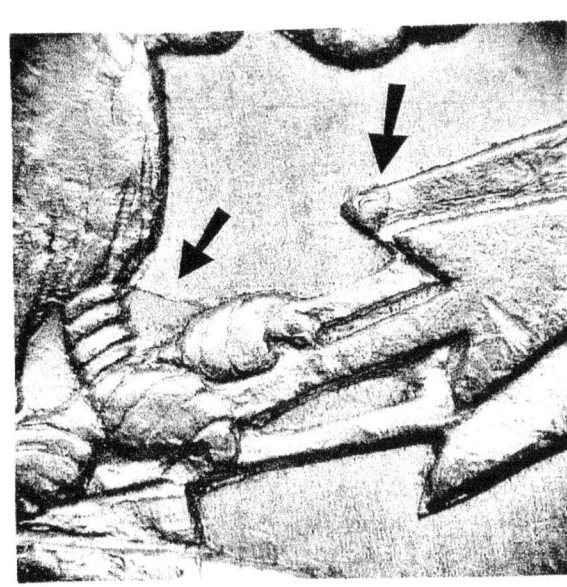

VAM 39 Gouge & Die Chip

VAM 39 Engraved Wing Feather

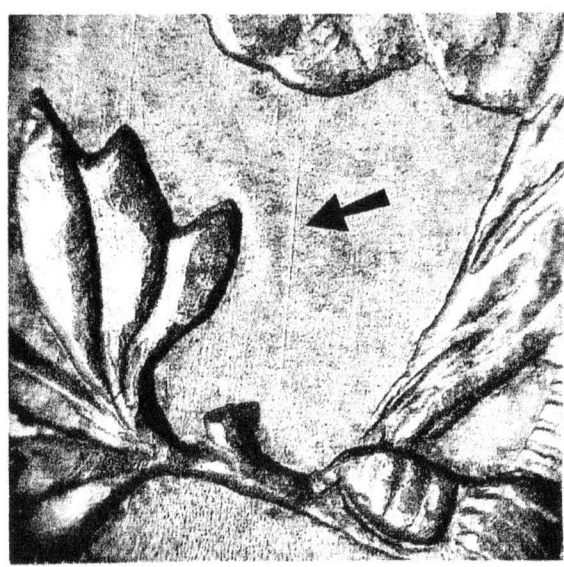

VAM 39 Polishing Line

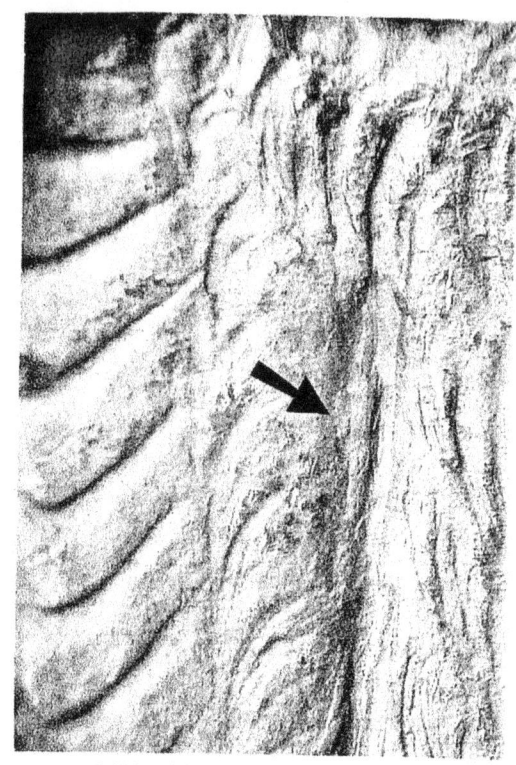

VAM 40 Engraving Wing-Body

VAM 40 Die Chips on Face, Line on Eye

VAM 40 Engraved Wing Feather, Chip
on some die states

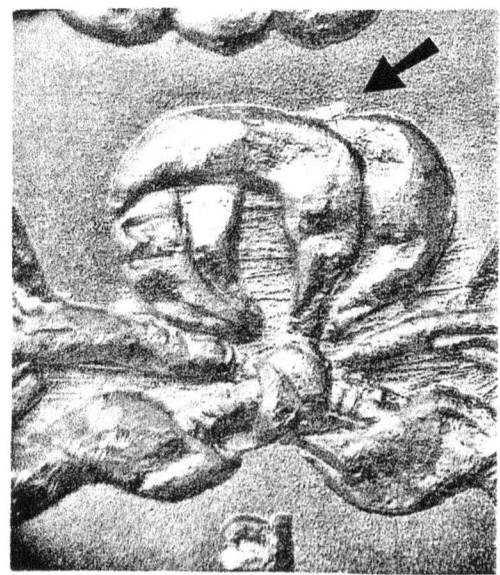

VAM 40 Die Chip Above Bow

VAM 41 Doubled LIBERTY

VAM 41 Doubled Cap Fold

VAM 41 Die Gouges

VAM 41 Lines in Wing

VAM 41 Doubled Nose & Lips

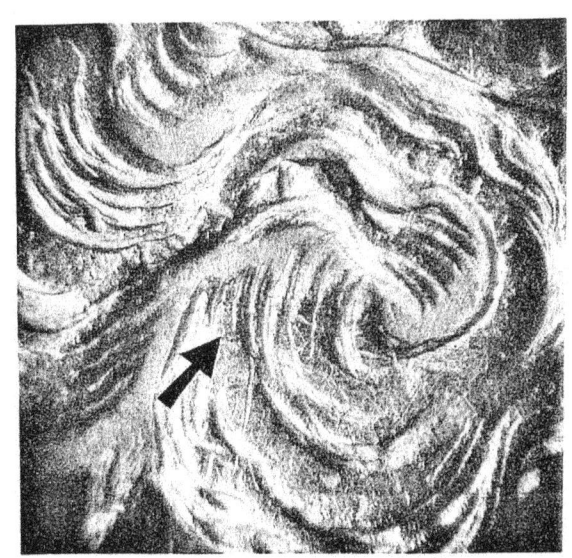

VAM 41 Doubled Lower Hair

VAM 41 Die Scratches in Wing

VAM 42 Spike Above Eyelid

VAM 42 Die Marks at DO

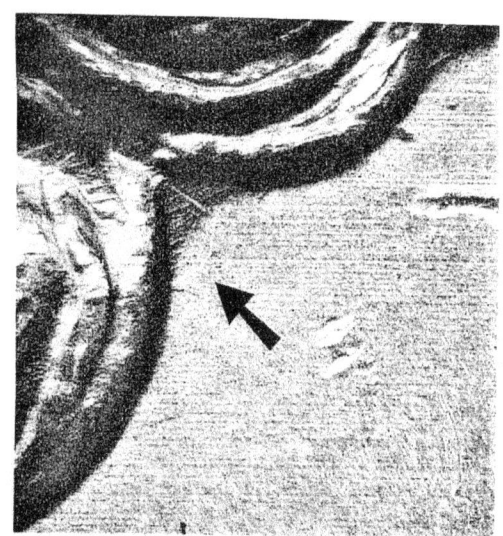

VAM 42A Clashed st

VAM 42 Hub Doubling NE

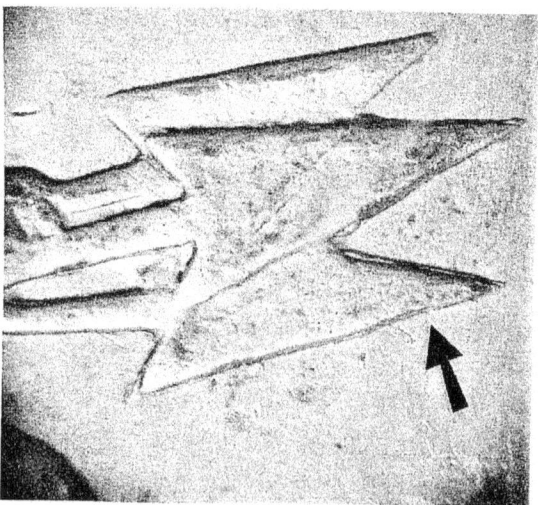

VAM 42 Hub Doubling Lower Arrow Head

VAM 43 Polishing in 8

VAM 42 Engraved Wing Feather

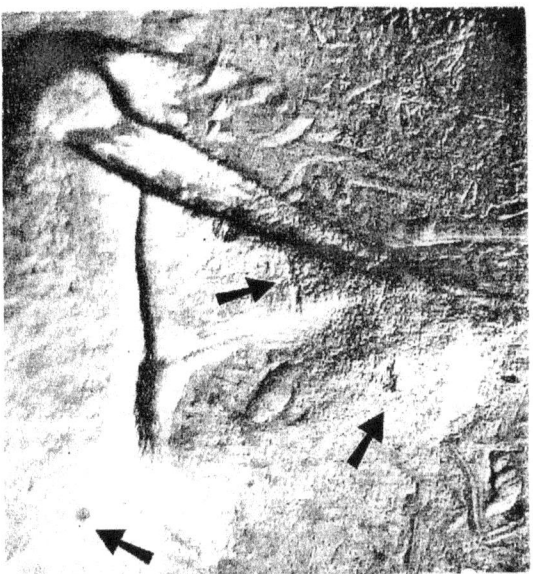

VAM 45 Die Chips Eye

VAM 45 Doubled STATES

VAM 45 Engraved Wing Feather

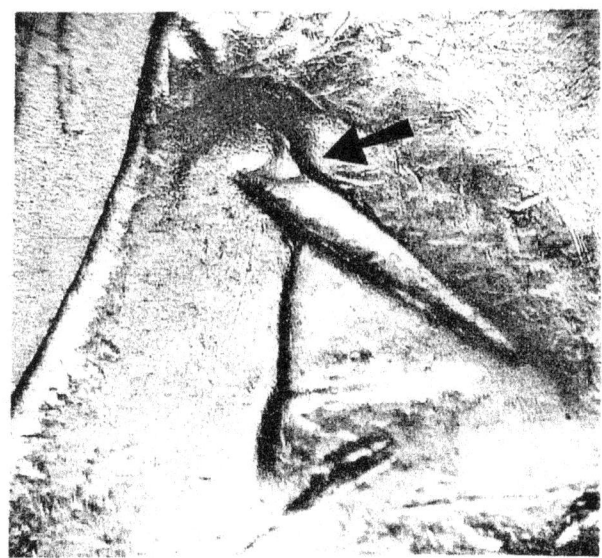

VAM 46 Die Gouge Eye

VAM 46 Worm Eye Die Break

VAM 47 Die 2 Polishing Lines 8

VAM 46A Die Break Wreath

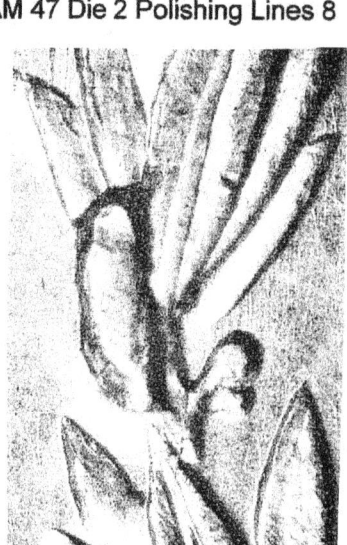

VAM 46A Die Break
Wreath, LDS

VAM 47 Engraved Wing Feather

VAM 47 Die 2 Polishing Line ER

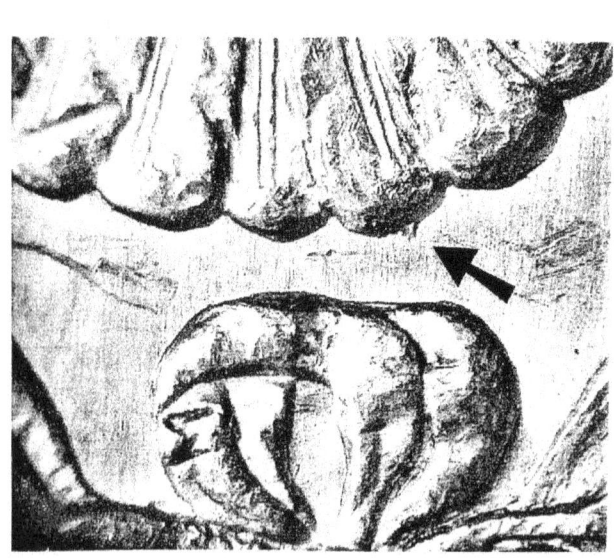

VAM 47 Tick Below Tail Feather

VAM 47 Doubled Legend

VAM 48 Over Polished Ear

VAM 48 Doubled B

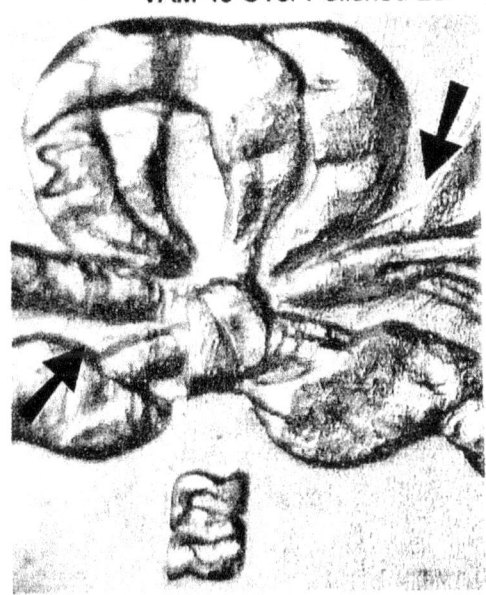

VAM 48 Scratch Bow

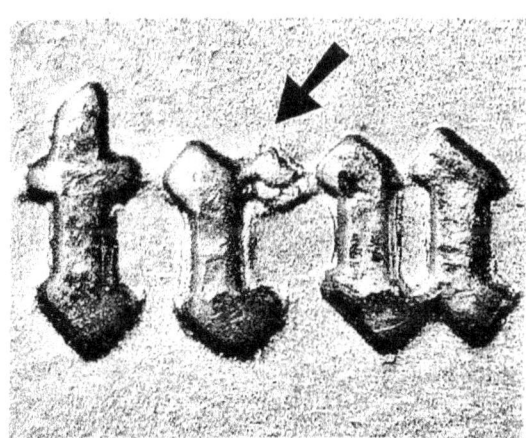

VAM 48 Broken r With Triangle

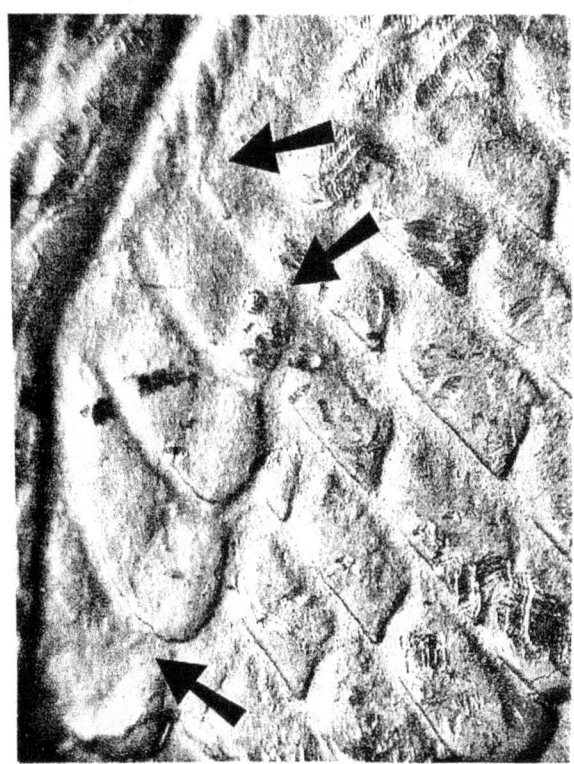

VAM 49 Dots & Lines

VAM 48 Engraved Wing Feather

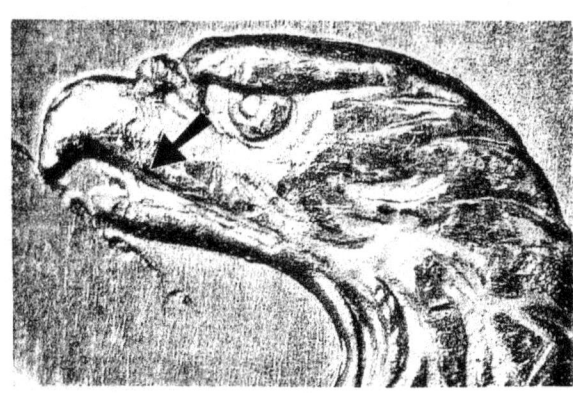

VAM 49
Gouge Mouth

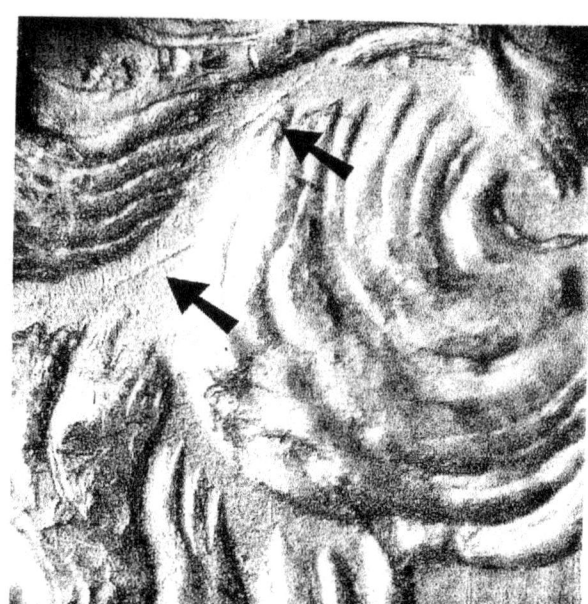

VAM 49 Die Scratches in Hair

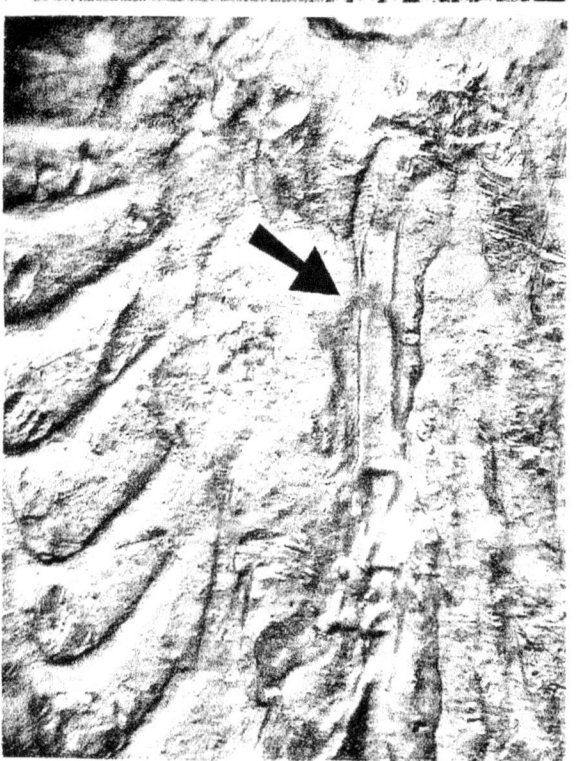

VAM 49 Acid Treated Wing-Body

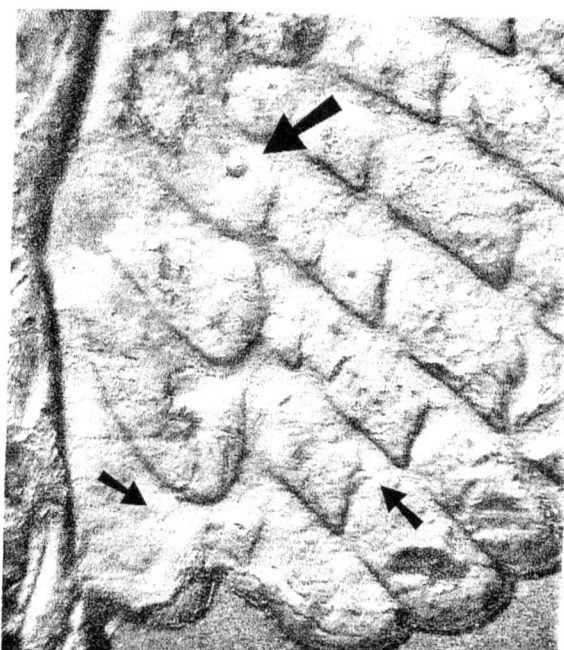

VAM 49 Dot Die Chip Wing

VAM 49 Acid Treated Wing Feather

VAM 49 Diagonal Line

VAM 50 Tripled Eyelid

VAM 50 Acid Treated Wing Feather

VAM 50 Shallow
STAT & Denticles

VAM 50 Acid Treated
Wing Feather

VAM 50 Lines in Middle of Wing

VAM 51 Polishing Lines Upper TF

VAM 50
S Tilted Left

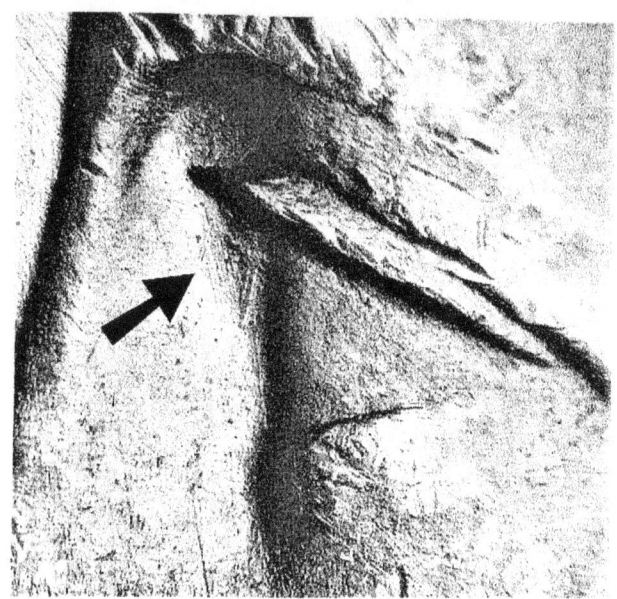

VAM 51 Spiked Eye

VAM 51 Over Polished Ear

VAM 51 Doubled ONE

VAM 51 Weak STAT

VAM 51 Engraved Wing Feather

VAM 52 Polishing Line Wing

VAM 52 Engraving
Wing-Body

VAM 53 Engraving
Wing-Body

VAM 52 Engraved Wing Feather

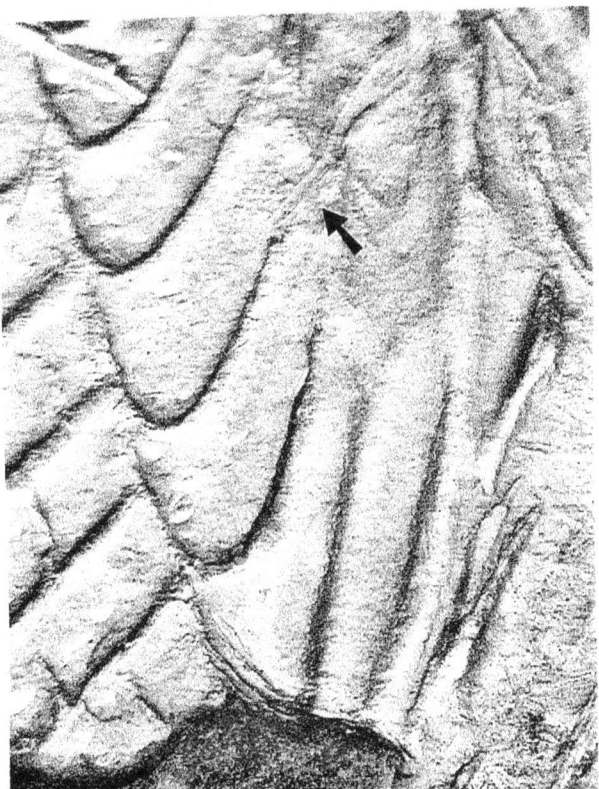

VAM 53 Engraved Wing Feather

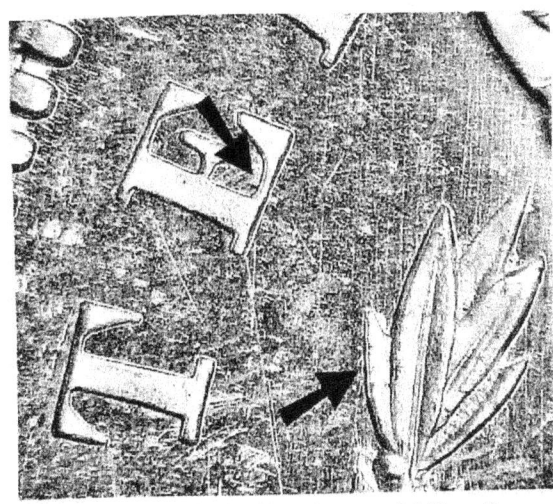

VAM 53 Doubled Legend, Wreath

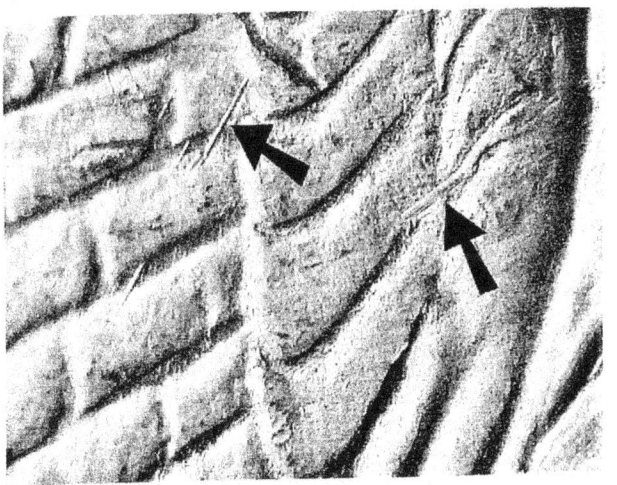

VAM 53 Die Scratches Wing

VAM 54 Doubled Profile

VAM 55 Acid Treated Wing Middle

VAM 55 Some Rust Pits (Possible Acid Treated)

VAM 55 Engraved Wing Feather

VAM 55 Dot on Tail Feathers

VAM 61 Doubled Motto

VAM 63 Polishing Line Below Cap

VAM 63 Die Scratch Eye Front

VAM 63 Beveled 8's

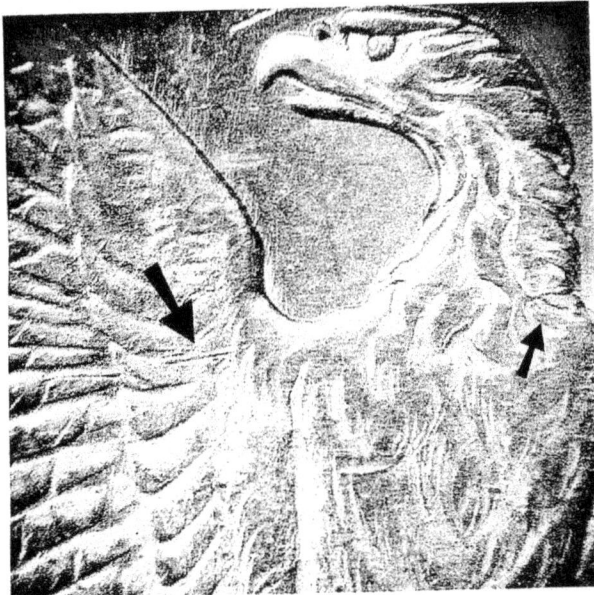

VAM 63 Die Scratch Thru Neck & Wing

VAM 63 S/S Right

VAM 64 Polishing Line LI

VAM 64 Engraved Wing Feather with Lines

VAM 64 Engraved Lines Wing Middle

VAM 64 Engraved Wing Middle

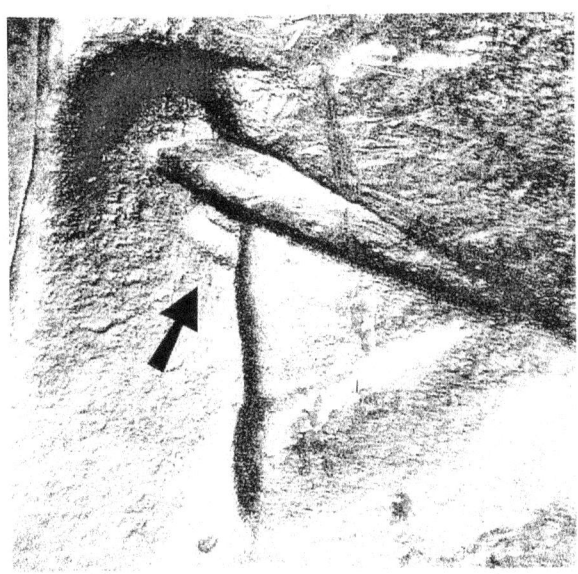

VAM 65 Double Spikes Eye

VAM 65 Doubled Motto

VAM 65 Doubled Motto

VAM 66 Die Scratch IB

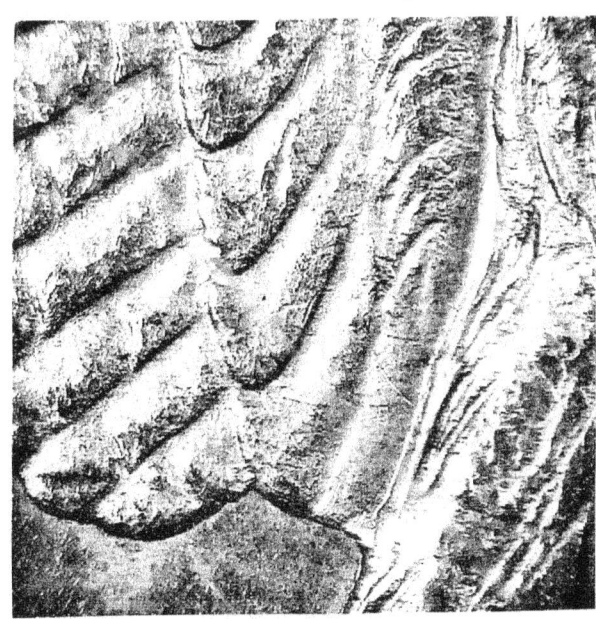

VAM 65 Engraved Wing Feather

VAM 66 Doubled Ear

VAM 66 Doubled Eyelid

VAM 67 Engraved Wing Feather

VAM 68 Doubled LIBERTY

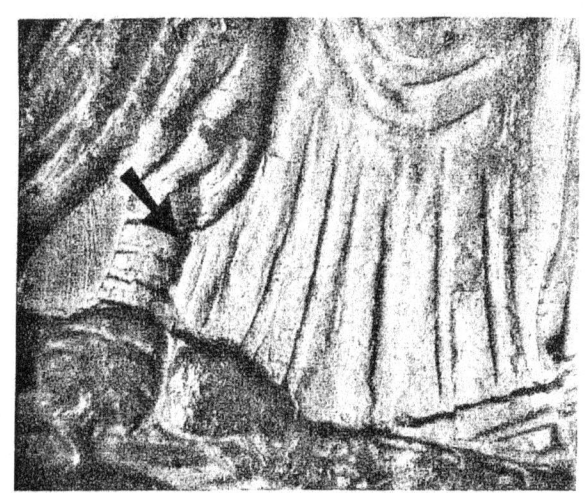

VAM 45/68 (1879 S Rev 78 VAM 9)
Two Engraved TF

VAM 69 Die Chip R

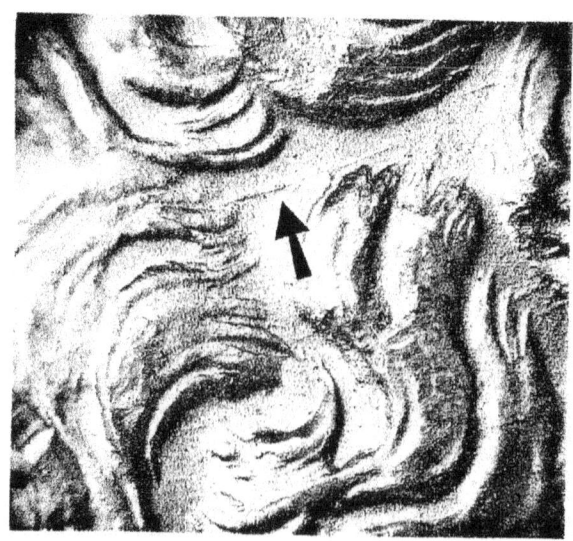

VAM 69 Die Scratch Hair

VAM 69 Die Chip Wing

VAM 69 Engraved Wing Feather

VAM 71 S Set High

VAM 73 Doubled Eyelid With Spike

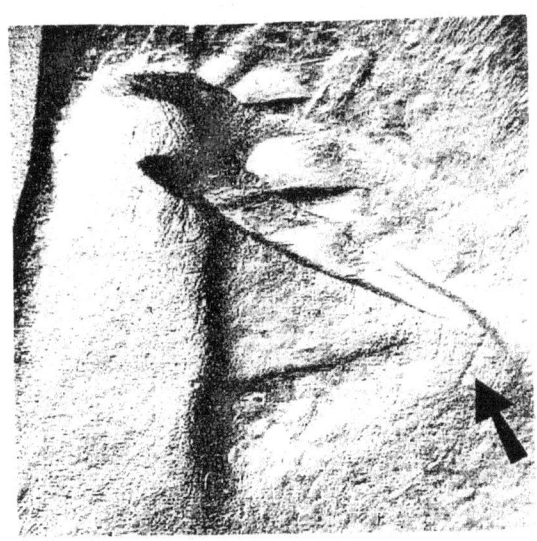

VAM 74 Line Behind Eye

VAM 74A Die Chip in Wreath

VAM 75 Doubled L

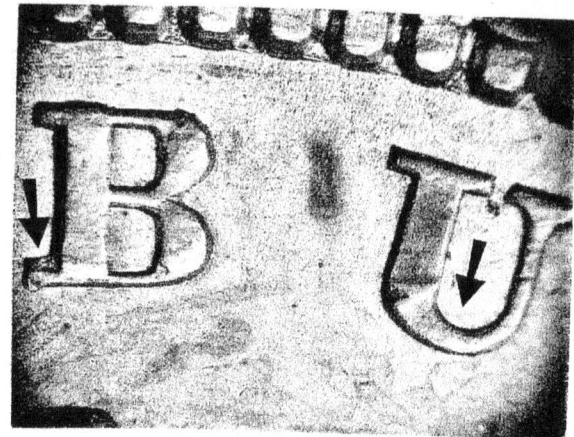

VAM 75 Doubled BUS

VAM 75 Die Flake Cap Top

VAM 75 Doubled UNUM

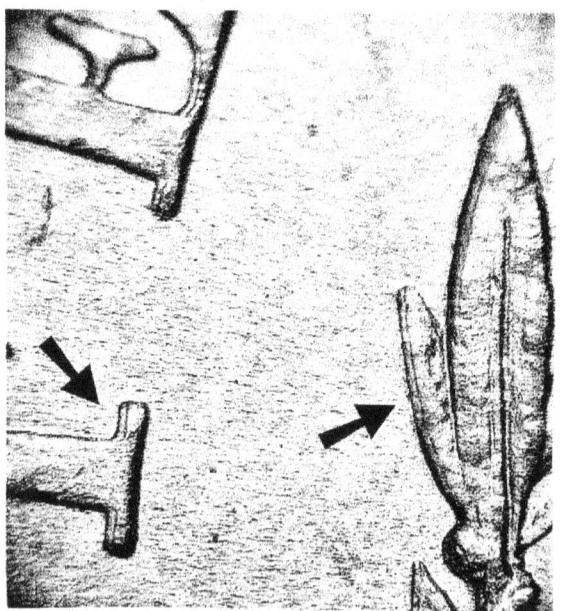

VAM 75 Doubled UNITED & Leaves

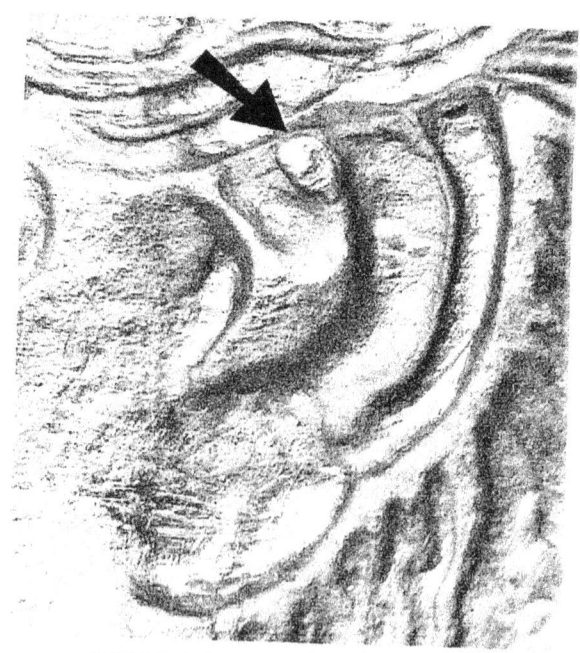

VAM 75 Comma Die Chip in Ear

VAM 75 Dot on Tail Feathers

VAM 75 Wing Center EDS

VAM 75 Engraved Wing Feather

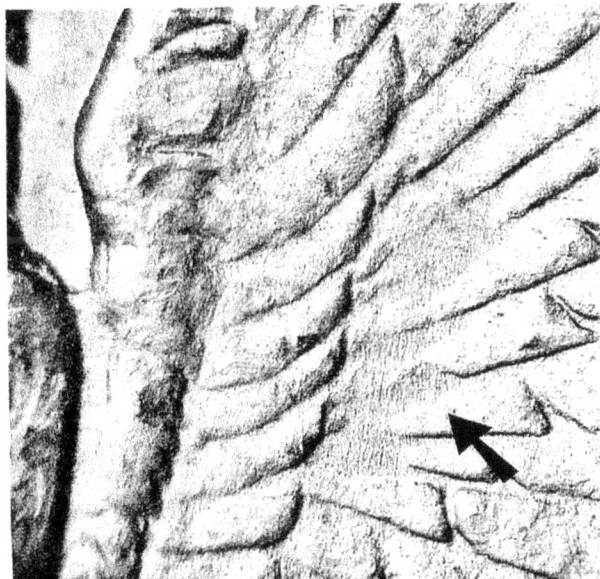

VAM 75 Over Polished Wing

VAM 75A Acid Treated Wing Middle

VAM 75 EDS Before Polishing

VAM 75 Over Polished Wing Center

VAM 75A Polishing Lines

VAM 75A Light Acid Treated?

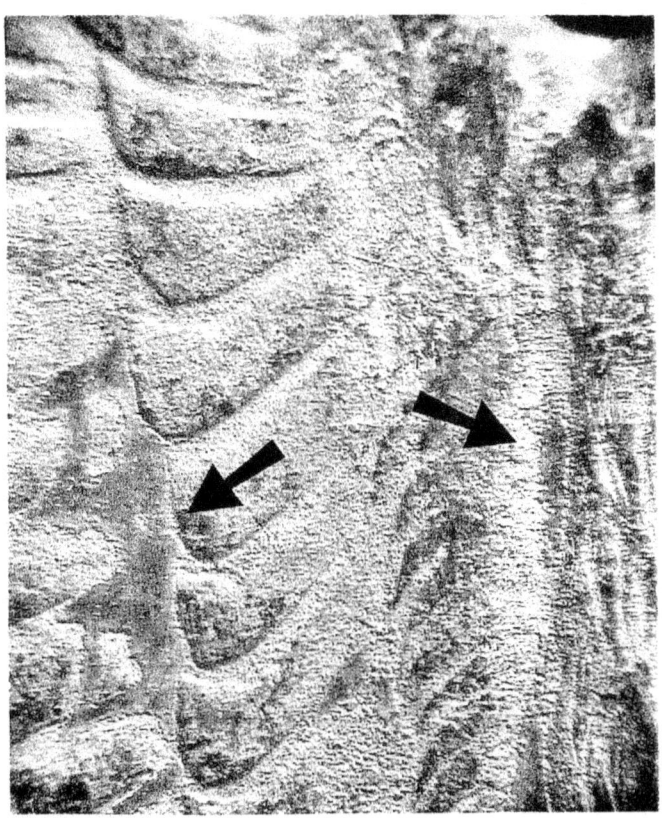

VAM 76 Acid Treated Wing-Body

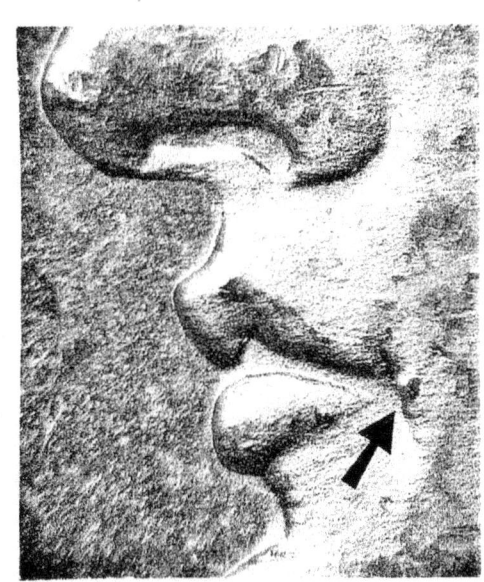

VAM 76 Die Chip Mouth

VAM 76 Acid Treated Wing Middle

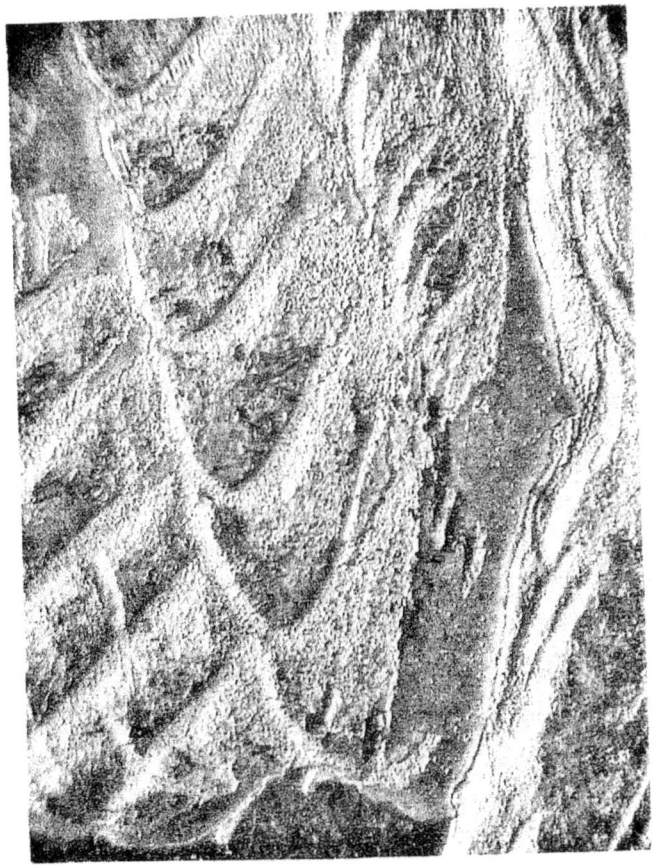

VAM 76 Acid Treated Wing Feather

VAM 76 Acid Treated Leg

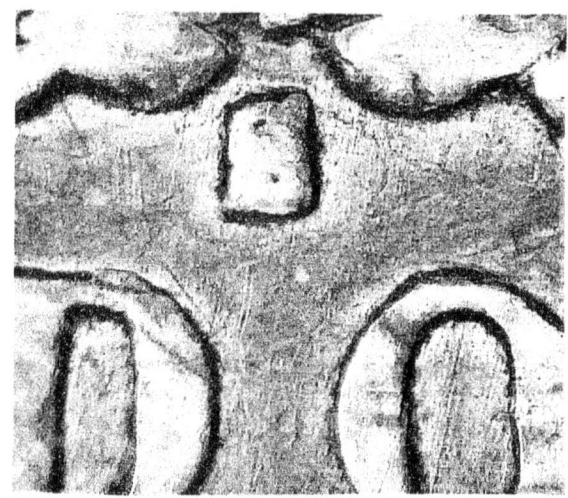

VAM 77 S Set High

VAM 78 S Set Left & Tilted Left

VAM 78 Die 1 Gouge Cotton Boll

VAM 78 Die 2 Doubled Eyelid

VAM 78 Die 3 Cap Ribbon, Chips

VAM 78 Die 4 Chips Ribbon End

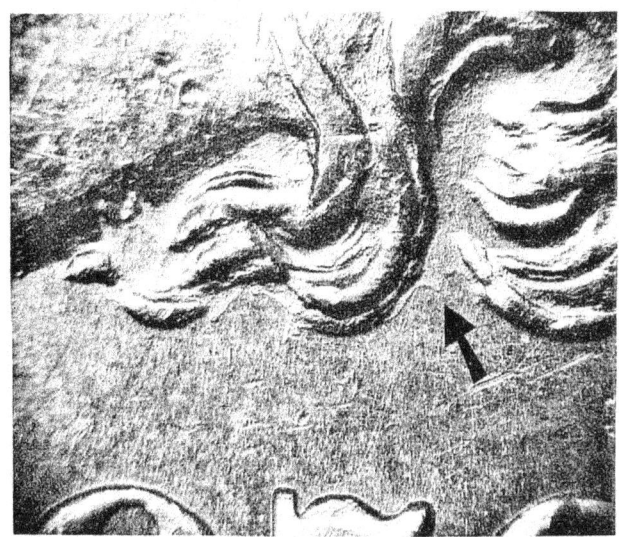

VAM 78 Die 1 Acid Treated Hair Edge

VAM 78 Die 3 Die Gouges in Ear

VAM 78 Lines in Feather

VAM 80 Doubled E

VAM 80 Line Eye Front

VAM 80 Double Lines Nostril

VAM 82 Die marker- Die Chips Lip

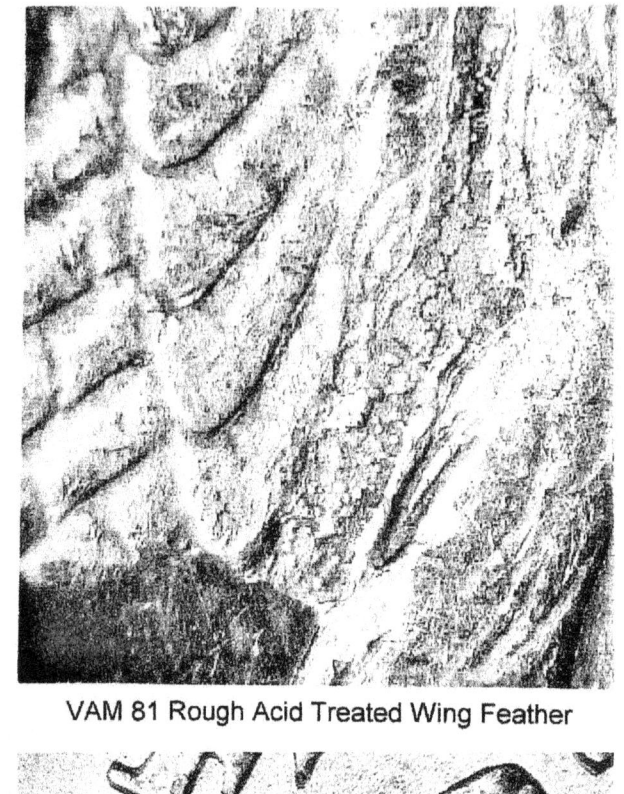

VAM 81 Rough Acid Treated Wing Feather

VAM 83 Lines in Wing

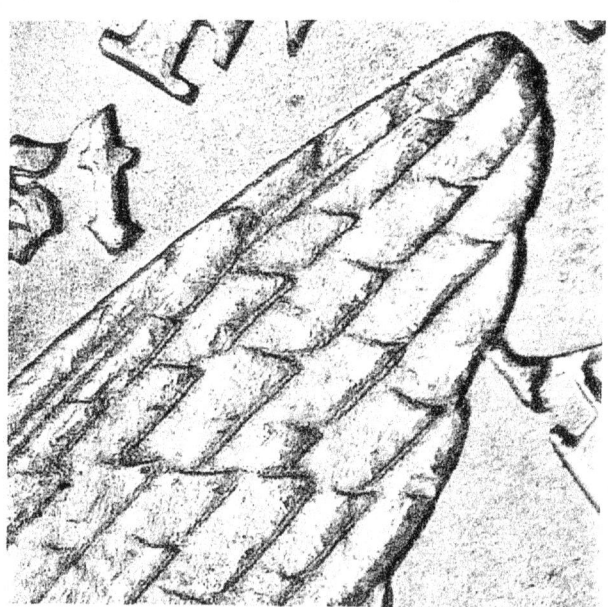

VAM 83 Doubled Eagle's Wing

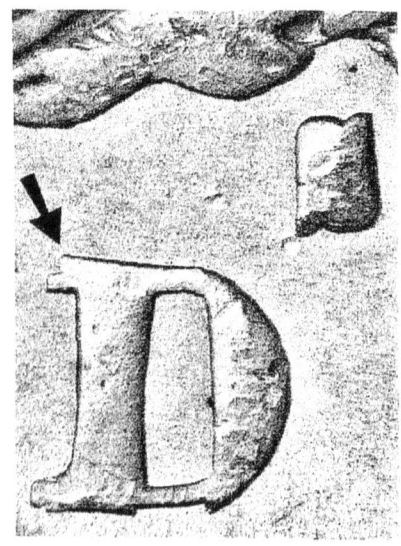

VAM 83 Doubled D

VAM 84 Polished, Doubled 878 & Hair

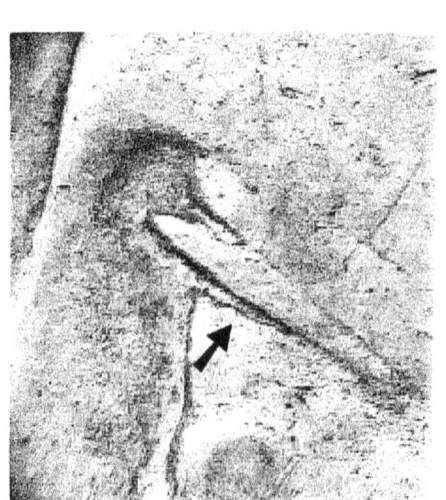

VAM 85 Doubled Eyelid

VAM 84 Acid Treated Wing Middle

VAM 84 Acid Treated Wing-Body

VAM 84 Acid Treated Upper Tail Feathers

VAM 84 Acid Treated Wing-Body

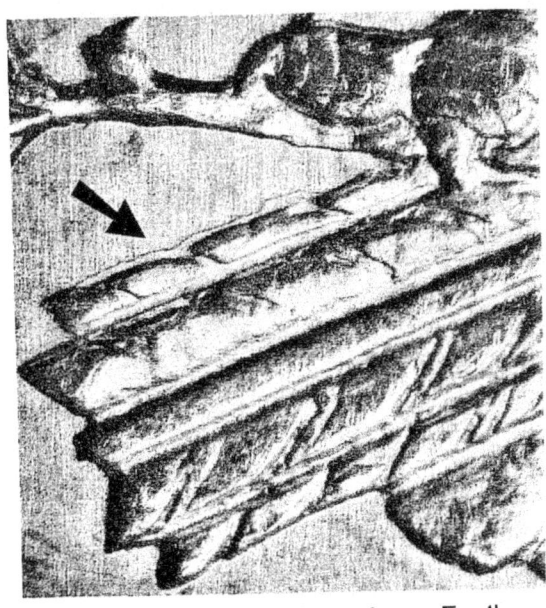

VAM 84 Acid Treated Upper Arrow Feather

VAM 84 Acid Treated Lower Tail Feathers

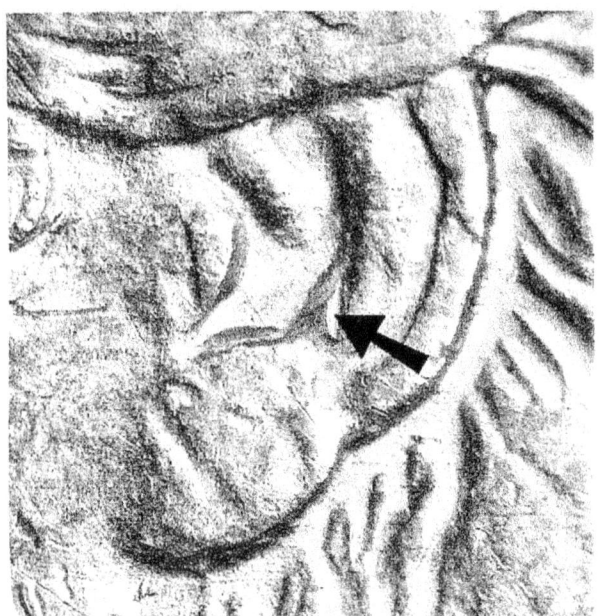

VAM 86 Doubled Ear

VAM 86 Die Scratches Cotton Bolls

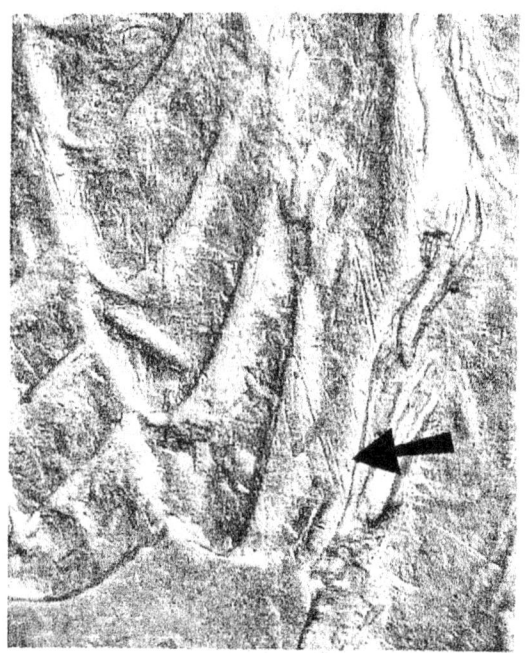

VAM 86 Die 1 Polishing Lines

VAM 86 Die 1 Die Scratches

VAM 86 Die 2 Die Chips in TF

VAM 86 Filled S Mint Mark

VAM 86 Die 3 Polishing Lines Wing

VAM 86 Die 3 Polishing Lines Wing

VAM 86 Die 3 Polishing Lines Tail Feathers

VAM 87 Doubled Motto

VAM 87 Spiked Eye

VAM 88 Engraved Wing Feather

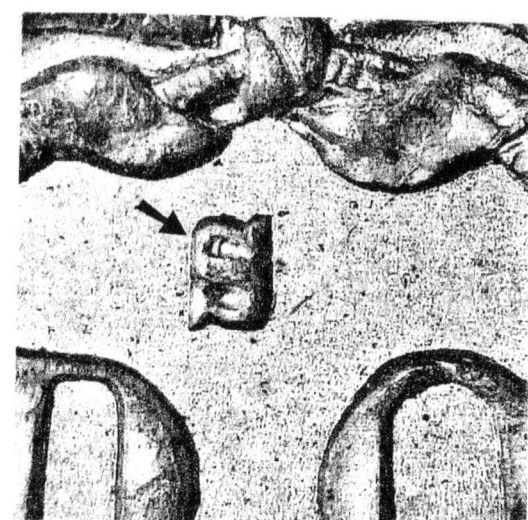

VAM 88 S/S Top Left Inside

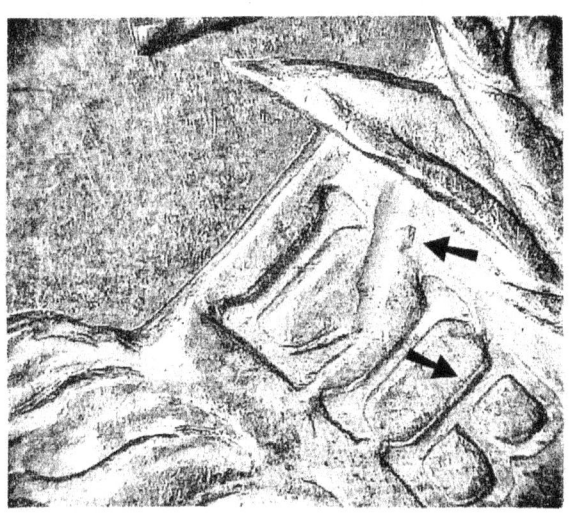

VAM 91 Doubled LIBERTY

VAM 91 Doubled Motto & Cap

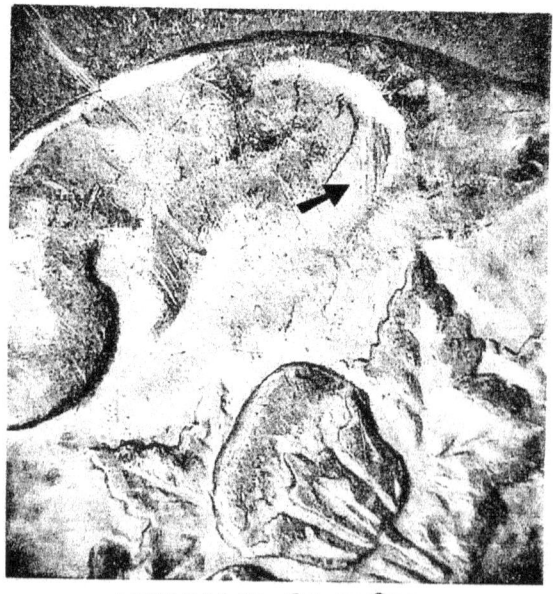

VAM 91A Die Gouge Cap

VAM 92 Die Gouges Wing

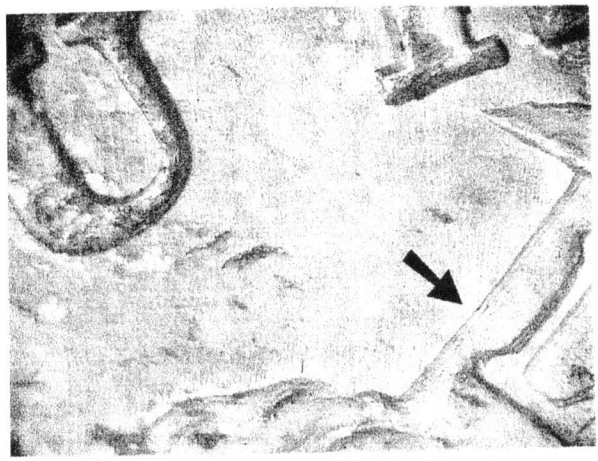

VAM 93 Doubled LIBERTY Band

VAM 93 Doubled L

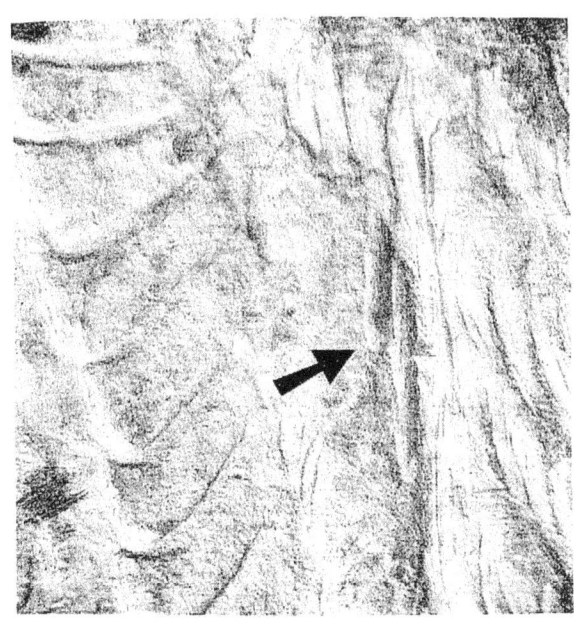

VAM 93 Engraving Wing-Body

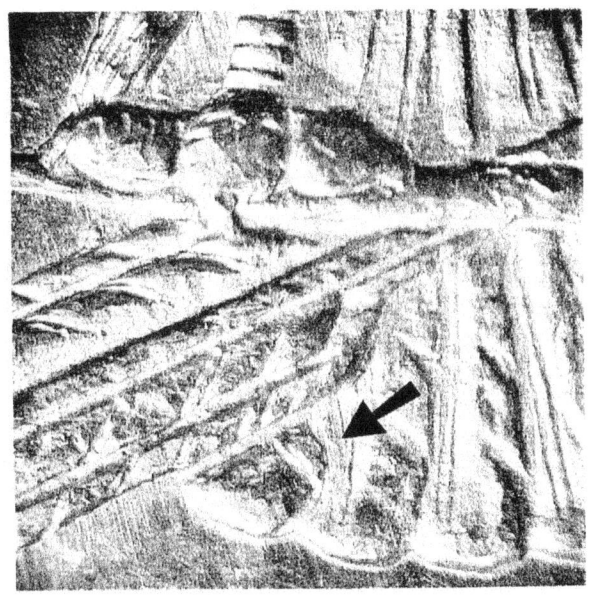

VAM 92 Die Gouge Tail Feathers

VAM 93 Line in R

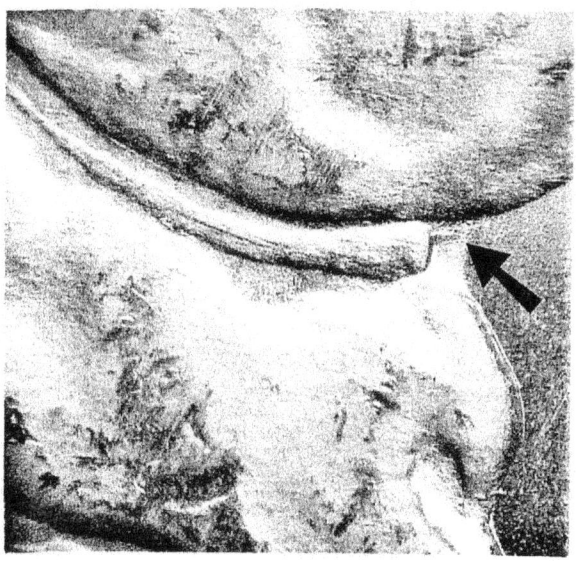

VAM 93 Line Ribbon Edge

VAM 94 Die marker- Wavy Line BE

VAM 94 Doubled UNUM

VAM 94 Doubled L

VAM 96 S/S Triangles

VAM 97 Engraved Wing Feather

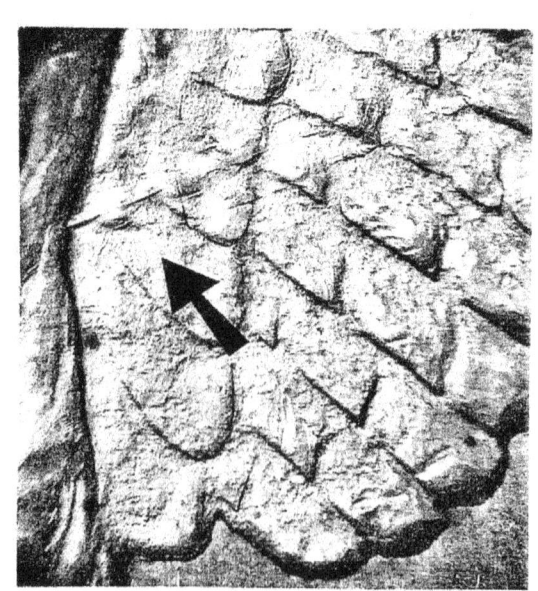

VAM 97 Die Gouge Wing

VAM 98 Doubled 878

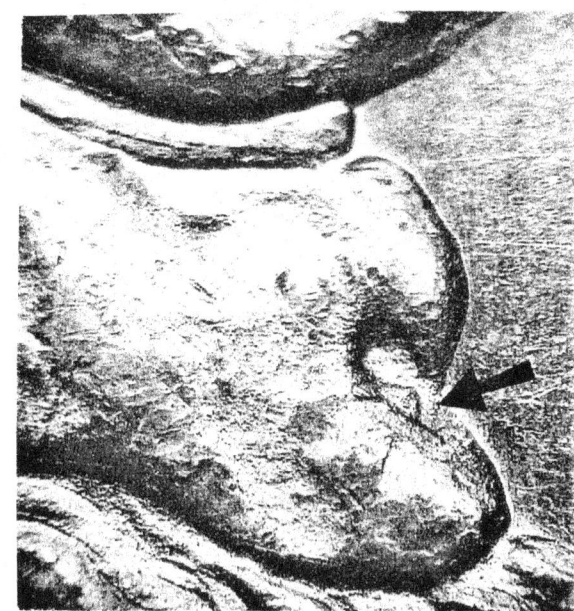

VAM 98 Die Chip Cap

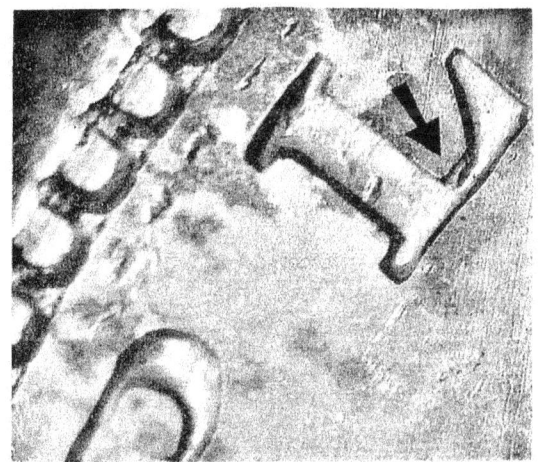

VAM 99 Doubled L, weakly struck letters

VAM 99 Lines Below Hair, on some die states

VAM 100 Engraved Wing Feather

VAM 103 Die Combo 1 Polishing Lines 8

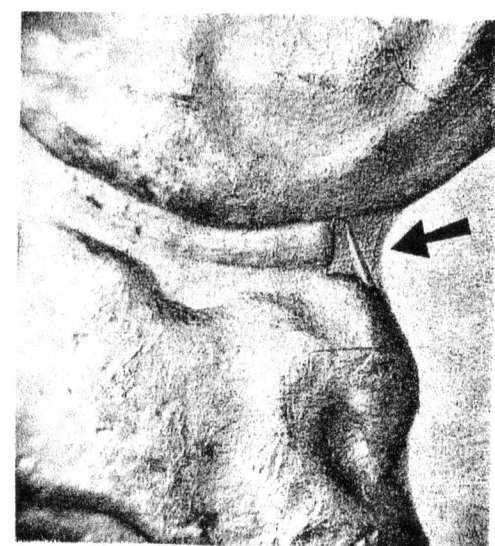

VAM 103 Die Combo 1 Die Scratch

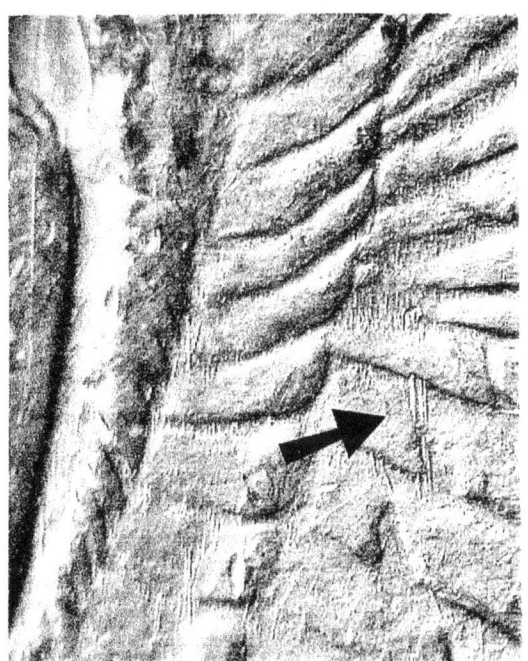

VAM 103 Die Combo 1 Double Die Scratches

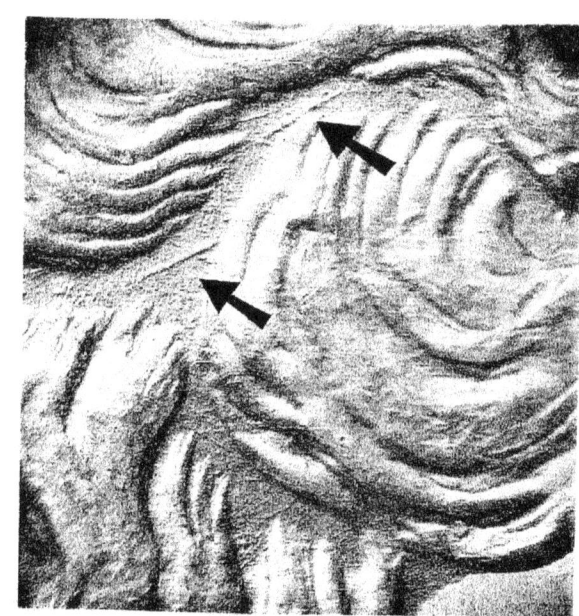

VAM 103 Die Combo 1 Two Die Scratches in Hair

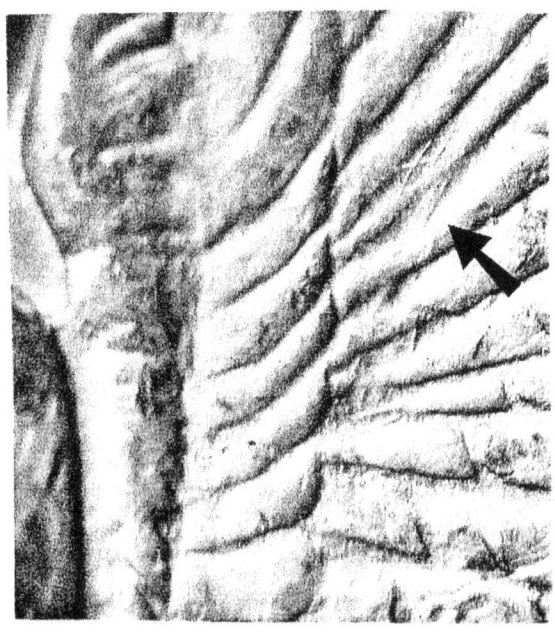

VAM 103 Die Combo 2 Polishing Lines

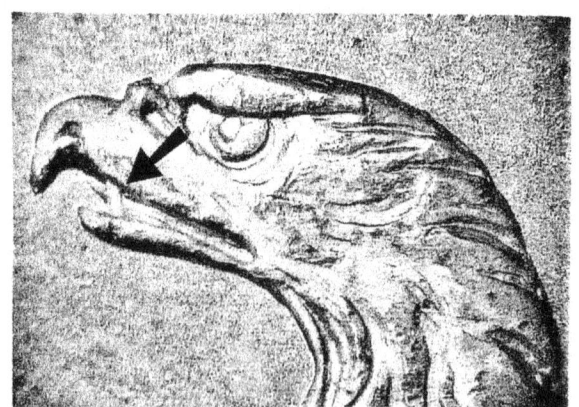

VAM 103 Die Combo 3 Gouge Mouth

-126-

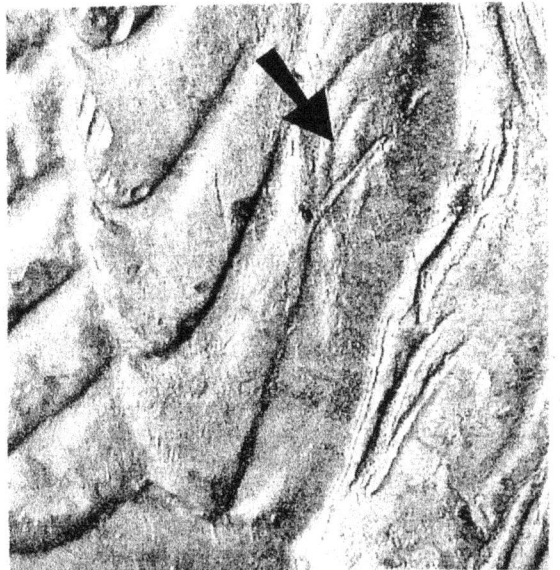

VAM 103 Die Combo 3 Polishing Line

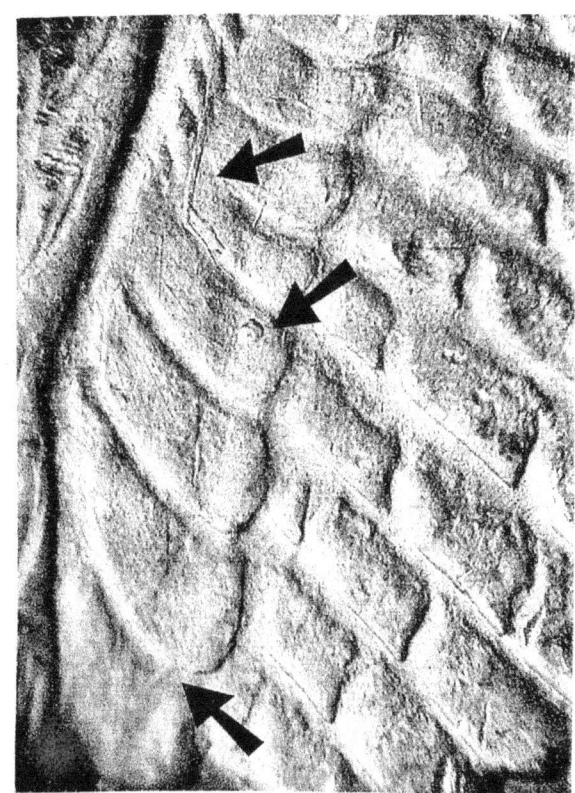

VAM 103 Die Combo 3 Dots & Lines

VAM 103 Die Combo 3 Diagonal Line

VAM 103 Die Combo 4 Polished 8

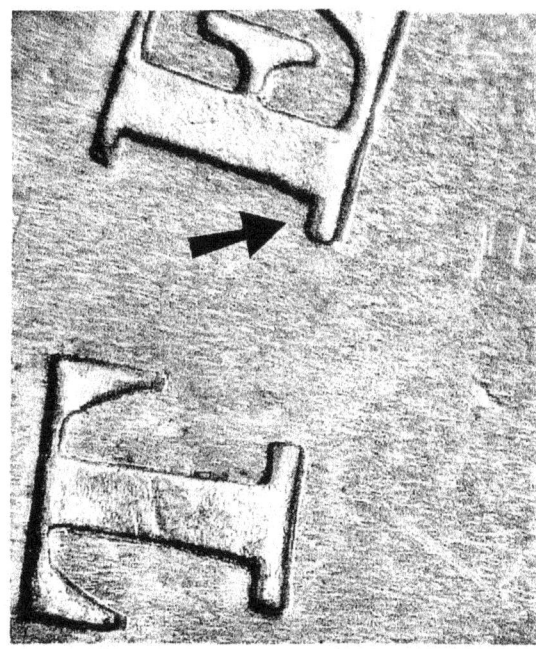

VAM 103 Die Combo 4 Doubled ITED

VAM 103 Die Combo 4 Double Polishing Lines

-127-

VAM 104 Die Gouges in Hair

VAM 104 Die Gouges in Wing

VAM 104 Engraved Wing Feather

VAM 104 Die Scratches on Wing

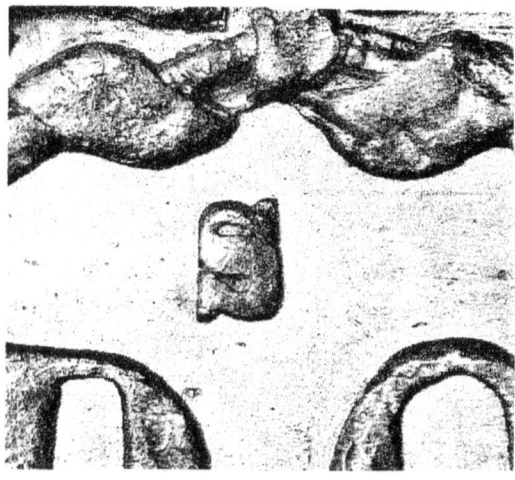

VAM 104 S Mint Mark Set Left

VAM 105 Die Scratch Nose Bridge

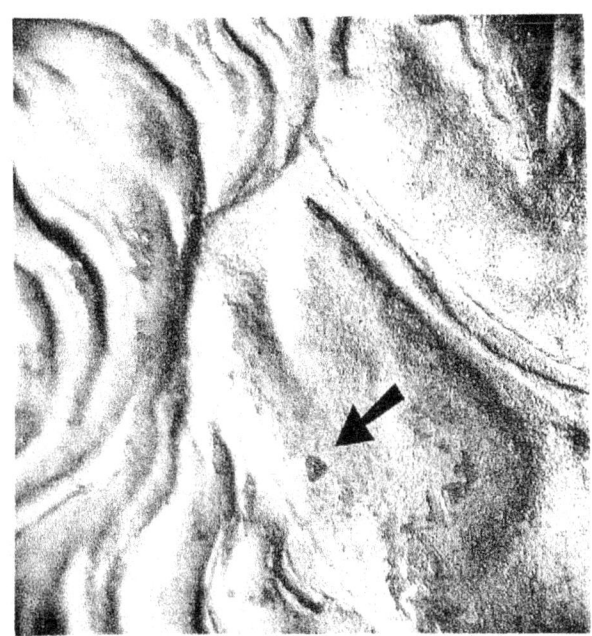

VAM 105 Die Chip Below Ribbon

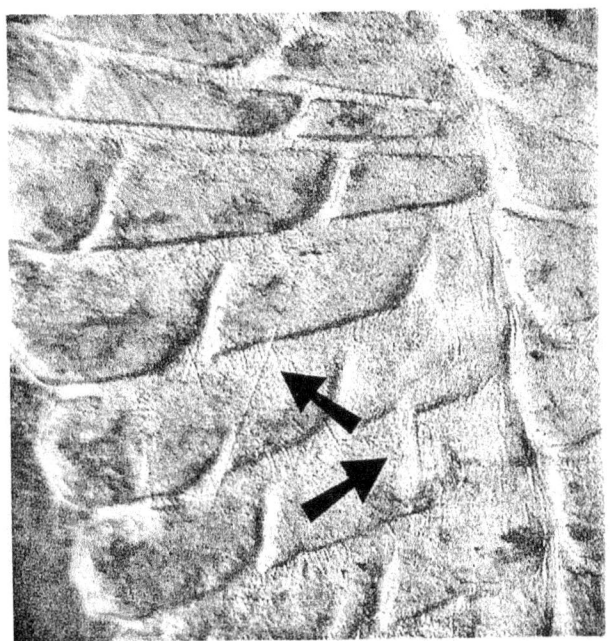

VAM 105 Lines in Wing

VAM 105 Broken r With Triangle

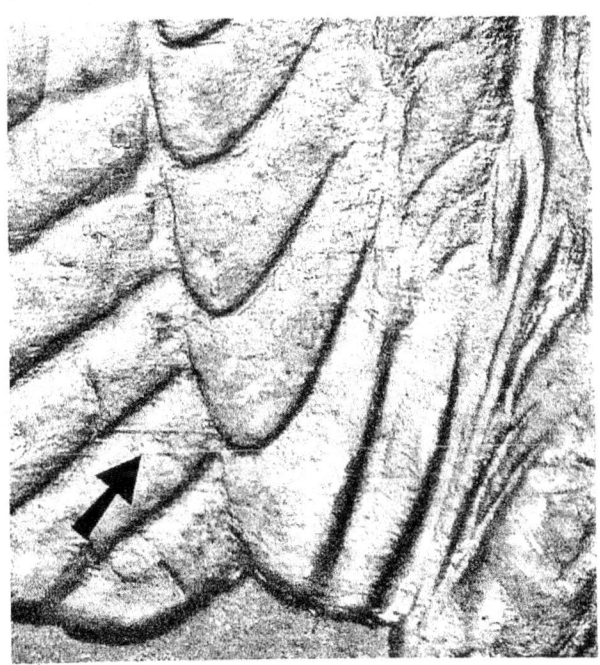

VAM 105 Engraved Wing Feather

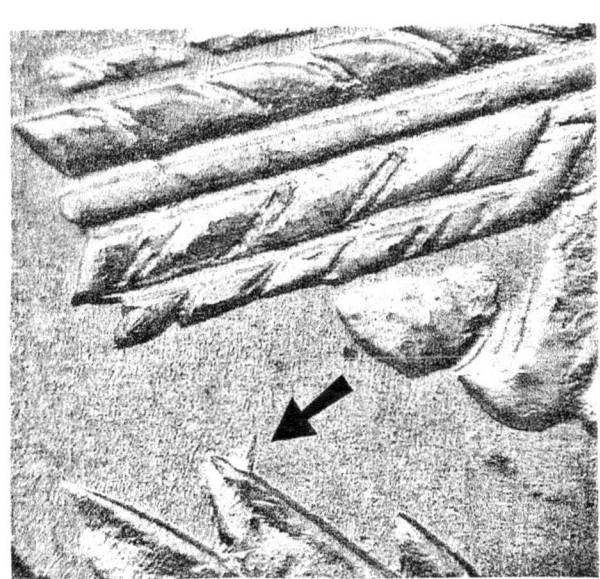

VAM 105 Triangular Die Gouge

VAM 105 Engraving on Feathers

VAM 105 Engraving on Feathers

VAM 105 Over Polished Tail Feathers

VAM 106 Over Polished TED & Denticles

-130-

VAM 106 Polishing Lines

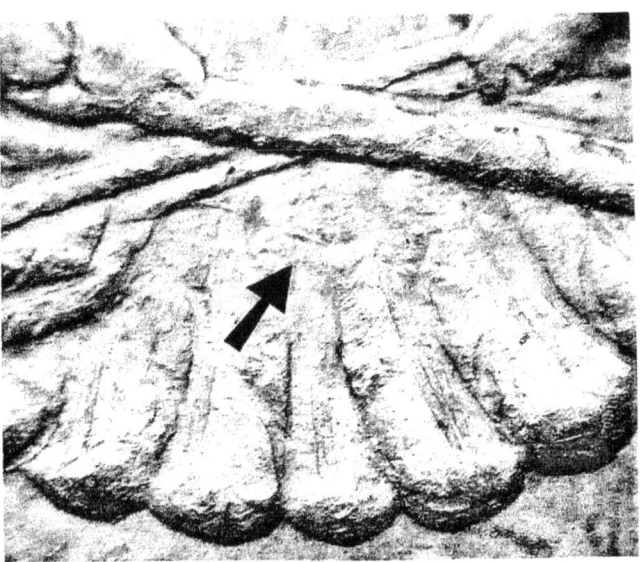

VAM 106 Line in Tail Feathers

VAM 107 Doubled Eyelid with Spike

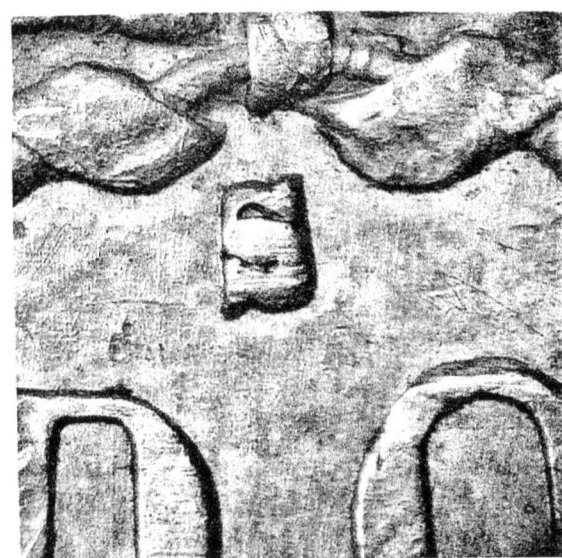

VAM 106 High S Tilted Left

VAM 107 Doubled D

VAM 107 Double Die Scratch

VAM 108 Die Chip Cap

VAM 108 Die Scratches Wing

VAM 108 Die Scratch Leg

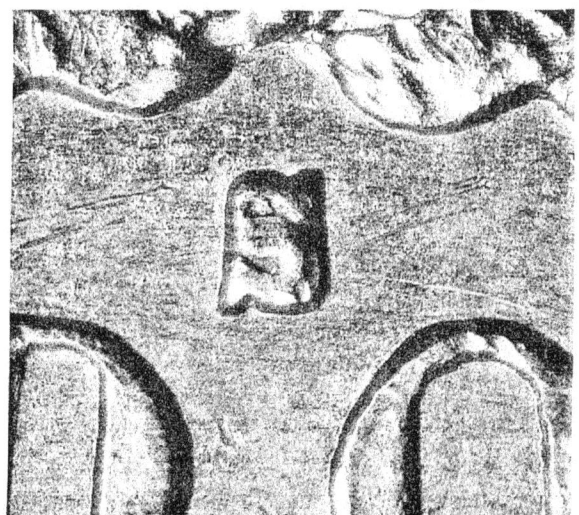

VAM 108 S/S Lines

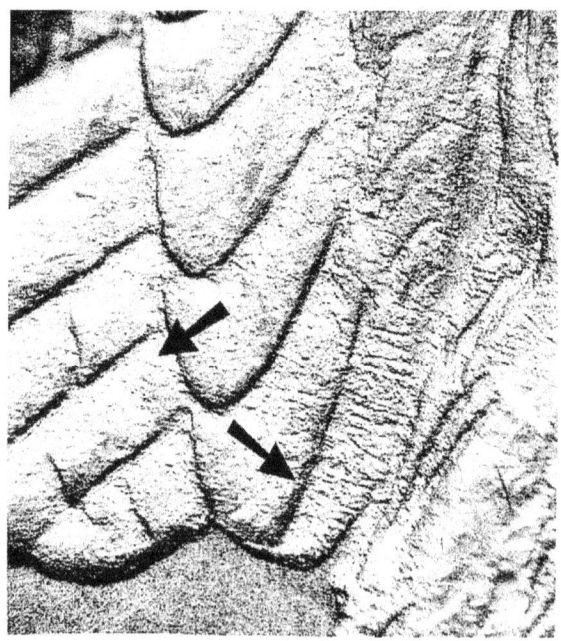

VAM 109 B^{2}a Reverse

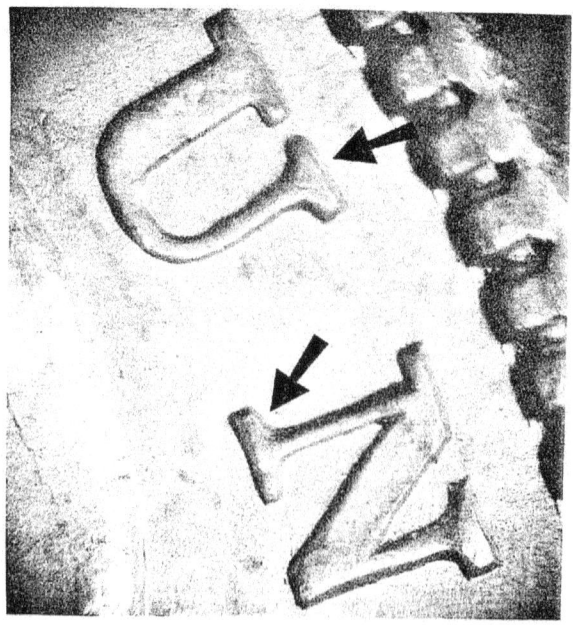

VAM 110 Doubled UNUM

VAM 110 Die marker- Line Forehead

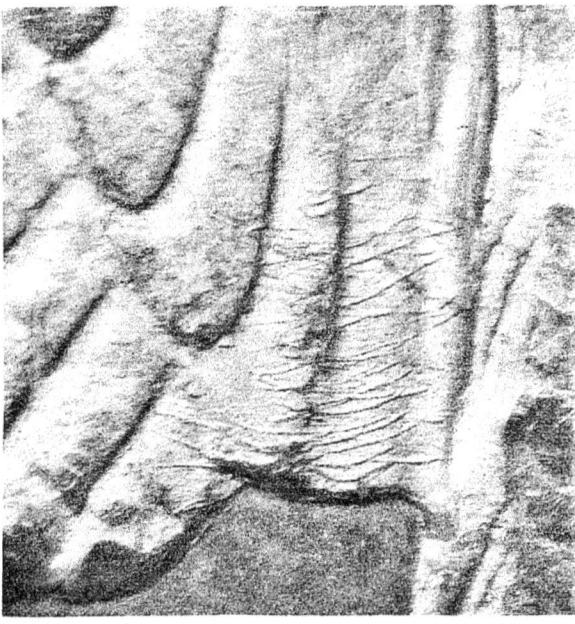

VAM 110 Engraved Wing Feather With Lines

VAM 110 Engraved Lines Wing Middle

VAM 110 Engraved 8th Upper Tail Feather

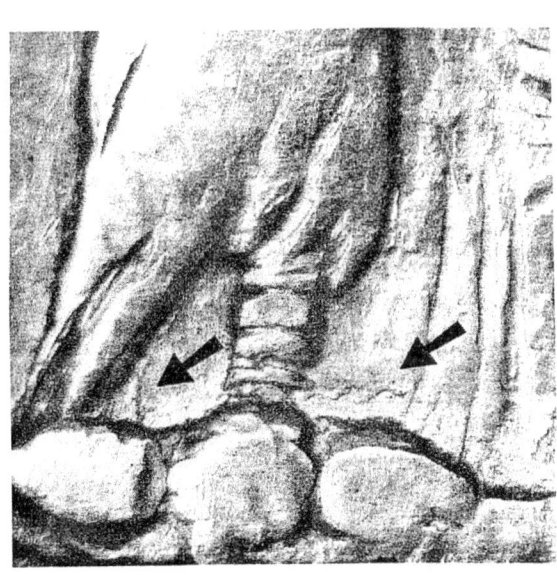

VAM 111 Die markers- Lines at Leg

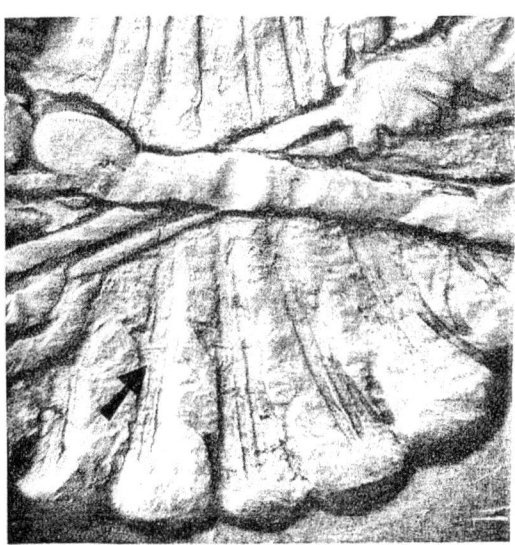

VAM 111 Die marker- Line in Tail Feathers

FURTHER REFERENCES

Please check Amazon Kindle for Michael S. Fey, Ph.D., and Leroy Van Allen & A. George Mallis publications. For hard copy print of books, please contact Dr. Fey at RCI, P.O. Box C, Ironia, NJ 07845 or eMail: Feyms@aol.com.

Hard copy books are also available at *The Institute for Silver Dollar Education and Research*, at website: *Ilovesilver dollars.org* or by contacting Executive Director John Baumgart at John.Baumgart@comcast.net

Amazon Kindle

Fey, Michael S. 2019. *The Complete Virtual Guide to Pricing Your Morgan Silver Dollars*. 286 pp. RCI

Van Allen, Leroy, & A. George Mallis. 2023. *Part I or II or III of Three. Comprehensive Catalog and Encyclopedia or Morgan & Peace Dollars*. RCI Total 520 pp.

Leroy Van Allen. 2011. *Wonders of Morgan Dollars*. 139 pp. RCI

Leroy Van Allen. 2013. *Wonders of Peace Dollars*. 273 pp. RCI

Leroy Van Allen. 2006. *Morgan Dollars 8 & 7 Over 8 Tail Feather Story*. 52 pp. RCI

Leroy Van Allen. 2010. *1878 P 7 Tail Feather Morgan Dollar Attribution Guide*. 130 pp. RCI

Leroy Van Allen. 2006. *1878 S Morgan Dollar Attribution Guide*. 139 pp. RCI

Fey, Michael S. 2009 The Top 100 Morgan Dollar Varieties: The VAM Keys

FURTHER REFERENCES

Hard Copy Books

Fey, Michael S. 2019. The Top 100 Morgan Dollar Varieties: The VAM Keys. 286 pp. RCI

Fey, Michael S. 2008. *A Decade of Top 100 Insights*. RCI 174 pp.

Van Allen, Leroy. 1991. *RotaFlip Die Rotation Booklet and Guide*. 1991. RCI

Kimpton, M.D., Mark. 2005. *Elite Clashed Morgan Dollars*. RCI 160 pp

Van Allen, Leroy, & A. George Mallis. 2023. *Comprehensive Catalog and Encyclopedia or Morgan & Peace Dollars*. RCI Total 520 pp.

Van Allen, Leroy 2011. *Wonders of Morgan Dollars*. 139 pp. RCI

Van Allen, Leroy 2013. *Wonders of Peace Dollars*. 273 pp. RCI

Van Allen, Leroy 2006. *Morgan Dollars 8 & 7 Over 8 Tail Feather Story*. 52 pp. RCI

Van Allen, Leroy 2010. *1878 P 7 Tail Feather Morgan Dollar Attribution Guide*. 130 pp. RCI

Van Allen, Leroy 2006. *1878 S Morgan Dollar Attribution Guide*. 139 pp. RCI

Van Allen, Leroy 2013. *Die Gouges and Scratches Peace Dollar Attribution Guide. 109 pp* RCI

Van Allen, Leroy 2008. *1921 Scribbles Morgan Dollar Attribution Guide*. 234 pp. RCI

Van Allen, Leroy. 2013. *Misplaced Date Digits Morgan Dollar Attribution Guide. 57 pp* RCI

Van Allen, Leroy. 2017. *Dashed Under 8 Morgan Dollar Attribution Guide*. 53 pp. RCI

Van Allen, Leroy. 2009. *Overdates and Over Mint Marks of Morgan Dollar Attribution Guide*. 53 pp. RCI

Van Allen, Leroy. 2015. *Denticle & Die Impressions Morgan Dollar Attribution Guide*. 109 pp. RCI

Van Allen, Leroy. 2009. *1921 P Infrequently Reeded or Wide Reeding Morgan Dollar Attribution Guide*. 31 pp. RCI

Van Allen, Leroy. 2011 *Amazing Changing 1921 S VAM 1B Thorn Head Morgan Dollar*. 2011. 22 pp. RCI

Van Allen, Leroy. 2009. *1889 P Doubled Ear Morgan Dollar Attribution Guide*. 32 pp. RCI

Van Allen, Leroy. 2016. *Micro o and Other Counterfeit Morgan and Peace Dollars*. 191 pp RCI

Van Allen, Leroy. 2005. *Micro o Mint Mark on Morgan Dollars*. 32 pp. RCI

Van Allen, Leroy. 2005. *Die Markers for 1921 Morgan and Peace Proof Dollars*. 9 pp. RCI

Van Allen, Leroy and Baumgart, John. 1992-Date Various VAM Book Yearly Supplements. RCI